Library of
Davidson College

STUDIES IN ENGLISH AND AMERICAN
LITERATURE, LINGUISTICS, AND CULTURE

VOL. 3

STUDIES IN ENGLISH AND AMERICAN LITERATURE, LINGUISTICS, AND CULTURE

Vol. 3

Editorial Board

Mary Carruthers, Leopold Damrosch, Jr., Richard Fallis, Thomas Garbáty, John L. Idol, Jr., Edward B. Irving, Jr., John E. Jordan, Jerome Klinkowitz, Carl R. Kropf, Albert C. Labriola, George Monteiro, William H. O'Donnell, Reeve Parker, Morse Peckham, Balachandra Rajan, John R. Reed, John R. Rickford, Jason Rosenblatt, Edward Stone, Michael Timko, Brian Wilkie, Robert Willson.

Managing Editor

Benjamin Franklin V

CAMDEN HOUSE
Columbia, South Carolina

Critic into Anti-Critic

Also by the author

The Art of Arnold Bennett, Bloomington, Indiana, 1963, and New York, 1973
The Author's Empty Purse and the Rise of the Literary Agent, London and New York, 1968
Confessions of an American Scholar (under the name Simon O'Toole), Minneapolis, Minnesota, and London, 1970

Editor

Arnold Bennett, the Critical Heritage, London and Boston, 1981
Father and Son (by Edmund Gosse), London, 1974
Letters of Arnold Bennett, 3 vols., London and New York, 1966, 1968, 1970
Sketches for Autobiography (by Bennett), London and Boston, 1980

Plays

(Produced at the Questors Theatre, Ealing, London)
Deaf, Dumb, and Blind, 1975
Magic 'n Tragic, 1975
Moonshipt, 1977
Poor Dumb Animals, 1971
Time, Life, Sex, and You Know What, 1972

Children's tale

My Fierce Tiger, London, 1970, New York, 1971

Critic into Anti-Critic

James Hepburn

CAMDEN HOUSE

Set in Garamond type
and printed on acid-free paper.

Copyright © 1984 by James Hepburn

CAMDEN HOUSE, INC.
Drawer 2025
Columbia, South Carolina 29202
Library of Congress Catalog Card Number: 84-70174
All Rights Reserved
Printed in the United States of America
First Edition
ISBN: 0-938100-33-5

Preface

THERE IS ONE MOTIVE that serves the critic and scholar best, and that is the motive of love—of authors, of understanding. The reader need go no further than my title to see that the motive has to some degree failed in me. It fails in everyone. We love showing off our knowledge, or we love demonstrating someone else's ignorance. Nevertheless, our common failure is no excuse, and I would like to offer my own particular excuse.

The essays printed here represent my major critical and scholarly interests over the past twenty-two years, aside from those that have already found expression in book form. Those in the title section record a progress or a change or a failure over those years, one that I did not plan in the beginning or see until it was well along. At the time I wrote the early essay "Deeper Chaos and Larger Order," I was moving away from psychoanalytical criticism. I still regarded Freud as a wise and subtle thinker, and as a literary artist and critic of art of considerable power. But the motive of love was failing. I did not think he understood as much as I had once thought he understood. More especially it seemed to me that some of his disciples among American literary theorists were not good theorists. The essay did not attack anyone explicitly, and it did not condemn either psychoanalytical criticism or any other fixed scheme for the critic. But it was sceptical enough to raise a storm at one of the Modern Language Association meetings, and the rumbles of the storm echoed for more than a couple of years. By that time I happened to be teaching the "Ode on a Grecian Urn" in a serious way. I was determined to get to the bottom of that poem's meaning, partly because I had once been embarrassed because of my ignorance of the problems of its meaning. But the more I thought about the meaning of the poem, the more I became convinced of the inherent deficiency of critical systems in getting at meaning, even though I still believed that academic critics and scholars stood on common ground. Several years later I arrived at my study of Swinburne, and by that time—to my surprise and dismay and pleasure—I had learned some scorn of modern academic criticism and scholarship, and it seemed almost a labor of love to try to prove that an old-fashioned critic like Edmund Gosse understood the poet better than his successors. Succeeding essays in the title section—those on the little tradition, Ottoline Morrell, and Thomas Hardy—argue my present view, which is that many of our shared values in literature are misconceived: we practice a recondite form of hero worship, an old Arnoldian idolatry that we ought to put by for the sake of civilization. My own exemplification of the follies and fantasies of such hero worship is recorded in part 5 of my essay on the verbal icon.

The motive of love, then, exists very impurely in these pages. But I hope it is seen to exist, as much in the recent essays as in the earlier, and nearly as much in scorn as in praise. I must add that insofar as my progress was inadvertent, insofar as I think critical systems do more harm than good, I in no way am offering here the development of a critical system of my own. The arguments of the title section are informal and unconnected, and rise from immediate problems. The most succinct statement of my views is in the essay on Keats and in part 5 of my essay on the verbal icon; the broadest expression of them is in the essay on the little tradition; the most elaborate single illustration is in the essay on Swinburne.

There is another way in which these essays fail to exemplify the great motive. Since my adolescence the lines "Red lips are not so red | As the stained stones kissed by the English dead" have been in my head and on my tongue. I need not apologize for the confused, sentimental, and youthful thoughts about men, women, death, and poetry that surrounded my love of these lines. It is a fact that Wilfred Owen meant a great deal to me then, and means a great deal to me now. If I had to single out the twenty brief passages of poetry that year in and year out strike me hardest, Owen's other lines from "Insensibility" would stand there beside those of Shakespeare, Donne, and others:

> We wise, who with a thought besmirch
> Blood over all our soul,
> How should we see our task
> But through his blunt and lashless eyes?
> Alive, he is not vital overmuch;
> Dying, not mortal overmuch;
> Nor sad, nor proud,
> Nor curious at all.
> He cannot tell
> Old men's placidity from his.

How strange, then, that my essay on Owen says little about this, but is mainly a discussion of certain technical aspects of his development. The love must be inferred. Our age, in criticism, is disinclined toward emotional outpourings, and perhaps rightly so. What I have written about Owen is something I thought needed to be said. The original reason for which I wrote, or what I felt when I read his manuscript poems in the British Museum, is something else. In any event, the essay on Owen and the other essays in sections 2 and 3 have nothing very directly to do with the development of anti-critical opinions. They exist for the best of reasons, even if the best of reasons is not always manifest in them.

The collection as a whole is a companion volume to a little book I published in 1970 called *Confessions of an American Scholar*, under the name Simon O'Toole.

Acknowledgments

I SHOULD LIKE TO thank the authorities of Bates College for a grant from the Hewlett-Mellon Fund in support of the publication of this book. About half the material here first appeared in periodicals. I have not made substantial changes in such material. "Deeper Chaos and Larger Order" appeared in *Literature and Psychology* (1961), "Stopping by Robert Frost" in *New England Quarterly* (1962), "Where Arnold Bennett Went Wrong" in the *Manchester Guardian* (1967), "Religion, Science, and Philip Henry Gosse" in the *Contemporary Review* (1978), and "Wilfred Owen's Poetic Development" in *Modern British Literature* (1979). I am grateful to the editors for permission to reprint.

"Ottoline the Terrible" and "Leda and the Dumbledore" first appeared in the *Sewanee Review* 84 (summer 1976) and 88 (winter 1980). Copyright 1976, 1980 by the University of the South. Reprinted by permission of the editor.

"The Notebook for *Riceyman Steps*," from *PMLA* 78 (1963), and "E. A. Robinson's System of Opposites," from *PMLA* 80 (1965), are reprinted by permission of the Modern Language Association of America.

Contents

I. Critic into Anti-Critic
  1. Deeper Chaos and Larger Order: Freudian Science and Art   3
  2. Stopping by Robert Frost   15
  3. Keats's Foster-Child and the Problem of Criticism   23
  4. Swinburne Corrupted   33
  5. Tennyson the Sadist   61
  6. A Shot at the Verbal Icon   75
  7. Mr. Pooter and the Little Tradition   93
  8. Ottoline the Terrible   109
  9. Leda and the Dumbledore   115

II. Other Essays
  10. The Notebook for *Riceyman Steps*   127
  11. Some Curious Realism in *Riceyman Steps*   135
  12. E. A. Robinson's System of Opposites   143
  13. Religion, Science, and Philip Henry Gosse   157
  14. Wilfred Owen's Poetic Development   167
  15. The Play that Oscar Wilde Failed to Write   179

III. Personal Sketches
  16. Where Arnold Bennett Went Wrong   201
  17. Dirty Words, Clean Poetry   209
  18. Thomas Hardy among the Americans   215
  19. Visiting Robert Frost in England   219

Notes   223

Index   235

I Critic into Anti-Critic

1 Deeper Chaos and Larger Order: Freudian Science and Art

I

IN THE LITERATURE OF psychoanalytical criticism there may be discerned two strains, the romantic and the scientific. Perhaps the most impressive example of the former is Freud's *The Moses of Michelangelo*. It is a personal essay, describing an encounter with an enigma and the unveiling of it. In the brief introductory section, Freud remarks that some of the great works of art are unsolved riddles. He acknowledges a personal limitation in confronting enigma: "some rationalistic, or perhaps analytic, turn of mind in me rebels against being moved by a thing without knowing why I am thus affected." That mysterious art of music he admits to be inaccessible to him. Then, in one of those astonishing passages that characterize the best of his writing, he describes the power that Michelangelo's statue has exerted over him:

> How often have I mounted the steep steps from the unlovely Corso Cavour to the lonely piazza where the deserted church stands, and have essayed to support the angry scorn of the hero's glance! Sometimes I have crept cautiously out of the half-gloom of the interior as though I myself belonged to the mob upon whom his eye is turned—the mob which can hold fast no conviction, which has neither faith nor patience, and which rejoices when it has regained its illusory idols.[1]

In section 1 of his essay, Freud reviews the earlier analyses of the statue, and he finds that the authorities do not agree on simple matters of physical detail. Are the tables of the laws slipping from the right hand of the statue or are they held securely? Is Moses grasping his beard or is he merely passing his hand over it? Nor do the authorities agree on matters of paramount importance. Does Moses display explosive wrath or majestic self-assurance? Is he shown at the moment when he discovers his people worshipping the golden calf or is he shown in a timeless posture? In section 2, Freud begins his own contemplation of the statue, and he realizes that the position of the tables of the laws and of Moses' hand upon his beard can be accounted for only by predicating a prior position. That prior position, it becomes evident, must be one of expressed anger (that itself was preceded by calm). The present position is not one of expressed anger, as Freud himself and most earlier authorities had thought; it is one of suppressed anger. In section 3 comes the full revelation. Freud perceives that Michelangelo has created not the wrathful Moses of convention but a Moses who has attained "the highest mental achievement that is possible in a man, that of struggling successfully against an inward passion for the sake of a cause to which he has devoted himself" (13:233). The mistakes of earlier authorities stem from confused perception of the actual statue that Michelangelo created and the prior position that is implicit in it.

The rhetorical form of the essay recapitulates Freud's own discovery of the meaning of the statue. On the fourth day of his first visit to Rome, in the year 1901, he wrote his wife that he had seen the statue, and added "*Plötzlich durch Mich. verstanden.*" In his *Life and Work of Sigmund Freud* Ernest Jones translates the phrase loosely, drawing upon Freud's opening remarks in the essay: "I have come to understand the meaning of the statue by contemplating Michelangelo's intention." Jones himself adds that Freud could not have come to his final interpretation on this first visit, and supports his view by citing the passage in the essay in which Freud remarks that for a long time he thought that the statue was about to start up in wrath. However, he does not suggest an intermediate interpretation that Freud might have made, and he ignores the possibility that Freud allowed himself some artistic license in the essay.[2] Eleven years passed before Freud was in Rome again to see the statue, and another few months elapsed before he began reading the literature dealing with it. Perhaps he did not discover the true meaning of the statue until he had conducted his scholarly investigation. If so, his essay preserves the chronological order of his experience. But rhetorically the essay recreates the romantic moment that he described to his wife. The introductory remarks express his awe before the statue; the review of the authorities in section 1 and his own reflections in section 2 express the intellectual puzzlement that the sense of mystery deteriorates into; then in section 3 comes the revelation: *Plötzlich durch Mich. verstanden.*

Such revealed truth is credited today more than it once was. The scientist who was believed to proceed by induction, assembling and adding up his facts until he arrived at the first law of thermodynamics or the uncertainty principle, is now seen as a man who usually leaps to conclusions. Often the leap is a revelation, and it may be many years before the revelation receives the scrutiny of uninspired analysis. It is tempting to think that Freud suddenly understood the statue of Moses when he first saw it in 1901, but hardly believed what he understood, and subsequently subjected it to the prosaic tests of critical investigation. One reflects that what is reckoned to be his most impressive single work, *The Interpretation of Dreams,* came not at the end of a long career of scientific investigation but near the beginning, at a time when he was most unscientifically interested in Wilhelm Fliess's numerology. Perhaps the subject, or nature, of psychoanalysis invites revealed truth. In *Surprise and the Psychoanalyst* Theodor Reik remarks upon its importance in psychoanalytic theory:

> If we thrust aside the doubtful communications from the unconscious, as being unreliable, indefinite, and contrary to our conscious judgments and prejudices, we shall, it is true, seldom be deceived, but then we shall seldom attain surprising knowledge.[3]

Contrasting to truth attained by revelation is truth attained scientifically; that is, truth that follows from known laws. Among Freud's own works, his monograph on Leonardo contrasts in such a way with his study of the statue of Moses. In part 1 of the monograph he both propounds and solves the riddle of Leonardo. The riddle is the artist who turned away from art to science and who when he returned to art did not complete his works and showed no concern for their physical permanence. The solution presents itself to the psychoanalyst who understands the laws that govern the behavior of men: "*There is only one way* in which the peculiarity of...[his] emotional life can be understood in connection with...[his] double nature as an artist and a scientific investigator" (11:73; emphasis supplied). The remainder of the monograph merely confirms and clarifies Freud's diagnosis. In part 2, Freud analyzes the fantasy that Leonardo had recorded as a true experience of his infancy. "While I was in my cradle," Leonardo had written, "a vulture came down to me, and opened my mouth with its tail, and struck me many times with its tail against my lips" (11:82). The interpretation comes easily: the fantasy is that of the passive homosexual, and also that of the child at its mother's breast. Freud then asks why Leonardo should have chosen the vulture as the instrument of his fantasy, and he turns for his answer to the Egyptian worship of a vulture mother goddess and to the notion that vultures are exclusively female. He shows that the fantasy signifies Leonardo's identification with his mother, with whom he lived alone during his first years, and that it also signifies his longing for his father.

In such a way the monograph spins itself out. Implicit in every line is the assumption that every properly trained psychoanalyst who was presented with the same evidence would interpret it in the same way and reach the same conclusion that Freud himself reaches. It is, one might say, a model for the scientific analysis that many psychoanalytic critics would like to see advanced in literary studies. And it is unconvincing. In his study of Leonardo, Sir Kenneth Clark observes that most Leonardo scholars have rejected Freud's argument; and although he himself is sympathetic to psychological explanation and does not directly attack Freud, he explains the development of Leonardo's art in cultural and intellectual terms that clash with the psychoanalytic explanation. Perhaps an art historian is likely to fail to appreciate the psychoanalytical viewpoint, and Sir Kenneth's admission that Leonardo scholars have rejected Freud's opinions "with horror" suggests reaction rather that reason.[4] But from within the psychoanalytical fold has come other evidence of Freud's failure. In his introductory remarks to the essay James Strachey points out that Freud relies upon a faulty translation of Leonardo's Italian. The scientific flight that he undertakes with the vulture should have been undertaken with a kite (11:61). Strachey argues that the mistake does not vitiate Freud's central analysis; but it does emphasize the frailty of Freud's reasoning in the essay. Consider, for example, Freud's use of the fact that Leonardo was once tried on a charge of homosexuality and his assertion that "it is doubtful whether Leonardo ever embraced a woman in passion" (11:71). Given the scantiness of biographical information on both points (as Freud himself notes, Leonardo was acquitted of the charge of homosexuality), some caution would be in order. But presently Freud is speaking dogmatically of "the atrophy of his sexual life (which was restricted to what is called ideal homosexuality)" (11:80). He takes the charge of homosexuality to be more significant than the acquittal, and he takes the acquittal to be adequate evidence that Leonardo was not an active homosexual. But if he had been more modest in his argument, he would not have been more convincing; for the important reason that the monograph is unconvincing is that it is scientific. Never for a moment does Freud give his reader the sense of Leonardo the man that he gives him of the statue of Moses. The monograph possesses its own rhetorical excellence, but it is untouched by the sense of revelation that persuades the reader of *The Moses*. It is a later work than *The Moses*—conceived, written, and published in 1909-10—the product of the scientist who is laying down the laws rather than of the inspired man who is uncovering them.

But if the scientific spirit is to be attacked, the romantic spirit must be attacked as well. *The Moses* needs to be looked at again. Although in the essay Freud no more than alludes to the matter, one of the most interesting problems that he raises is the bearing that one's own psyche has upon the way one sees things. Why did so many nineteenth century authorities see incipient wrath in the statue rather than restrained wrath? Why were some so bemused by their feelings that they described the details of the statue inaccurately? Did Moses seem like a stern father to them? But Freud himself should not be exempt from the laws of human psychology that he believes in, and there is evidence aplenty to suggest that his reaction to the statue was predetermined. Without questioning the legitimacy of that reaction, Ernest Jones observes that it coincided with the dispute with Jung, a dispute which Freud wished to conclude without destroying the psychoanalytic movement. (Jones is assuming that Freud's final interpretation came in 1912-13 rather than in 1901.) "One cannot avoid the pretty obvious conclusion," Jones writes, "that at this time, and probably before, Freud had identified himself with Moses and was striving to emulate the victory over passions that Michelangelo had depicted"—a victory, in Freud's words describing the statue, "for the sake of a cause to which he has devoted himself" (2:366). One can hardly avoid another conclusion: that Freud attributed to the statue the victory that he himself wanted, not merely a victory in suppressing his anger at Jung (assuming that Jones is right about the date of the interpretation), but a victory such as that which his development of psychoanalytic theory represented in the whole of his psychic life, the submitting of the unconscious to reason. Two pages earlier in his biography Jones remarks that Freud's first feeling that the statue was gazing angrily at him must have reflected feelings about an angry father. Again one is tempted to think that Freud's final interpretation reflected his wish for his father to put away his wrath. Many pages further on, Jones remarks upon a connection between Freud's interest in the historical Moses and his relationship with his younger brother Julius, whose Jewish name may have been Moses. Jones notes Freud's jealousy of his brother, and his feeling of responsibility for his brother's death; and at another point he quotes Freud's remark to a translator of *The Moses* that "my feeling for this piece of work (the statue) is rather like that towards a love-child" (2:367). One is inclined to believe that Freud's version of the meaning of Michelangelo's statue was compounded of the images he wanted to see in his father, in himself, and in his younger brother. His interpretation was so personal that he published the essay anonymously and did not acknowledge authorship for ten years.

Jones quotes Freud saying in his early years, "I always find it uncanny when I can't understand someone in terms of myself"; and he quotes him writing the very opposite to Arthur Schnitzler, although it may be the same thing: "I think I have avoided you from a kind of awe of meeting my 'double'.... Your determinism and your scepticism..., and the extent to which your thoughts are preoccupied with the polarity of love and death; all that moves me with an uncanny feeling of familiarity" (1:320; 3:443). The uncanniness of that which he cannot interpret in terms of himself and the uncanniness of the person who seems to be his double are, in part, the subject of his essay, "The Uncanny," that he wrote in 1919. He asserts in that essay that the capacity for doubling gives man his powers of self-observation, and that the uncanniness of the double must stem from the fact that it calls to mind "a creation dating back to a very early mental stage..., a stage, incidentally, at which *it wore a more friendly aspect*" *(17:236; emphasis supplied)*. Who can doubt that Freud's contemplation of the unsolved riddle of the great work, his awe before it, and his interpretation of its expression constituted an uncanny experience? Who can avoid thinking of Oedipus confronting the Sphinx? Those German words are puzzling: *Plötzlich durch Mich. verstanden.* What has been understood through Michelangelo? Suddenly through Michelangelo I have understood the statue of Moses? Or suddenly through Michelangelo (through the statue of Michelangelo) I have understood myself? *Plötzlich mich verstanden. Plötzlich durch Mich., mich verstanden.* When Freud went to Rome for the first time, he was completing the major part of his self-analysis.

II

If the danger of romantic analysis is that it may have more to do with the author of the analysis than with the object he is discussing, and if the danger of scientific analysis is that it is usually unconvincing and often unscientific, the solution must be to find a proper balance between the two. (Assuredly no piece of analysis is purely one or the other.) Before such a course is recommended, it will be useful to look at the problem from another standpoint. In the opening lines of *The Moses* Freud says:

> I am no connoisseur in art, but simply a layman. I have often observed that the subject-matter of works of art has a stronger attraction for me than their formal and technical qualities, though to the artist their value lies first and foremost in these latter. I am unable to appreciate many of the methods used and the effects obtained in art (13:211).

This becoming modesty does not characterize the main body of the analysis. Within four paragraphs Freud has forgotten that he is a layman, forgotten too that his layman's interest is narrowly limited to subject matter. He writes: "In my opinion, what grips us so powerfully can only be the artist's *intention*...; what he aims at is to awaken in us the same emotional attitude, the same mental constellation as that which in him produced the impetus to create" (13:212). And soon enough he is saying that he will uncover "all that is most essential and valuable for the comprehension of this work of art" (13:211). This ambivalence of attitude has been hinted at by Ernest Jones in another context. Jones remarks in his biography that "Freud always had an immense respect for artists, possibly tinged with some envy. He seemed to take the romantic view of them as mysterious beings...but he tried at least to comprehend the source of their inspiration" (2:344). In discussing the monograph of Leonardo, Jones asserts that Freud probably saw the conflict in Leonardo between artist and scientist to be very much his own conflict. Subsequently he argues that in Freud the passion to get at the truth, the passion of investigation, submerged the artist that he might have been. Assuredly Freud responded to the statue of Moses with his esthetic sensibilities, with more than his announced interest in subject matter, and then he gave rein to his scientific passion. He was aware of mystery, and then he sought to master it.

But the modesty of the opening of *The Moses* not only suggests a romantic reverence for art; it also expresses something of the scientific attitude itself. The scientist sits down like a child before the unknown; he rises like a master. (If he is a good master, he rises with a gracious gesture. Thus Freud concludes his essay by wondering whether he himself has "shared the fate of so many interpreters who have thought they saw quite clearly things which the artist did not intend either consciously or unconsciously" (13:236). Such a dual attitude can be seen in most of the psychoanalytic writing on art that is avowedly scientific. In the opening pages of *Fiction and the Unconscious,* Simon O. Lesser remarks that it is perhaps "not feasible to develop a truly scientific esthetic of response to fiction," but the main body of his discussion offers scientific certitude:

> We read fiction to secure richer fulfillment of desires no more than partly satisfied by life and to allay the anxieties and guilt feelings our experience arouses.
>
> . . . .
>
> The aspects of narrative art we assign to form have three essential functions: to give pleasure; to avoid or relieve guilt or anxiety; and to facilitate perception.[5]

In *Psychoanalysis and American Literary Criticism,* Louis Fraiberg begins his discussion of the views of Ernst Kris by noting Kris's objection to the certitudes of Jung and Rank: "their urge for certainty has blinded them to the complexity of the subject." But the Kris whom Fraiberg offers to us has his own certitudes:

> The tremendous variety of art arises from the (unconscious) secondary revision, which softens objections, supplies transitions, finds points of similarity, and in general provides at least a patchwork of temporarily acceptable organization of the fantasy. The way is thus prepared for the artist's deliberate manipulation of the fantasy according to the requirements of his basic idea, his medium and his audience, all of which constitute the conscious exercise of his craft. But before it is ready for his hand, the raw material has first come from unconscious sources— the whole sequence may have been initiated by some conscious idea which then associated itself with suitable unconscious material—and it has been processed by unconscious forces.[6]

These contrasting attitudes can be seen to be consistent with each other. Lesser's observation that it may not be feasible to develop a truly scientific esthetic of response to fiction suggests a practical difficulty or impossibility—comparable, it may be supposed, to the impossibility of man's observing the outer limits of his expanding universe. It does not imply that the response to fiction fails to obey universal laws. One or more functions of form may not be ascertainable, but they exist, and they operate under the laws of psychoeconomics. In a similar way the complexity that Kris speaks of may render certitude difficult or impossible, but it does not deny the actuality of universal law that certitude presupposes. The language in which Fraiberg couches his central discussion of Kris's view of artistic activity—"revision," "supplies," "provides," "patchwork," "manipulation," "requirements," "exercise," "craft," "raw material," "sources," "processed"—compares the human mind to an industrial system operating according to the laws of classical economics and physics. It implies a closed system. Elsewhere Fraiberg writes:

> Psychoanalysis insists that there are no accidents in psychic life; everything has meaning and purpose, if only we can discover what these are. (102)
>
> . . . .

[Edmunk] Wilson understood that emotional life follows universal laws. (172)

. . . .

Wilson knows that psychoanalysis is a branch of biological science. (179)

The historical connection of Freudian psychology to romantic thought—to the preoccupation with the self, with the passions, with the dark side of human nature that characterizes romanticism—has often been remarked upon. No less noticed has been its connection to materialistic, mechanistic thought. These two currents united in the man who, as Jones describes him, was both artist and scientist, and who allowed the scientific self—the investigator, the searcher after the final truth about sexuality—to dominate the artist to a much greater degree than had Leonardo. Freud's tribute to the mystery of art and the artist expressed the artist-romantic in him, but his uneasiness before the enigma, that "rationalistic...turn of mind in me," always triumphed (13:211). *The Moses* begins in mystery and ends with science, begins with art and ends with science. In a similar way most psychoanalytical writing pays tribute to the mystery of art, and then proceeds into science.

III

Although it was suggested that the dual attitude of modesty and certitude need not reflect inconsistent assumptions, there is a possibility that it does. Do Freudian critics acknowledge that art is mysterious and free, or do they acknowledge only that it may be impenetrable, ineluctable? Do they settle, finally, for mystery or for universal law? The weight of evidence suggests the latter, and there may be no problem. But Freud's famous statement in "Dostoevsky and Parricide" comes to mind: "Before the problem of the creative artist analysis must, alas, lay down its arms (21:177). And Mr. Fraiberg speaks of "mysteries of esthetics...beyond the reach of psychoanalysis" (28). Such statements may seem to press in the direction of mystery rather than of universal law.

What are the implications of subscribing to the notion of universal law—whether that law be penetrable or impenetrable? One implication is a version of relativism. It can be seen, in part, in Freud's analysis of the statue of Moses. The statue derives its particular quality from Michelangelo's own struggle to control the violence of his temper; reaction to the statue depends upon the psyche of the individual critic. Carried further than Freud carries it, such a view implies that Freud understood the statue only in terms of his own psyche, and that other Freudian critics will necessarily contemplate the statue differently. Such a view underlies much Freudian analysis of artists and their art. Will it do? In contemplating the statue of Moses, may not Freud have stood above the law, observing others obeying the law, observing himself bowing before his father, himself, and his younger brother? Perhaps he possessed the capacity of doubling, of creating a self to stand outside of the obedient self. In such a self there lurks the possibility of violation of the law. If, as Freud acknowledged, great artists have long been capable of the detached observation that he himself achieved in agony, then the door is opened—it seems—to chaos, to mystery.

The other implication of universal law commonly appears in Freudian esthetics. It is an implication that has been pursued from other vantage points. In *The Mathematical Basis of the Arts* Joseph Schillinger writes: "If art implies selectivity, skill and organization, ascertainable principles must underlie it. Once such principles are discovered and formulated, works of art may be produced by scientific synthesis."[7] One sees a similar end in view when Lesser remarks that narrative form serves the three functions of giving pleasure, avoiding guilt, and facilitating perception. To be sure, the mathematical theory envisages an art produced by a computer, whereas the psychological one assumes that the unconscious mind of a human being must always be the source; but the notion of prescription underlies both. It is this implication that has elicited the common criticism that Freudian critics think that if a piece of literature deals with the Oedipus complex it must be great art. Lesser responds to such criticism by distinguishing between the Oedipal theme in *Hamlet* and in an unimportant work:

> In the first place, no one could claim that the Oedipal theme is more than one component of the subject-matter of *Hamlet*. But the essential point is that the contribution this one theme makes to the appeal of the play has been obscured by a particularly savage form of reduction: the theme had been contracted...to...an opprobrious label.... To show the part the theme does play in our response to *Hamlet,* we would have to do justice to the theme *in its fullness*. We would have to suggest the infinite cunning with which it is orchestrated in nearly all the play's key relationships and in innumerable actions and speeches. (74)

Yet the implication seems to remain: if a writer will take the great theme and orchestrate it cunningly, he will have a great play. Lesser disposes of an inadequately stated objection to a common Freudian view; at the same time he appears to subscribe to the view that when the universal laws of the mind are followed in certain complex ways the result is great art. Lesser may not acknowledge that his thinking points in such a direction, and other psychoanalytic critics may not accept the implications that their scientific approach suggests. The question, then, is whether the underlying assumption of most Freudian critics is romantic rather than scientific. Is it believed that great art is inherently mysterious?

A variety of evidence indicates an answer in favor of the romantic outlook. It is evidence of a sort that Freud sometimes favored: evidence that we might normally scorn. We who are Freudians might ask ourselves how we arrived at our wisdom. Did it come from an objective, exhaustive reading of Freudian, anti-Freudian, and non-Freudian literature, or did it come through a romantic revelation? On what evidence were we convinced that we, the Trobriand islanders, and Neanderthal man had endured the Oedipus complex? Secondly, on what basis do we accept or reject the various and often conflicting views of psychoanalysts? Psychoanalysis may be a science, just as medicine is a science; but much medicine is unscientific, and much psychoanalysis must be. Consider Edmund Bergler's five-layer structure of sublimation, offered in *Psychoanalytic Quarterly* in 1945:

> The starting point in sublimation is not an id wish *per se*, but the result of regression. In other words, it is in itself the result of a conflict. That conflict is presented (layer one), immediately counteracted by a superego reproach (layer two), which necessitates the establishment of a defense mechanism (layer three). The superego objects, however, even to the defense mechanism (layer four), which in turn forces the unconscious ego to sublimate (layer five), which represents the defense against the defense.[8]

Some of us may say that criticism of such a theory lies beyond our province, and leave it to the psychoanalysts. (Yet we may have been willing to make a judgment on the Oedipus complex.) But some of us, perhaps most of us, will feel the way Kepler is said to have felt in contemplating the intricate mathematics of his time that described the movement of the stars: the art of the Creator could not have been so clumsy, so inelegant. The modern description of such movement is more complicated than it was when Kepler stepped in to simplify it; and therefore Bergler may be right. Nevertheless, one wonders whether any of the artists whom Bergler analyzed had produced a grand, overwhelming work—an unsolved riddle—such as the statue of Moses. Perhaps most of us reject Bergler's theory as being at once too complex and too simple. We are not experts in psychoanalysis; but the whole of our knowledge in every realm gives us a viewpoint from which we say as authoritatively as possible: that piece of psychoanalytic theory does not fit. The viewpoint may be a romantic one, in which the notion of fitting is itself suspect.

Consider two psychoanalytical discussions of music:

> The esthetic effect of music is the result of three factors: compulsive repetition, pleasure in economy and the force of attraction exerted by the unconscious.
> . . . .
>
> The external world of the infant is alien, dangerous. Associated with it is the chaos of external sounds, against which the infant cannot protect itself. Music is the formal control and knowledge of sounds which once threatened destruction.[9]

Who will doubt that the second passage speaks more truly about the significance of the opening bars of Beethoven's Ninth Symphony? The authors of the second view quote one of Rilke's Duino Elegies to support their argument: "For Beauty's nothing/but beginning of Terror we're still just able to bear." Some people will doubt it. Will not their judgment, too, be an intuitive, romantic one?

A similar attitude prevails in judgments upon art itself. When Freud remarks in *The Moses* that "some of the grandest and most overwhelming creations of art are still unsolved riddles" (13:211), he seems almost to be saying that a work of art that is a riddle is a great work; and he is unquestionably acknowledging the fact that men pass the judgment of greatness upon works which escape rational analysis. The judgment is intuitive, romantic. In the introduction to his translation of Euripides's *The Bacchae,* William Arrowsmith writes:

> Of itself *The Bacchae* needs neither apology nor general introduction. It is, clearly and flatly, that unmistakable thing, a masterpiece.... Elusive, complex and compelling, the play constantly recedes before ones's grasp, advancing, not retreating, steadily into deeper chaos and larger order....[10]

The play has a disconcerting transparency. It yields to psychoanalytic investigation its themes of homosexuality and castration, of id wish and ego control, much more readily than, say "Death in Venice" yields its similar themes. But when one compares the two works, one sees that "Death in Venice" is a complex psychological story and that *The Bacchae* is clearly and flatly a riddle. Similarly one comes away in bafflement from that greater work than *Hamlet, King Lear*. No critic has touched its center. Even *Hamlet* eludes us. At one time, when the commentaries of Schlegel, Bradley, and others proved inadequate, the essay of Jones came like a revelation. But time passes, and though we may still regard the essay highly, it seems less and less central. *Hamlet* reasserts its mystery, and we turn elsewhere for a new effort to penetrate it.

IV

What should Freudian criticism be? A nice balance between romanticism and science? Science unveiling the mysteries? Are we brothers to those scholars—some of whom gaze scornfully upon us—who are scientists laboring in the vineyards of the humanities? Possibly another approach is more useful: that of a reasonable critic moving always in the direction of mystery, and content to end there. What is Freud's study of the statue of Moses? Surely we reject the notion that it is merely a reflection of his own mentality or of early twentieth century Austrian mentality. Surely we reject the notion that it is merely the last scientific word on the statue. Despite Freud's inadequate confession of humility, it is, perhaps, an approach to mystery rather than an unveiling of it; and its chief merit as a piece of analysis may be that it succeeds in conveying something of the mystery that the statue possesses. It provides in itself a parallel to that mystery. Not being a great artwork, it presently surrenders its own mystery—expressed through its sense of revelation—and another essay must attempt to approach the statue in another way. The same fate overtakes Jones's essay on *Hamlet*. Not many years ago the chief means of conveying the mystery of great art was enthusiastic and impressionistic commentary; it has been succeeded by a criticism that is drier, more cautious, a criticism that at its worst—while being most scientific—is dust and ashes, and that at its best succeeds in approaching mystery.

Fraiberg remarks in his book that Ernest Jones "believes that the more deeply the artist goes into his unconscious for inspiration... the more profound the result is likely to be" (61-62). No Freudian critic is likely to disagree with the opinion, but it needs elucidation. What is the difference in meaning between deep and profound? Will it do to say that the more profoundly the artist goes into his unconscious the more profound the result is likely to be? Or that the more deeply he goes the deeper the result is likely to be? The language begins with classical mechanics—with the notion of depths, with the notion of an unconscious that occupies physical space; and it ends with mystery—with a word that has lost both literal and metaphorical meaning in order to express the inexpressible. The division of the mind into id, ego, and superego is a mechanistic reduction, perhaps a more useful reduction than Jung's fourfold division, but inevitably simplistic. Ultimately we must say that the more profoundly an artist thinks, the more profound the result is likely to be.

It is not to be believed that mankind merely cringes under the eternal gaze of Moses who carries the unbreakable tables of the laws. The mass of us may cringe, but Freud was that free, mysterious man who met the gaze and broke the laws. And so is the great artist: that man whose masterpiece constantly recedes before one's grasp, advancing, not retreating, steadily into deeper chaos and larger order.

2 Stopping by Robert Frost

MANY YEARS AGO, William Rose Benét called Robert Frost a "wise old woodchuck," and more recently Lionel Trilling called him "a terrifying poet." Trilling explained that the universe that Frost depicts is a "terrifying universe"; but even as he was speaking, Robert Langbaum was saying that "Frost takes into account nature's destructiveness, but his examples of it are seldom very frightening." To Yvor Winters, Frost was incapable of grasping the predicament of modern man; to Hyatt H. Waggoner, he understood the predicament and made a "strategic retreat"; to James M. Cox, he "forced a clearing in the woods," braved "the alien entanglements of experience."[1]

Consider the variety of interpretations of a single poem, "Stopping by Woods on a Snowy Evening." Some earlier writers see the poem as a tribute to the New England sense of duty; Lawrance Thompson sees it as an epitome of the journey through life, with hardships (the dark and cold evening), beauties and pleasures (the woods), duties, and death. Leonard Unger and William Van O'Connor think that the traveler's choice is between estheticism and moral action; John Ciardi prefers the woods to represent the death-wish. Most critics do agree—tacitly—on one aspect of the meaning of the poem: that it ends with a rejection of whatever the woods represent and an affirmation of whatever is implied by "promises." An attempt to resolve some of the differences among such critics cannot do better than to begin at this point at which they are in agreement.[2]

For their agreement seems no more satisfactory than their disagreement. To say that "Stopping by Woods" ends with an affirmation is to ignore the tone in which the literal or symbolic meaning is given. Unger and O'Connor in their commentary on the poem assert that the effect of the repeated last line is to emphasize the choice made for moral action; but in fact the lulling rhythm and repetition, of both rhyme and phrase, deprive the assertion of force. The mood that the poem induces in the reader nullifies his acceptance of the intention expressed by the traveler. The sum of the reader's experience of the poem is different from the meaning of the traveler's experience of the woods. Presumably the traveler goes home to supper, to his duties, and to the rest of his journey through life; but these things are not the poem.

To put the matter differently, a distinction must be made between the spell of the woods that the traveler experiences (and that the reader of the poem may once have experienced) and the spell that develops in the poem. Each of the first three stanzas begins flatly; each rises, with the last line or two lines, toward the spell; but not until the end of the third stanza is the rise powerful, and not until the opening of the fourth and final stanza is the rise sustained rather than broken. The spell is clearly and firmly achieved only in the final stanza, both in the lines in which the traveler acknowledges the spell of the woods and in the lines in which he rejects it. According to Reginald L. Cook, Frost composed "Stopping by Woods" after he had spent a whole night working on another poem: "He went outside to look at the sun and it came to him. 'I always thought,' he explains, 'it was the product of autointoxication coming from tiredness.'"[3] Presumably, then, Frost began not with the spell of the woods but with a mood; he referred his mood to a remembered spell of the woods, and referred it as well to particular rhythms, rhymes, and language. Frost's own statements on his art support such a view, not only as it applies to the process of composition, but as it applies to his chief poetic aims: poems "begin in something more felt than known" ("Education by Poetry"); the poet's "intention is of course a particular mood that won't be satisfied with anything less than its own fulfillment" ("The Constant Symbol"); the outcome of a poem is "predestined from the first image of the original mood—and indeed from the very mood" ("The Figure a Poem Makes").[4] At any rate, "Stopping by Woods" is, for the reader, not so much a recreated experience of the spell of the woods as it is an experience of words, images, rhythms, and rhymes; the action that its narrator commends to himself is contradicted by the spell of language.

A similar conflict between meaning and mood occurs in many Frost poems, notably in "Come In." On the symbolic level, this poem presents more difficulties than "Stopping by Woods," for the choice between woods and stars is not nearly so clear a choice as one between woods and promises. The woods may be the same in both poems, but are stars promises? Most commentators on "Come In" do not discuss the problem. They accept the implication in the poem that the stars represent something different from the woods; and they assume—on the basis of parallelism with "Stopping by Woods," "Into My Own," and other poems—that the stars represent human or social values. But the mood of the poem contradicts any such symbolic meaning. Although the narrator refuses to come into the dark and lament, the poem is a lamentation, and the narrator's refusal is a lamentation. In contrast to "Stopping by Woods," the dominating stanza in "Come In" is the penultimate stanza. Almost everything that precedes it builds directly toward it, and the fall in the final stanza is a dying fall. The poem begins with a solitary narrator, a darkening woods, and a lonely bird. The second and third stanzas present deepening images of melancholy: the bird singing bravely and futilely, the light of day fading. With the heightened language of the fourth stanza, the melancholy mood is fully established. The last stanza diminishes—but does not break—the mood. The narrator says that he is "out for stars"—and although the stars do not possess explicit symbolic meaning, they do carry the suggestion of loneliness and isolation.[5] The tone of the stanza is only slightly playful (no more playful than the tone in the second stanza); it is a tone of melancholy bravado, like the bird's, a tone of injured pride and renunciation:

> But no, I was out for stars:
> I would not come in.
> I meant not even if asked,
> And I hadn't been.

The renunciation in the stanza is a mood rather than an act. As a mood it is close to the mood of the rest of the poem. Superficially, the renunciation is stated more firmly than the renunciation that closes "Stopping by Woods," but the power of the fourth stanza, the absence of a clear distinction in the choice, and the tone of the renunciation override the gesture.

The reverie, regret, melancholy, and renunciation that pervade "Stopping by Woods" and "Come In" are common to much of Frost's poetry. Their typical accompaniment is the spell, the dream, the tableau, the withheld action. In *A Boy's Will*, "Into My Own" sets the tone for several poems. The narrator expresses a wish to enter the woods, but he does not enter. He says that "I should not be withheld," but the poem expresses only a yearning for darkness and isolation. In "Storm Fear" the narrator may—like the traveler in "Stopping by Woods"—go about his tasks the next day; but the poem ends with the mood of surrender: "And my heart owns a doubt | Whether 'tis in us to arise with day | And save ourselves unaided." The titles of such poems as "Ghost House," "A Dream Pang," and "Reluctance" suggest their moods. In "Reluctance" the narrator does not wish to "bow and accept the end | Of a love or a season"; but the poem affirms nothing except desolation. In "Pan with Us," Pan forsakes his pipes, his joys: "Play? Play?—What should he play?" *A Boy's Will* concerns romantic weltschmerz rather than will—even a wind's will. Many of the lyrics in later volumes are similar: "After Apple-Picking," "An Old Man's Winter Night," "The Sound of the Trees" (compare "I shall make the reckless choice" with "I should not be withheld" in "Into My Own"), "To Earthward," "Acquainted with the Night," "Desert Places," "Moon Compasses." Of course, these poems differ from each other significantly. The detailed daytime scene of "After Apple-Picking" is hardly to be confused with the impressionistic nighttime scene of "Desert Places." Nevertheless, both poems are reveries, tableaus, dream poems.

Such qualities may not seem to include the dramatic quality that critics characteristically speak of in describing Frost's poems. Lawrance Thompson mentions the "drama-in-miniature ... with setting and lighting and actors and properties complete" (25) of "Stopping by Woods," and John Ciardi analyzes the poem as three scenes set against each other. But the poem presents a dramatic tableau rather than a dramatic action; the only action is the horse's shaking its harness bells. In "Come In," the narrator renounces action. "The Pasture" describes a gesture. In "Reluctance" and "Acquainted with the Night," the action consists of walking. Of course, these are lyric poems, but Frost's monologues, dialogues, and dramatic narratives reveal much the same quality. The situation in "Mending Wall" moves toward no conflict and toward no resolution. The narrator "could say 'Elves,'" but he does not do so much as that. "The Death of the Hired Man" avoids a clash between Warren and Silas; it offers no genuine clash between Warren and Mary, but rather a revelation of the stubbornness of the one and the generosity of the other; it moves toward a conclusion that obviates a quarrel and an action. The poem is the coda to an action. "Home Burial" much more nearly approaches dramatic action, but it ends on the verge of an action that probably there will be no need for: "I'll follow and bring you back by force. I *will*—." "The Subverted Flower" depicts the failure of youth to act in its own behalf. In these four poems, farmer and neighbor, husband and wife, and boy and girl confront each other; but the tension builds toward the establishment of a subdued, somber, or savage mood rather than toward an action. Other poems with a radically different tone possess something of the same quality. The narrator in "Two Tramps in Mud Time" does no more than maintain his stance against the tramps. In "A Drumlin Woodchuck," the woodchuck commits himself to a defensive posture, and nothing in the poem recommends a different attitude to the reader. The narrator in "An Empty Threat" expresses a desire to abandon civilization, but he does not go ("I stay," he says in the opening line of the poem) and he does not want to stay.

Awareness of these qualities of mood and image runs through all of the critical arguments that address themselves to meaning and action. No commentary on "Stopping by Woods" fails to acknowledge the spell of—or in—the poem. The differences of opinion arise through the transformations that the spell undergoes according to the poetic, psychological, or social presuppositions of the individual critic. James M. Cox, for example, speaks of the "haunting rhythms" of the poem; he then goes on to describe the poem as a "counter-spell" against the woods: "the act by which the traveller regains dominion of his will. The intricately interlocking rhyme scheme... and the strict iambic tetrameter, while they imitate and suggest the hypnotic power of the forest, also form the basis of a protective charm against that power" (82, 83). Apart from the questionable identification of the traveler within the poem with the poet making the poem (and presumably with the reader reading the poem), Cox's interpretation depends upon a reductive psychological theory that links "Stopping by Woods" to true incantatory verse and to nursery rhymes. The individual poetic quality of the poem—the haunting rhythm (of only the latter part of the poem, it should be noted)—has been lost sight of. Earlier in his essay, Cox makes his point from another perspective. Noting the prevalence of woods imagery in Frost's poetry, he says: "Frost... sees the drama of existence as man's willingness to risk himself before the spell of the dark woods. For him self-reliance becomes self-possession, and the victory lies not in the march forward into the wilderness but in the freedom he feels while patroling the boundary of consciousness" (80). In this venture into poetic biography, he implicitly aligns himself with Lionel Trilling, whose address to Frost on the occasion of Frost's eighty-fifth birthday is another essay in psychological-esthetic theory: "When I began to speak I called your birthday Sophoclean and that word has, I think, controlled everything I have said about you. Like you, Sophocles... was the poet his people loved most. Surely they loved him in some part because he praised their common country. But I think that they loved him chiefly because he made plain to them the terrible things of human life: they felt, perhaps, that only a poet who could make plain the terrible things could possibly give them comfort" (452). Surely there is truth in what Trilling says, and it is perhaps because there is that Robert Langbaum can say that Frost's world is "seldom very frightening." The reader at the end of "Stopping by Woods" and "After Apple-Picking" is nearer to being sleepy than to being frightened by or purged of the terrors of the universe. In some remote, abstract way he may be shocked by the world that is depicted in "A Drumlin Woodchuck"; but the poem is a delightfully grim poem (not at all like *Oedipus Rex*), and much of the success of it is that momentarily the reader becomes a wise old woodchuck like the one who wrote the poem. Trilling loses Frost's poetry in talking about poetry in general. At the same time, one cannot assent to Langbaum's expectations that the people in "Storm Fear" will have the strength to carry on the next day. The catharsis is in the experience of the poem, not in the experience that the poem refers to. And were the latter sort of catharsis relevant, the reader might yet wonder about the fate of Frost's particular farmer. Two of Frost's fellow New Englanders, Amy Lowell and R. P. Tristram Coffin, see such poems as "Storm Fear," "Home Burial," and "The Fear" as accurate reflections of a society that had lost its vitality. In her review of *North of Boston* Lowell speaks of the "left-overs of the old stock, morbid, pursued by phantoms, sinking slowly to insanity."[6]

The problem of survival, in and out of the poems, is scrutinized from another standpoint by Yvor Winters, who wonders how well the farmer can withstand the storm if he dwells upon his fears, and how well the reader can confront the modern world if he reads poetry that is dedicated to weltschmerz. Fine word though catharsis is, Winters argues that sensibility leads to sickness: the society that devotes itself to feeling and imagination loses vigor. Winters notes "the vague melancholy" (165) of "The Sound of the Trees," and he reflects that a poem that rests with vague melancholy is a bad, confused poem; for a poem ought to help the reader to comprehend the human situation. Of all of Frost's critics, Winters perhaps comes closest to an explicit recognition of the mood that dominates the poetry; but he is much more interested in prescribing the proper social function of poetry than in describing the actual quality—individual or collective—of the poems.

Not many critics believe that understanding a poet and his poetry amounts to a game in which the critic chooses his assumptions and works out an analysis that follows from them. Allowing for inevitable differences of perspective and value, most critics would probably assume that some general agreement could be reached about whether Frost has confronted or retreated from social responsibility and whether "Stopping by Woods" is a poem that is devoted to the problem of moral choice. At the same time, most critics would be hesitant about setting up a single inviolable set of assumptions to insure agreement; and occasionally someone attempts to show the merits in approaching a poem from differing assumptions. Applying in turn the assumptions of the new criticism and those of the Chicago critics to the analysis of a single poem, Charles A. McLaughlin writes:

> It would seem that the reader or critic, instead of being dismayed at the apparent opposition of these two views of poetic form, should be grateful that a variety of methods are available to enrich his reading of poetry and that he should regret those occasions when any single method attempts to set itself up as the exclusive or "new" way of solving all the questions about poetry or as the only fruitful way of unveiling the humanistic values of great works of art.

The poem that McLaughlin analyzes from the two standpoints is "Stopping by Woods," and his analysis from the Chicago standpoint (he uses Unger and O'Connor to represent the new criticism) is interesting: he describes a dramatic development of attitudes on the part of the narrator, from casual interest to momentary fascination to rejection. But the significant fact about both of his analyses is not that they proceed from different assumptions, but that they proceed from the same one. "Now I take it," Mclaughlin says in beginning the Chicago analysis, just after he has completed his presentation of Unger and O'Connor's view, "that there is little disagreement that 'Stopping by Woods' presents us with a dramatic situation, a moment of moral choice on the part of the speaker of the poem, as was presupposed even in the dialectical analysis just outlined."[7] Since the presupposition is questionable, the light that the Chicago criticism throws upon the poem is likely to distort it as much as the light of the new criticism. McLaughlin is presumably right that a single method is too restrictive; but a multiplicity of methods may be a snare and a delusion. The poem is there, and whether the critic uses a single or a double set of standards, his task is to illuminate the poem.

When John Ciardi published his analysis of "Stopping by Woods" in *Saturday Review*, he was beset by an outraged public. The response that most pleased him, Ciardi remarked later, came from a man who said only, "Get your big clumsy feet off that miracle."[8] It may be questionable whether the poem is a miracle or a minor lyric, but there is little doubt that it has been trampled down by poetic, psychological, and social theories. Even if the poem does make a choice of social responsibility over estheticism or the death wish, it makes the choice so slightly, so undramatically, that to discuss the choice as the essence of the poem is to distort the poem. It is a poem of undertones and overtones rather than of meaning. Frost once remarked about another lyric, "Neither out Far nor in Deep": "Poetry is implication. Let implication be implication. Don't try to turn implication into explication. If I had wanted to say anything definite I would have put it into the poem."[9] Being a poet rather than a critic, Frost perhaps undervalues explication. And he perhaps—in this statement—overvalues implication. He is primarily a lyric poet; and, as he says elsewhere, the aim in lyric poetry is not mainly implication: the aim is song.

3 Keats's Foster-Child and the Problem of Criticism

THE COMMONEST FACT ABOUT literary criticism is the perennial confidence with which it is conducted. We see that no critic before us has said the right things about the "Ode on a Grecian Urn," but we do not suppose that we ourselves will fail. Perhaps it is our very sense of past failure that gives us confidence. And then in the event we are proved only half right. Can we console ourselves with the thought that we are no less wrong than our predecessors? Can we bemuse ourselves with the proposition that criticism is always impossible and always necessary? Or can we bring ourselves to believe that the critical game is misconceived, and that we should always be more modest than we are likely to be? I would like to look at some aspects of the "Ode" with these questions in mind. In particular I would like to suggest that part of our difficulty lies in the gap between critical perception and experience, between what we can seem to say about the poem and what the poem means to us in our experience of it.

Consider the fact that according to the canons of modern literary criticism there are defects in the poem that modern literary critics have hitherto failed to see, even though more attention has been given to the poem than to almost any other in the language. Such a defect lies in the metaphor of the foster-child, the second of the trio of metaphors with which the poem opens. Cleanth Brooks, who is one of the few critics who have paused before the metaphor, says only, in *The Well Wrought Urn:*

> The exactness of the term can be defended. "Silence and slow time," it is suggested, are not the true parents, but foster-parents. They are too old, one feels, to have borne the child themselves. Moreover, they dote upon the "child" as grandparents do. The urn is fresh and unblemished; it is still young, for all its antiquity, and time which destroys so much has "fostered" it.

His remarks extend and transform the metaphor rather more than they justify it; they certainly do not criticize it. A few other critics provide similar paraphrases. E. C. Pettet, in *On the Poetry of Keats,* speaks of the urn as the "child" of "some forgotten artist...; but it has survived because it has been fostered and cherished by time." Earl Wasserman writes in *The Finer Tone*: "On the literal level, the urn has existed in the physical world, in which all things are mutable, and so is related to aspects of time and sound. And yet, by enduring long, it has... caused them to become secondary factors in its existence (an unravish'd *bride*, and a *foster-child*)...."[1] Other recent critics have little or nothing to say.

The defect of the metaphor is that in contrast to its companion metaphors of the unravish'd bride and the sylvan historian it has no significant development. In the subsequent lines of the first stanza we see unravish'd maidens and sylvan history: the characterizations of the urn in lines one and three are transformations of the scenes depicted on it. Stanzas 2 and 3 continue the contemplation of unravish'd maidens on the urn; stanza 4 depicts sacramental activity that might include marriage; the final stanza speaks of beauty that a bride exemplifies. Similarly the notion of legend, or history, underlies stanzas 2 and 3; in the fine modulation of images in stanza 4 it replaces the bride in importance; in the final stanza the historian speaks. If we like to think of the maiden and the historian as of equal importance, we can say that the closing lines depict their marriage, a union of beauty and truth. In his essay, Brooks chooses to dwell at greater length upon the historian. Wasserman gives more attention to the bride. They are silent about the foster-child.

It is of course true that Brooks and Wasserman approach the poem from different critical perspectives, but they and most other modern critics are agreed that the merit of a poem rests in large part upon its organic unity. Brooks's essay attempts to defend the last two lines of the poem on the basis that they are prepared for dramatically and rhetorically: "the assertions made in a poem are to be taken as part of an organic context" (152). Wasserman's lengthy analysis attempts "a reading of the total imagistic grammar of the poem" (14)—a grammar which, for Wasserman, includes a complex relationship of a trio of images: lover-tree-song. How imperfect will the lonely foster-child seem to such critics? Will it be to the extent of suggesting that Keats tore the metaphor unconsciously from its rightful context in the "Immortality Ode" (The homely Nurse doth all she can| To make her foster child, her Inmate Man,| Forget the glories he hath known")? It may be conceded that the metaphor has other virtues for Keats than the exactness that Brooks speaks of and the loose thematic propriety that Wasserman and others allude to. Its loveliness of vowel color complements that of "unravish'd bride"; its suggestion of innocence and frailty is appropriate; the line as a whole has the heightened tone, the calm and just extravagance, of the other language of the poem. Do these virtues defeat, or merely conceal, the defect? Is the defect visible (eventually) to criticism but not to experience? Is such a defect real? By the same token, if a virtue is visible only to criticism, is it a real virtue?

I

A good poem, it is commonly believed, controls the experience of the reader; or, as I. A. Richards puts it in *Practical Criticism*, a good reader allows a good poem to control his experience. If the "Ode" is a good poem—aside from an unnoticeable defect or two—should not our critics mainly agree with one another? or should not their varying interpretations seem to be based upon like experience? or should not the careless experience of one critic be forever exposed by the carefulness of another? An examination of some discussions of the poem suggests chiefly that criticism often bears very little relation to experience.

It would seem on the surface that Cleanth Brooks's defense of the last two lines of the poem is based on experience, translated into terms of dramatic and rhetorical propriety. He dismisses the old objection that these lines state an absurdity that mars the poem, and shows that the paradox that "beauty is truth" is consistent with a series of paradoxes throughout the poem: an urn speaks, the historian is sylvan, ecstasy is static, and so forth. Presumably the reader is led through the earlier paradoxes to accept the last one—in context. But Brooks's paradoxes exist mainly as a critical "fabrication" (to use E. C. Pettet's description of them); they are not evident in experience of the poem, and Brooks creates some of them through transformations of metaphor, irony, ambiguity, and illogic. He says, for example, that the statement that unheard melodies are sweeter than heard melodies is "a rather bold paradox" (144); but it is instead an old familiar notion out of Plato. To the extent that the reader is conscious that Keats is offering him a proposition, he is likely to feel—without necessarily surrendering to Platonism—that it is true rather than that it is paradoxical. It speaks of a particular human experience—or sentimental belief, if you will—similar to Shelley's "memory of music fled" and Wordsworth's "music in my heart." As Keats would say, it appears almost a remembrance. Brooks himself makes a backhanded concession to the fact when he remarks that "even the dulling effect of many readings has hardly blunted" the paradox. (144)

Wasserman's discussion presents a similar problem. The vocabulary of his analysis often seems to concern another poem than the "Ode." He speaks of "the startling force" of "unravish'd," the "nervously taut" empathy in the repetition of "happy," the "staccato" of the questions in the first stanza; he describes the movement of the poem as a "drama," with "action" and "climax" (15-29). This comes to more than infelicitous phrasing. In interpreting the fourth stanza, Wasserman writes: "the now dimension-bound mind of the poet, no longer able to hold mortal and immortal in oxymoronic fusion [as in the first three stanzas], divides it imaginatively into its component symbols: the heaven-altar and the world-town. And he thrusts them to the opposite extremes of the scene" (43). If the reader is unaware of thrust (if instead he is conscious of linked sweetness and parallel phrasing: Who are these coming...? To what green altar...? What little town... ?), he sees no separation; and he perforce rejects Wasserman's view that altar and town are opposed symbols of heaven and earth. "Thrust" is in keeping only with Wasserman's dramatic terminology.

An article by Jacob Wigod in 1957 points up this particular conflict between criticism and experience. Wigod is in basic agreement with Wasserman's approach: he wants to read the poem in the light of Keats's ideas, and he finds language such as "tension," "urgency," and "climax" suitable for describing the poem. But because he thinks that Keats had put the notion of the pleasure thermometer behind him by 1819, he rejects Wasserman's reliance upon it in interpretation. His own understanding of Keats's ideas leads him to conclude that "the climax occurs... in the final stanza. Wasserman is surely wrong in assuming that the climax occurs at the end of the 3rd stanza."[2] How does one know where a climax occurs? Wigod's confidence must rest upon his experience of the poem: there is no climax in the third stanza. The fact damages the entire structure of Wasserman's argument. But is there a climax in the final stanza? Does the metaphor of dramatic action do anything but misrepresent the poem—even as it presumably confuses perception of the poem?

When we turn to less systematic studies of the poem, we do not expect to find such consistent distance between criticism and experience. Nevertheless, an essay like Leo Spitzer's, in 1955, which purports to offer a "down-to-earth" analysis to contrast with Wasserman's, displays similar remoteness. Spitzer begins by asking and answering some elementary questions. "*What is the whole poem about*, in the simplest, most obvious terms... ? It is first of all a description of an urn—that is, it belongs to the genre, known to Occidental literature from Homer... to... Rilke, of the *ekphrasis*, the poetic description of a pictorial or sculptural work of art." He is thus led into his own description of the urn: it represents three scenes, "wild pursuit" (stanza 1), "tender wooing" (stanzas 2 and 3), and "solemn ceremony" (stanza 4). He then asks a second question: "What has Keats *failed* to discern clearly in the frieze?" He answers that Keats's questions in stanzas 1 and 4 express uncertainty, and he infers "that this uncertainty is centered about *historical identity*. Keats simply does not know who precisely the Greek protagonists are in the scene of the pursuit and of the sacrifice." Surely it will be an extraordinary reader of the poem who is satisfied with Spitzer's answers. His response to his first question is hardly the inevitable one. It is instead a historian's answer, and anticipates the historian's answer he provides for his second question. Perhaps also like a historian he ignores a second question that might preclude his own: is the described urn to be thought of as real? His automatic assumption of its reality leads him not only to describe the scenes and infer Keats's puzzlement over details, but also to conclude that Keats has "come upon a newly discovered (and unexamined) Greek urn," and that "still unravish'd bride" means "the urn... has not yet been violated by *archaeological or historical scholarship*."[3]

Experience of the poem suggests other answers. The poem concerns thought and feeling aroused by thinking about—possibly observing but also remembering and imagining—an urn. To the extent that scenes are evoked, two scenes rather than three are suggested, the second stanza beginning as a reflection upon what has been contemplated in the first, and both the second and third stanzas recalling images from the first. Keats's questions in the first stanza are exclamatory rather than interrogative; those in the fourth are meditative. The unravish'd bride is not threatened either by an archaeologist or by Quietness: both ingenuity and syntax yield before an image that comes as naturally as the leaves to a tree and that suggests shy and tender beauty. The most crucial of these points concerns Keats's questions in the first stanza. In his discussion Spitzer elaborates upon what he supposes to be Keats's uncertainty: "the first stanza contains a series of unresolved paradoxical oppositions as the bewildered, restless, nearly anguished and breathless seven questions of the poet show. His own quest...for historical identity...still prevents him from taking in the whole beauty of the work of art" (209). Spitzer repeats the point at another stage of his discussion. Yet he himself says in a footnote, wherein he objects to Wasserman's arbitrary association of a particular degree of empathy with interrogative constructions: "As to our St. I, the questions are interrogative in form alone; they have in reality the emotional value of exclamations ('What wild ecstasy?' could be printed 'What wild ecstasy!')" (212n). In this concession to experience, Spitzer undermines his general interpretation of the poem as an expression of conflict between historical and esthetic impulses.

II

If I. A. Richards is right about good poetry, it would seem that either the "Ode" is a bad poem or it has had bad readers. But the fact is that the critics in large part agree with one another. After having analyzed his paradoxes and interpreted the final lines of the poem, Brooks acknowledges that his "interpretation...differs little from past interpretations" (151). If we set several comments on the last lines side by side, they may seem more similar than different.

> If we know anything of human life we know that words which contain a message of peace in moments [of anguish] such as Keats was then enduring will not be easy words. They may be simple, but they will not be easy...; they must contain a great renunciation. Such a message is in the words: "Not my will, but Thine be done".... It is meaning of this kind, and of this order, that we must seek in "Beauty is truth, truth beauty," if we are ever to know what they meant to Keats or what Keats meant by them.
> . . . .

> The Beauty of which Keats speaks, or rather the priestlike consecrated Urn, is spiritual beauty, divine beauty; the beauty of eternal essence or spirit which is of God, in whom truth and beauty, beauty and truth are one.
>
> . . . .
>
> If a man is to "know" that beauty is truth, he must learn it not by direct experience, but indirectly; it must be told him by the urn ("to whom thou say'st"), for otherwise he could not know it, since it is not true of the sphere of his direct experience, and since no soul ever returns to tell the purpose for which the soul must abandon the mortal sphere.... The very bourne of heaven does not noisily cry out to man its existence; knowledge of its nature is forever available, but man can gain it only by a self-annihilating entrance into the bourne itself.
>
> . . . .
>
> The inference is, in effect, that imaginative constructions are valid glimpses of truth, and hence that the poet can commit himself to the visionary imagination.[4]

Broad agreement, agreement that ignores differences, ignores precision, is not likely to satisfy the individual critic; but it does in this case accord with the fact that Keats was a young man without fixed ideas. He could say that what the imagination seizes as beauty must be truth, but he could also say that poetry is not so fine a thing as philosophy. He could speak of the pious frauds of religion and also long for immortality and the finer tone. He was, as John Taylor said, a man of fits and starts—a man, that is, of negative capability. If we examine the language of a single letter, that to Benjamin Bailey of November 22, 1817, we arrive at contradiction rather than certainty. In the letter, Keats says that the imagination *seizes* beauty, which is truth; that the imagination *is* truth; that the imagination is a passion; and that all our passions (which include imagination, love, and other unnamed things) *create* essential beauty.[5] What we can be sure of is that despite Keats's admiration for consecutive reasoners—including the heirs of sensationalist psychology—he makes no effort either to put aside objections or to sift paradoxes. His metaphors—beauty, truth, imagination, sensation, passion—rush to express the knowledge that he feels in the pulse of his life. It seems probable that consecutive reasoning on our own part will express his belief less adequately than he does himself.

Some of his fellow romantics and successors can be observed indulging in a similar rush of metaphor to express similar views. In the preface to the *Lyrical Ballads* Wordsworth writes that the object of poetry is truth, and he seems momentarily to be saying what Kenneth Burke in *A Grammar of Motives* wants "beauty is truth" to mean: poetry is science. But then he goes on to say that the only restriction upon this object is that the poet must at the same time provide pleasure, and he refuses to think of this as a demeaning function: "Nor let this necessity of producing immediate pleasure be considered as a degradation of the poet's art. It is far otherwise. It is an acknowledgement of the beauty of the universe...." Having thus linked truth, pleasure, and beauty, he concludes: "we have no knowledge, that is, no general principles... but what has been built up by pleasure, and exists in us by pleasure alone...." In Shelley's *Defence of Poetry* occurs the same sort of language, most notably when he says that "to be a poet is to apprehend the true and the beautiful, in a word, the good...." When Matthew Arnold reviewed Keats's poetry, he had no trouble understanding what Keats meant: "To see things in their beauty is to see things in their truth, and Keats knew it." When that seemingly anti-romantic novelist Arnold Bennett wanted to describe art, he spoke romantic language: "The first and noblest aim of imaginative literature is... to render a coherent view of life's apparent incoherence, to give shape to the amorphous, to discover beauty which was hidden, to reveal essential truth."[6] We need not suppose that any of these men believed quite the same thing as Keats—or necessarily believed something different—but it is evident that they all took their views seriously. Consecutive reasoners might not be satisfied with their equations and substitutions, might find them absurd or paradoxical, might feel the need to translate them into rational thought. That is neither here nor there. It seems likely that Keats expected readers of his poem to apprehend its truth immediately. Perhaps they do. The range of religious, philosophic, esthetic interpretations of the poem are more or less satisfactory paraphrases of the nondiscursive wisdom that the poem reaches toward.

III

In speaking of Keats's ideas, we have gone outside the experience of the poem, and we have ignored the several problems posed by the last lines. Perhaps Keats believed that beauty is truth except on the occasion when he wrote the poem; perhaps he believed it but the poem fails to express it; perhaps he believed and intended everything that Wasserman wants of him but the poem says less or more. Discussions of the last lines concern the textual problem (how much does the urn say?), the grammatical problem (to whom does "ye" refer? to what does "that"?), the rhetorical problem (in what way do the lines relate to the rest of the poem?), the philosophical problem (what does the assertion mean?), and the biographical problem (what relationship does the assertion bear to Keats's ideas expressed elsewhere in and out of poetry?). No general agreement on any of these points appears imminent. In 1953 Alvin Whitley writes that "the transcripts [of the poem] obviously infer a single statement uttered by the urn without any interference on the part of the poet." In 1958 Jack Stillinger argues otherwise. Again in 1953 Wasserman asserts that we cannot, as Brooks would do, read the poem in isolation but must bring to bear upon it everything we know about Keats's thought; and he so arms himself. In 1958 Robert Berkelman suggests that those letters commonly linked to the poem—such letters as

Wasserman uses, which speak of imagination, beauty, and truth in one breath—refer to views that Keats was rejecting at the time he was writing the poem. But perhaps these problems will yield to some degree to experience of the poem. Among all the comments on the last lines, the most extraordinary is Robert Adams's opinion, in 1953, that "the force of the last lines is vindictive": the poet is turning upon the urn and its figures and saying, that's all *you* know. Such an improbable opinion points the way, for the lines have a tone that is the reverse of vindictive. They have the same calm slow rhythm, the same repetition of phrasing, the same heightened language, the same loveliness of sound, the same high and solemn thought of most of the rest of the poem. They exist in the context of the earlier lines, and sustain and complete them. These qualities of tone count for more than the position of quotation marks or the reference of a pronoun—just as they count for more than question marks in stanza one. Their weight has helped to make most of the interpretations end by saying very much the same sort of thing. Given the calm strength of rhythm throughout the poem, it is easiest to believe with C. M. Bowra, Perkins, Whitley, and others that the last two lines belong to the urn, which speaks a high thought for Keats.[7] But given the slight coloring of melancholy throughout the poem, it is also easy to believe that some sort of qualification is implicit—one which inclines Murry, Wasserman, and others to give the last part of the lines to Keats, who makes clear that the thought is indeed a special one. If we ask whether Keats's opposition to didacticism in poetry could have allowed him to speak the last part in his own person, or even allowed him to let the urn speak for him, we answer that the tone of the last lines is simply nondidactic. If we ask whether "ye" refers to the urn and its figures or to mankind, we answer that the tone makes either reference yield the same implication of a truth at once complete and partial. Perhaps more than anything else, the argument over the last lines has reflected each critic's refusal to be satisfied with the inadequate paraphrases of his predecessors. Nothing less than the poem will suffice except his own paraphrase.

IV

Apparently the critic should be a poet: he must find the right metaphor. Keats asks whether the unravish'd bride, foster-child, and sylvan historian illuminate his urn; the critic must ask whether paradox, drama, and interrogation describe the poem. The critic has even the opportunity to write an organic poem: he can extend his metaphor. But criticism is not poetry: the urn in Keats's poem is at once described and created by his metaphors, whereas the poem the critic writes about exists outside his essay; poetic metaphor has an autonomy that critical metaphor must eschew. The critical task is more modest—less poetical, less scientific—than we would like it to be; it must divide attention between its own language and the independent poem that it cannot create, duplicate, or alter.

Though the critic may want to come armed to the poem, he must constantly surrender to the poem; he must refuse to create his own poem.

An important critical poem of our day is organicism. But will organicism really tell us whether the image of the foster-child is a defect? Or can it really assure us that Wasserman's discovered trinity of tree-lover-song is a virtue? If we have a hard time answering such questions, we can console ourselves with the thought that all the while Keats's poem waits for us.

4 Swinburne Corrupted

IN 1953 JOHN S. MAYFIELD, collector of literary manuscripts and latterly curator of same, published an essay entitled "Swinburne's Boo" in which he presented some new facts about Jane Faulkner, the woman in Swinburne's life. Edmund Gosse had told the story of the disastrous love affair all too briefly in his biography, and Mayfield set out to learn more. What he discovered—and he surely deserves thanks for providing light relief in a world that inclines to be serious—was that Jane Faulkner was ten years old at the time of Swinburne's proposal. He offered the fact to various Swinburne experts, and more than one of them said that they would not be surprised at anything Swinburne did. But they were being frivolous, and *Lolita* was still in the future. Mayfield was certain that Gosse was wrong, as Gosse had been wrong before, and Jane Faulkner was not the woman of the case. He did not say anything in his essay about Swinburne's fondness for children, which reached extraordinary poetic depths in the Putney years, and he presumably did not know of the letter to Richard Monckton Milnes of 27 December 1862 (the same year as the Jane Faulkner affair) in which Swinburne says of Milne's seven-year-old daughter, "I hope Florey has not forgotten her conditional engagement to me in ten years' time *if* I am rich enough to give her a trousseau of rubies." Later investigators have followed Mayfield and have gone on to identify and describe the actual lucky woman. I think they and he have gone wrong. I think the more facts we have acquired about Swinburne, the more we have corrupted him.[1]

I

The major piece of work was done by Cecil Lang in an article published in 1959. His first task was to deplore the original carelessness of Gosse:

> A generous man would commiserate rather than condemn him for venturing a guess that must have seemed to have substantial and visible foundations, and, though this is more difficult, one can even forgive him for asserting as fact what he ought to have tendered as hypothesis. Far, far more culpable than his hapless misidentification of

an infant girlchild as the inaccessible Innominata is, as we shall see, his misreading of "The Triumph of Time," the well-known poem in which Swinburne laments his unhappy fate.²

The main line of Lang's argument runs thus. First, it is certain that Swinburne did have an unhappy love affair. Gosse reports Swinburne telling him so, and a letter to Gosse in 1875 about Gosse's marriage says so: "It must be the best thing that can befall a man to win and keep the woman that he loves while yet young; at any rate I can congratulate my friend on his good hap without any too jealous afterthought of the reverse experience which left my own young manhood 'a barren stock'" (3:51). Secondly, it is clear that "The Triumph of Time" is exactly autobiographical, and the evidence again lies with Gosse, who says Swinburne told him so, and with a letter to William Michael Rossetti of 9 October 1866 which says so (1:197). Now, says Lang, the love-situation described in the poem is as follows. The woman does not love the poet ("O love, my love, had you loved but me?"); she has chosen another man ("Flesh of his flesh, but heart of my heart"); the poet's hopes have been destroyed at one blow ("Whose whole life's love goes down in a day"—presumably at the announcement of betrothal or marriage to the other man); but the poet will say nothing, not even declaring his own love ("I will say no word that a man might say" and "Yea, if I could, would I have you see | My very love of you filling me?"); and the woman does not even suspect that the poet loves her ("I shall never tell you on earth"). These details, says Lang (the first of which is implicit rather than explicit in his argument), contradict the details that Gosse reports Swinburne telling him, namely that he declared his passion and the woman laughed in his face. Gosse used scattered phrases in the poem to embellish the story as Swinburne gave it to him, but he did not see the contradictions.

Lang then extracts from the poem a few details that might be helpful in identifying the woman of the case, notably that she seems to be associated with music ("I shall loathe sweet tunes," "I shall hate sweet music"). A cancelled draft of a line for stanza 20 suggests that she and the poet may have composed songs together: "Songs we had written." Lang then goes to Swinburne's late play *The Sisters*, whose hero, Reginald Clavering, Swinburne admitted was a self-portrait. The hero is loved secretly by a cousin who grew up with him, rode horses with him, and climbed with him; and he secretly loves her, but in language reminiscent of "The Triumph of Time" he refuses (for a while) "to say what any man may say."³

Who was the woman? Lang suggests Mary Gordon. She was Swinburne's cousin, about three years younger than he, and the two of them grew up together on the Isle of Wight, riding and climbing together many a time. She and Swinburne composed verses together and she often played music for him. A letter of his of 31 December 1863 says that her playing of Handel put him into an ecstasy. It was possibly during his visit with her at this time—presumably after the end of the year—that she told him she was going to be married. She did marry in 1865. The poem was composed between 1862 and 1866. Lang also points to two other poems which tell of a disaster in love: "Thalassius," the admittedly autobiographical poem of some years later, and "A Leave-Taking," which seems to have been composed at the same time as "The Triumph of Time" and in which is emphasized the unawareness of the woman that the poet loves her.

Lang thinks that the case for Mary Gordon is "almost irresistible," but he does admit that it is far from perfect, and he points to some things that can be said against it, mainly Mary Gordon's own disclaimer that there was any romantic attachment between her and Swinburne, and the utter absence of any direct evidence. She herself describes a seemingly prosaic letter that Swinburne wrote to her upon her betrothal, and no correspondence between them exists for the next quarter of a century (though she did have the opportunity to destroy any letters she wanted to destroy). According to Gosse, she rarely saw him after the early 1860s. All of this, of course, may bespeak the ignorance of the beloved and the vow of the poet never to tell her on earth.

II

Nine years after Lang's article, Jean Overton Fuller published her critical biography of Swinburne. She follows Mayfield and Lang and contributes some fascinating information about Mary Gordon. Part of her task is to trace the flagellant element in Swinburne's life. She offers no clear evidence that either as a child at home or as a boy at Eton Swinburne himself was beaten or that at either place he enjoyed being beaten or enjoyed seeing other boys beaten. But there is material from later life to suggest the possibility, and Fuller accepts it. When Swinburne was thirty years old he wrote to George Powell, who likewise was interested in flagellation, that if he visited Eton again there were two things he would most like to see, the river and the flogging block. In an earlier letter to Monckton Milnes, a letter devoted to flagellation, he says: "I can boast that of all the swishings I ever had up to seventeen and over, I never had one for a false quantity in my life.... One comfort is, I made it up in arithmetic, so my tutor never wanted reasons for making rhymes between his birch and my body" (1:78). Late in life he published an ode to celebrate the 450th anniversary of Eton, and privately he wrote another one about flagellation there. He did have difficulties of a "rebellious kind" (Gosse's words) at Eton, and Fuller surmises that he had to leave because his perverse pleasure in flagellation became apparent to the authorities. She makes the same surmise about his leaving Oxford.[4]

It is evident, at any rate, that with the beginning of Swinburne's life in London in 1860 he became involved with people who had a most active interest in flagellation. He wrote numerous letters to friends on the subject, he wrote near-pornographic novels and poems on the subject, he wrote serious poems in which the sadomasochistic element is only more heavily veiled, and he visited brothels where flagellation was performed. Of all this material that Fuller refers to, two items are crucial. The first comes from the novel *Love's Cross Currents*. One of the two heroes of the novel is Reginald Harewood, who as a boy is often beaten by his father. Fuller quotes what may be a trial fragment that describes the feelings of Redgie's sister for him:

> But her liking was for her brother Reginald.... Each of Redgie's flogging was a small drama to her; she followed with excitement each cut of the birch on her brother's skin, and tasted a nervous pleasure when every stroke drew blood. (72)

The same fragment describes a later occasion when after witnessing the death of an admirer she meets Redgie and "took him round with her arms and kissed him, laughing" (73). The other is "Dolores":

> Cold eyelids that hide like a jewel
> Hard eyes that grow soft for an hour;
> The heavy white limbs, and the cruel
> Red mouth like a venomous flower;
> When these are gone by with their glories,
> What shall rest of thee then, what remains,
> O mystic and sombre Dolores,
> Our Lady of Pain?

Fuller thinks that the disguise in *Love's Cross Currents* is as thin as the disguise that Lang see through in *The Sisters*. Redgie's sister is Swinburne's cousin—for did not Mary Gordon and Swinburne grow up together almost as brother and sister? And if Mary Gordon is Redgie's sister, she is also Dolores as well as the beloved in "The Triumph of Time." Fuller caps her point by referring to the crucial letter to William Michael Rossetti that Lang uses all too casually. Rossetti, says Fuller, was proposing to Swinburne a special edition of three poems that seemed intimately related: "Dolores," "The Garden of Proserpine," and "Hesperia." Swinburne replied to the proposal: "I should not like to bracket 'Dolores' and the two following ('The Garden of Proserpine' and 'Hesperia' as they appeared in *Poems and Ballads* that year) as you propose. I ought (if I did) to couple with them in front harness 'The Triumph of Time' etc., as they ('The Triumph of Time,' etc.) express that state of feeling the reaction from which is expressed in 'Dolores.' Were I to rechristen these three as trilogy, I should have to rename many earlier poems as acts in the same play" (1:197). Thus "The Triumph of Time" and "Dolores" describe two aspects of the affair with Mary Gordon.

Along with this analysis, Fuller tells us some things about Mary Gordon that other biographers did not emphasize or did not know. Two items are of special importance. First, on 2 October 1864 Swinburne wrote to Mary Gordon about an accident he had while bathing in the sea, and he said he was buffeted about "and got so thrashed and licked that I might have been ——— in ——'s clutches." Mary Gordon published this letter in her memoir of Swinburne's boyhood and said that the blank spaces referred to two characters in a story. The story was in fact Swinburne's recently written and as yet unpublished novel *Lesbia Brandon* (so called). In it Bertie Seyton is a much beaten pupil of Mr. Denham's. Clearly Mary Gordon had read the novel in manuscript and might have been able to infer from it, if from nothing else, Swinburne's proclivities. What else might she have read? What else might have passed between her and Swinburne? What sort of woman was she? Secondly, Fuller brings forward some unpublished letters from Mary Gordon to Swinburne dating from the nineties. They are addressed, childish fashion, to "Cy merest dozen" ("My dearest cousin"). The body of each letter continues in much the same manner. One letter reads in part:

> You will be scored to death of so much dribbling but one point in your last letter to me I must observe on. Cow, my nousin, do you meally rean to *stand there*, and tell me that the timehonoured and traditional pode of nunishment is disused at Eton? I am more upturbed and perset than you can imagine. I fear . . . that we may expect a capid deradence of England's screatest ghool (272).

Fuller is not ready to say that Mary Gordon was Dolores in a full sadistic sense, but it is clear to her that Mary Gordon was like Redgie's sister and that she and Swinburne consciously shared an interest in flagellation. To what extent Swinburne elaborated upon their interest and their relationship in his enflamed imagination is impossible to say. But Fuller can add some reasonable conjecture to the story that "The Triumph of Time" tells. She emphasizes the consanguinity and closeness of the Swinburne and Gordon families and the mutually known fact of Swinburne's nervous constitution. Perhaps Mary Gordon's family told her that marriage to Swinburne would be inadvisable. Perhaps she had some degree of intimacy with him, or encouraged him unwittingly, and then was forced to turn away. ("Had the chance been with us that has not been".)

To round off her argument Fuller examines the physical scene of certain poems, chiefly "The Triumph of Time," "Hesperia," and "The Sundew," and concludes that it is the Isle of Wight, the home of both Swinburne and Mary Gordon. The lovers held hands at the sea there, as "The Triumph of Time" says they did.

At about the same time as Fuller's book there appeared a series of articles by F. A. C. Wilson, who accepts the identification of Mary Gordon as the beloved and who provides further details on the flagellant element in Mary Gordon's career and offers to show that characters and situations in her novels are veiled allusions to her relationship with Swinburne—so heavily veiled as to bear the right meaning only to the already persuaded. Latterly there has been published Philip Henderson's biography, in which Lang, Fuller, and Wilson are accepted virtually without question and entirely without addition.[5]

In sum Mary Gordon is now ensconsed as the innominata, although there is not a shred of direct evidence of an attachment that was more than cousinly, superficial, and slightly naughty. The fatal event in Swinburne's life is thereby very nearly reduced to the parting of two flagellants. Surely for even the most sympathetic person there is much to criticize and scorn in Swinburne, and the juvenile perversities he indulged with Simeon Solomon, George Powell, Mary Gordon, and others—in letters, in conversation, and possibly in action—are vulgar to say the least. So are many of the poems that reflect this aspect of his life. Yet Swinburne was a great poet, and unless he constructed high poetic emotions out of superficial experience, "The Triumph of Time" and other poems reflect an anguish that the silly Mary Gordon could not have aroused with either a friendly or a parting blow.

III

The argument against Lang, Fuller, and Wilson begins with the letter to William Michael Rossetti. Two important points can be seen in the passage quoted above: first, that there may have been more than one woman in the "play," so that the women in "The Triumph of Time" and "Dolores" are not necessarily the same woman, a possibility that Fuller is content to ignore, and secondly, that a good many poems are involved—"Dolores," "The Garden of Proserpine," "Hesperia," "The Triumph of Time," and some unidentified ones that come under the rubric "etc." How curious that Lang should rest his case with little more than an examination of "The Triumph of Time"! It would seem necessary at the very least to look at several poems for their mutual implications, and it would also seem wise to bear in mind Swinburne's remark in the "Dedicatory Epistle" in the first volume of his poems that some of the poems in *Poems and Ballads* are "photographs from life" and others are "sketches from imagination" and that his critics had absolutely no success in distinguishing the one kind from the other (1:vii). Whether all the poems identified in the letter to Rossetti are to be thought of as photographic would seem to be open to question, and so likewise whether "The Triumph of Time" is to be thought of as more exactly photographic than other poems, named or unnamed.

With these things in mind, I would like first of all to look at "A Leave-Taking." It is commonly thought to deal with the affair, and it is the only poem other than "The Triumph of Time" that Lang himself makes more than the most perfunctory use of.

> Let us go hence, my songs; she will not hear.
> Let us go hence together without fear;
> Keep silence now, for singing-time is over,
> And over all old things and all things dear.

She loves not you nor me as all we love her.
Yea, though we sang as angels in her ear,
   She would not hear.

Let us rise up and part; she will not know.
Let us go seaward as the great winds go,
Full of blown sand and foam; what help is here?
There is no help, for all these things are so,
And all the world is bitter as a tear.
And how these things are, though ye strove to show,
   She would not know.

Let us go home and hence; she will not weep.
We gave love many dreams and days to keep,
Flowers without scent, and fruits that would not grow,
Saying, "If thou wilt, thrust in thy sickle and reap."
All is reaped now; no grass is left to mow;
And we that sowed, though all we fell on sleep,
   She would not weep.

Let us go hence and rest; she will not love.
She shall not hear us if we sing hereof,
Nor see love's ways, how sore they are and steep.
Come hence, let be, lie still; it is enough,
Love is a barren sea, bitter and deep;
And though she saw all heaven in flower above,
   She would not love.

Let us give up, go down; she will not care.
Though all the stars made gold of all the air,
And the sea moving saw before it move
One moon-flower making all the foam-flowers fair;
Though all those waves went over us, and drove
Deep down the stifling lips and drowning hair,
   She would not care.

Let us go hence, go hence, she will not see.
Sing all once more together; surely she,
She too, remembering days and words that were
Will turn a little toward us, sighing; but we,
We are hence, we are gone, as though we had not been there.
Nay, and though all men seeing had pity on me,
   She would not see.

Recall now the five central elements of the affair that Lang draws from "The Triumph of Time": the woman does not love the poet; she has chosen another man; the poet's hopes have been destroyed at one blow; the poet will say nothing, not even declaring his own love; and the woman does not suspect that the poet loves her. "A Leave-Taking" can at most be said to allude to only the first and fourth of these. It also bears some similarity to "The Triumph of Time" in its image of the drowning poet. In other respects it is different. The woman is not at all "my sweet" as she is in "The Triumph of Time." She seems incapable of love and is certainly incapable of pity. Perhaps she is incapable only of loving the poet, though the emphasis suggests a general incapacity; but a woman who cannot love a man might still be able to pity him, and she cannot do this. Secondly, the poet seems to be the better person of the two, which reverses, it would appear, the situation in "The Triumph of Time." He is worthy of pity here, and the woman is pitiless, and in "The Triumph of Time" her life is as "sweet as perfume and pure as prayer" and his deserves no pity: "For the worst is this after all; if they knew me, | Not a soul upon earth would pity me." Thirdly, the poet's silence includes rather more than a withholding of a declaration of love, and perhaps does not include that at all. His silence is the conventional poetic silence that poets have long professed to fall into, or have urged upon themselves, with the failure of love. Love inspires their song; with the failure of love their song will die. In "A Leave-Taking" there is no evidence that the poet did or did not declare his passion; all that we know is that he is unloved and will give up poetry. He seems further to say that the woman's inability to love, inability to be moved by lovesong, is reason for his silence. If it were otherwise with her, perhaps he could go on singing—presumably of unrequited love—and move her to love him. The last stanza suggests that he might touch her with an altogether glorious expression of his love. The poet may well have declared his passion and he would certainly even now declare it poetically if he saw any hope that the woman would respond.

If it is curious how different the poem is from what Lang thinks it to be, what is still more curious is that it describes a situation rather like that which Gosse reports in his biography: Swinburne proposed, and the woman laughed in his face. The poet was worthy of love or pity, and the woman was pitiless and loveless. Perhaps all that Gosse had wrong was the name?

The contradictions in detail between "A Leave-Taking" and "The Triumph of Time" make clear how difficult our task is. If "The Triumph of Time" is not necessarily more exactly autobiographical than certain other poems, and if aside from the poems mentioned in the Rossetti letter (and perhaps "Faustine," of which more later) we cannot say positively which other poems are involved, we seem to have two unsatisfactory possibilities open to us: (1) to construct the affair relying solely on the named poems, and assume that other poems that support them are also exactly autobiographical, and others that contradict are sketches from imagination, or (2) from a judicious culling of poems that seem to have an autobiographical note, to construct the outline of a situation that affords no contradictions. Lang himself says that no one could read "The Triumph of Time" "without the moral certainty that it is an authentic *cri du coeur*" (125) and thus one could say of "The Triumph of Time" and "A Leave-Taking" (if the latter seems like a *cri du coeur* too) that they do not contradict each other if they concern two different women in the "play." The hazard of this approach is that one critic's moral certainty is not another's. I would say that of all Swinburne's poetry the one poem that cries most powerfully and authentically is "Anactoria." And how could I read it as exactly autobiographical without doing some sort of psychological transformation? The poem must be at once a photograph from life and a sketch from imagination. And what a strange poet it is whose most powerful feeling comes through a free translation of another poet's work! The difficulties are, I think, insuperable, at least if one wants the sort of fact that Lang, Fuller, and Wilson are after.

A glance at a few other poems may seem to multiply the problems. "The Triumph of Time" itself does not afford so clear a reading as Lang supposes. The first stanza is crucial.

> Before our lives divide forever,
> While time is with us and hands are free,
> (Time, swift to fasten and swift to sever
> Hand from hand, as we stand by the sea)
> I will say no word that a man might say
> Whose whole life's love goes down in a day;
> For this could never have been; and never,
> Though the gods and the years relent, shall be.

Lang seems to read this stanza so that "this" in line 7 refers to saying no word that a man might say. The exact autobiographical meaning, then, is that the love that has preoccupied all of Swinburne's youth and manhood has gone down in a single day, perhaps with the revelation of betrothal or marriage, and he will never say a word about his loss, never declare to the woman the fact that he has loved her. It does seem easy, though, to read the stanza differently, so that "this" refers to consummated love, and the autobiographical meaning becomes something else. Swinburne's attachment is one that he sees could never have been consummated, and he will say nothing of the sort that a man might say whose position was otherwise—who had reasonable hopes and saw them dashed. The occasion perhaps remains the same—the woman's betrothal or marriage. We may assume, then, that the woman knew of his love, if not of the depths of it, but may not have loved him. Later in the poem we see that he has dreamed of fulfillment even though fulfillment was impossible ("Had the chance been with us that has not been"). His silence mentioned in later stanzas is rhetorical, as in "A Leave-Taking," and it refers to a refusal to vex the woman now either with his continued love or with the disaster to his soul that has overtaken him (lines 165ff., 187ff., and the last two stanzas). Such an interpretation does not seem to be altogether satisfactory, but it does seem at least as satisfactory as Lang's. It suggests that we may not be able to see straight even if we have the exact photograph in hand.

Another poem of considerable interest in the case is "Félise." This poem has no more certain a claim than "A Leave-Taking" to belong to the "play," but two lines in it are similar to the third and fourth lines in "The Triumph of Time": "We stand on either side the sea,| Stretch hands, blow kisses, laugh and lean." If the echo has any force (and I think it has as much as Lang's echo from *The Sisters* quoted above), it provides further confusion in the affair. But in a poet notable for recurrent phrasing, argument from echo is hazardous (even though there are at least two other phrases in the poem that recall "The Triumph of Time": "the gulf is strait" and "one ruined thing"), and there is additional reason that will be mentioned later for thinking that "Félise" is relevant. The confusion is this. Swinburne refers to the woman in the poem as his "sweet" and he has loved her unavailingly, as with the woman in "The Triumph of Time"; but she is also his "snake," Dolores-like, and between them has lain "the dust of many strange desires." She is also Gosse's laughing woman in the respect that "Love was a jest last year, you said." And there is no other man between them: today the poet's own love is dead and the woman loves him.

Next in the sum of problems is chronology. Swinburne was almost as closemouthed about the composition of his poems as he was about the supposed love affair, and very few of the poems in *Poems and Ballads* can be dated with any precision. Lang gives the terminal dates for the composition of "The Triumph of Time" as 1862 and 1866, and even if he is right about Mary Gordon it remains a surmise on his part that Swinburne wrote the poem immediately after his visit to her late in 1863, presumably at the beginning of 1864. Now in the progress of the "play" the relationship with Dolores follows chronologically upon that with the beloved—assuming or even not assuming that they are two different women; but one of the relevant poems about a Dolores figure does not fit easily into the scheme if we use Lang's dating. The poem is "Faustine." In "Notes on Poems and Reviews," written in 1866 in reply to the critics of *Poems and Ballads*, Swinburne links "Faustine" with "Dolores,"[6] and the women in the two poems are cut from the same cloth as actual and mythological ladies of pain. The actuality of Faustine is certainly the greater, and the account of her closes with a bitter comment about the hapless man who might love her with a real love. "Faustine" cannot be dated precisely, but its terminus ad quem is May 1862, for it appeared in the *Spectator* for May 31st of that year. This gives the first four months of 1862 or before for Mary Gordon to tell Swinburne she cannot have him and for Swinburne to turn for solace to Faustine-Dolores and write for the *Spectator*. Such chronology would upset Lang's surmise that "The Triumph of Time" was written in white heat after the 1863 visit, if nothing else. Lang does not explain why he gives 1862 as the terminus a quo for "The Triumph of Time," and the argument here suggests that early 1862 is the likely terminus ad quem. Perhaps slightly contributory to such dating is Swinburne's reference to his "young manhood" in his letter to Gosse about the disaster in love, and his assertion in "Hesperia" that "too soon did I love it, and lost love's rose." He was already twenty-five in 1862. Gosse in his *Life* gives 1862 for the date of composition of "The Triumph of Time," though without evidence. In support of Lang's surmise and a later date for the composition, it must be said that "Dolores" was composed in the spring of 1865. Of the date of composition of "Félise" all that is known is that it was written at least some while before 21 March 1866, on which date Swinburne wrote to Ruskin that it was "rather a favourite child of mine" (1:160). All these chronological problems are further complicated by the fact that Swinburne was writing about cruel ladies well before 1862, and the psychological course of his sexual life—which will be elaborated upon below—doubtless has a more subtle chronology than the limited, reasoned chronology of the "play" implies.

Lastly something must be said about the supposed setting of the love poems on the Isle of Wight. I am inclined to grant considerable force to this argument of Fuller's, partly because of ignorance on my part of the English landscape; but there are doubtful aspects of it. Swinburne's settings tend to be more poetical than realistic, and the sea's edge is a conventional poetic place for lovers. Furthermore, he was profoundly attached to the sea and to his home on the Isle of Wight. Had he fallen in love with a woman at Blackfriars Bridge, it is not improbable that he would have transported the affair to the seaside. There are poems like "The Triumph of Time" and "Félise" in which the lovers are beside the sea but the setting is otherwise imprecise. There are poems like "A Leave-Taking" in which love is a sea and the poet flees seaward, but it might as readily be the North Sea or the Atlantic. And there is "Dolores," which has no setting in the ordinary sense but which implies city rather than country or seaside for contemporary worship at the shrine: "Fierce midnights," "house not of gold but of gain," "chapels unknown of the sun." Of course it is true that Swinburne saw Mary Gordon in Northumberland and London as well as on the Isle of Wight, but the matter remains unclear.

If with all these problems in mind we return to Swinburne's letter to Gosse on the disaster, we see how little help this most reliable of all documents in the case is in describing his love. We cannot begin "reversing" the details of Gosse's situation as described therein without running into difficulty about how exactly and completely the reversal can and ought and was meant to be taken.

IV

Before trying to resolve these problems, I would like to consider the question that is at the heart of Fuller's analysis: whether the women of "The Triumph of Time" and "Dolores" are one and the same. Fuller herself makes no detailed comparison of the poems or of other related poems, nor does she ask herself whether her view stands in fundamental contradiction to Lang's. But Dolores is surely a woman who laughs to scorn ("O lips full of lust and of laughter," "The life and the love thou despisest," "Wilt thou smile as a woman disdaining," etc.), and in this respect she belongs rather more to Gosse's account than to Lang's; and her "house not of gold but of gain" seems at the very farthest remove from the "life sweet as perfume and pure as prayer" of the woman in "The Triumph of Time." So profoundly different are the two women that they could be the same woman only to a much more wildly enflamed imagination than Fuller ascribes to Swinburne. If the two poems refer to the same woman, it would suggest that Swinburne could not be trusted at all to distinguish between photograph and imagination, and that any reliance upon his word would be folly.

Yet something has to be said for Fuller's view that she herself has not said. In "The Triumph of Time" itself there are two curious passages. The first begins at line 179.

> My thoughts are as dead things, wrecked and whirled
> Round and round in a gulf of the sea;
> And still, through the sound and the straining stream,
> Through the coil and chafe, they gleam in a dream,
> The bright fine lips so cruelly curled,
> And strange swift eyes where the soul sits free.

I think the sense of this (and it will be strengthened by some later comment) is that in the death of love the poet is drawn toward lust; his beloved is succeeded in his thoughts by Dolores. But the passage is so intimately interwoven with the poet's address to his beloved, especially in the lines that immediately follow it, that they seem to be addressed to her, and the reader might be forgiven for thinking so in spite of assurance to the contrary. Then in the next to last stanza of the poem comes an image that clearly concerns the beloved but that describes a kind of love that seems at least halfway in the direction of lust for Dolores:

> But if we had loved each other—O sweet,
> Had you felt, lying under the palms of your feet,
> The heart of my heart, beating harder with pleasure
> To feel you tread it to dust and death—

It is assuredly not the pure love through which the poet "might have stood with the souls that stand | In the sun's light" earlier.

To meet these embarrassments within "The Triumph of Time," one might say (provisionally) that Swinburne's pure love for his beloved had its admixture of impurity, as happens with all men; and if his impure feeling inadvertently disrupts the unity of the poem, it does not either turn the woman into Dolores or render Swinburne unreliable in his perception of character. The lapse is a lapse of feeling. Such a solution keeps the woman of "The Triumph of Time" distinct from Dolores.

But then there is Félise. She is neither so pure as the woman of "The Triumph of Time" nor so impure as Dolores. Last year she was certainly thought worthy of love, but in the very inception of love the poet wanted her "subtly warm, and half perverse." And again one has to say that if all these women are one woman, Swinburne was madder than we think and utterly unreliable. Or is Félise a third woman, and is it simply coincidental that part of the relationship there (the man loving and the woman not loving) is the same as the situation as rendered with variations by Gosse and Lang?

My own basic assumption is that Swinburne was not mad and that the radical differences in portraiture of the women in the three poems imply different women insofar as the poems can be taken, or were meant, as photographs from life from which we can infer biographical fact (though not necessarily biographical fact about Swinburne). Relying in this way upon Swinburne's sanity, I would then go to his essay "Notes on Poems and Reviews" for some elucidation of the problem. Neither Lang nor Fuller makes any use of it, though it is an essential document. There, in a discussion of "Dolores," he says:

> I have striven here to express that transient state of spirit through which a man may be supposed to pass, foiled in love and weary of loving, but not yet in sight of rest; seeking refuge in those 'violent delights' which 'have violent ends,' in fierce and frank sensualities.... (12)

This passage itself suggests that at least two women are involved. Swinburne then goes on to comment upon "The Garden of Proserpine," which, he says, describes a succeeding state of spirit: "that brief total pause of passion and thought when the spirit, without fear or hope of good things or evil, hungers and thirsts only after the perfect sleep." And this state is followed by one other, an unstable condition from which there are lapses into the situation described in "Dolores." This last state offers "a stingless love, an innocuous desire" such as is described in "Hesperia":

> The worship of desire has ceased; the mad commotion of sense has stormed itself out; the spirit, clear of the old regret that drove it upon such violent ways for a respite, healed of the fever that wasted it in the search for relief among fierce fancies and tempestuous pleasures, dreams now of truth discovered and repose attained. (12-13)

In all the discussion Swinburne offers no clarification of the foiled love and the weariness of loving except possibly in a reference to "the martyr's ardour of selfless love, an unprofitable flame that burnt out and did no service" (13), which seems meant to describe the foiled lover's attitude and its gradual descent into weariness.

All the poems that have been analyzed here fall into the "play" as outlined in the "Notes." "Félise" is the one poem that dilates upon the double situation of the man foiled in love and weary of loving. "The Triumph of Time" and "A Leave-Taking" are preoccupied with the foiled lover, and "The Triumph of Time" looks ahead briefly to the descent into lust (in the passage beginning at line 179). Admittedly the loves in "Félise" and "A Leave-Taking" remain different from the love in "The Triumph of Time," even though Swinburne's broad outline covers all three, and an explanation of that aspect of the matter is still to be found. The next state is that described in "Dolores" and also "Faustine," and it figures largely in the latter part of "Hesperia," where Swinburne describes again his subjection to Dolores and his flight from her. In the "Notes" he says that the huntress Dolores "follows her flying prey" (13).

The succeeding state, the "perfect sleep" of "The Garden of Proserpine," presents no immediate problem. It is in "Hesperia," which describes the final state, that the identity of the beloved comes into focus again. It might appear that the woman of the poem is the same woman as in "The Triumph of Time." "O my sweet," the poet says to her; in the last lines she is "holy"; and "out of the distance of dreams... comes back to me... the delight of thy face." The relationship, though, has changed, in the manner that "Notes" describes, and the beloved has pity for him and can succor him with her pity in a way that seemed impossible in "The Triumph of Time." There, though he was "swift to follow," he could not; and he did not deserve pity. It is uncertain, however, whether the poet and his beloved are together except in imagination. "Not a dream, not a dream is the kiss of thy mouth," he says, but this is perhaps an expression of the intensity of his thought. Is the woman the beloved of the past reunited with him? Is she a memory of that woman? Or is she a goddess arising out of the poet's spiritual death and inevitably owing something to his earlier loves and aspirations? She seems like a ghost, and the poet himself and the love in his heart are like "a ghost rearisen."

It is evident that the "Notes" have not solved our problems, but their helpfulness may be more apparent if we look at one further poem in their light. "Thalassius" was written a dozen or more years after the other poems, and it may be thought to be less trustworthy in its autobiographical reference, and the mythical mold into which the material is cast may seem to be uninviting. But Swinburne regarded it as a spiritual autobiography, and the mythical element is no more pronounced than that of "The Garden of Proserpine" and perhaps "Hesperia" and "Dolores." What is striking indeed is that in the "Notes" Swinburne gives "Dolores" quite as mythical a quality ("symbolic" is the word he uses, 12) as "Hesperia" and "The Garden of Proserpine," and it is doubtless the psychological cynicism of latter-day critics and readers that refuses to take the poem as much more than a disguise for perverse sexuality. In any event, one can abstract from "Thalassius" something of the same story that appears in the other poems. The poet loves, and love fails, and he descends into lust, and is redeemed.

But there are differences and additions. The most striking of these is that the account of love is described as a meeting with the young god Love, and the god himself has the snake-like hair and tongue that have been associated with the impure Félise and the vicious Dolores and that have even seemed to mar the portrait of the woman in "The Triumph of Time." There would appear to be two main implications of the use of the god rather than the goddess for the reader to choose between. The first is that Swinburne's sexual interests were homosexual. If he was a homosexual, the *cri du coeur* of "Anactoria" might have a more apparent explanation, and the story of a fateful proposal or withheld proposal to one woman or another would be a fabrication or an exaggeration or the precipitant of true love, and the sex of the beloved in the other autobiographical poems would be mere disguise. I doubt if this view need detain us long. Lang says in his edition of the *Letters* that he does not know whether Swinburne was "overtly homosexual" (1:xlix), and what he presumably means is that in the course of many years of study he has not found documentary evidence that Swinburne ever had sexual relations with another man. By the same token we do not know whether Swinburne was overtly heterosexual. He was supposed to have been a virgin at the time that D.G. Rossetti set Adah Menken upon him, and that lady said she could not bring him "up to the scratch." What went on in the brothels is unknown (except that, on Gosse's word, Swinburne was whipped), and a letter in 1865 which dilates upon "Dolores" also dilates upon male flogging. It is of course a fact that such flogging is not necessarily accompanied by direct sexual activity, and Swinburne's writings on flagellation tend to be pure in that respect. At any rate, insofar as Swinburne had any sexual interests at all, (and Gosse in his private essay on him thinks that his "generative instinct was very feebly developed"), the total volume of poetry outwardly concerned with variations of heterosexual love and the number of letters that suggest homosexual interest would seem to argue that he was bisexual.[7] The reliance upon the young god Love in "Thalassius" does not in this respect mean that the search for the beloved woman is a mistake.

What seems to me to be the likely alternative reason for the use of the male god is that Swinburne wants to keep clear of the ordinary heterosexual implications of a meeting with Love and also—in the succeeding lines—of any perverse heterosexual implications. He wants to say clearly and unequivocally that love in its actuality is corrupting and deathly, and that the course of true love must ever run thus:

> I am he that was thy lord before thy birth,
> I am he that is thy lord till thou turn earth:
> I make the night more dark, and all the morrow
> Dark as the night whose darkness was my breath:
> O fool, my name is sorrow;
> Thou fool, my name is death.

Such a view of love gives a larger implication to Swinburne's phrase "foiled in love" in the "Notes." Swinburne need not have been rebuffed by a woman; he need not have seen a loved woman choose unwittingly another man; he was before anything else an inevitable victim of a cruel god. As he and the god walk together in "Thalassius," "suddenly Love's face turned, | And in his blind eyes burned | Hard light and heat of laughter." Lang picks up this phrase and couples it with two or three out of "The Triumph of Time" to argue that Gosse embellished the Jane Faulkner story with details from the poems; but Swinburne is certainly not describing a callous woman here, and Gosse's story seems rather to bear an emblematic relation to Swinburne's bitter truth. John Mayfield suggests that Swinburne himself misled Gosse with the Faulkner story, but I think Swinburne instead gave him the real truth—that love laughed in his face.

Following the revelation in "Thalassius" of what love is, comes the weariness (ll. 306-14) that Swinburne also describes in "Félise" (which poem itself discourses upon "God's intolerable scorn"), and the descent into lust (ll. 315-400). Since this weariness and descent are implicit in the nature of love, the separate elaboration of them in the poem is to be regarded as dramatic, allegorical. Our lady of pain is herself a scornful deity. It is of course in this respect that the several apparently different women of "The Triumph of Time," "A Leave-Taking," "Félise," and "Dolores" have their collective unity, and that the flickering images of Dolores in "The Triumph of Time" are most fully explained and perhaps justified—and in reading "The Triumph of Time" in this light one will give more than usual attention to the state of the poet's soul as he speaks: he knows already the cruel face of the young god, he has succumbed to the cruel god, he is damned ("the gait is strait; I shall not be there"). It is likewise in this respect that the individual love poem can be taken as a photograph even if one or another detail contradicts the details of other poems. The truth to be photographed is the truth that "Thalassius," the "Notes," and the "play" tell. The poems render this truth with examples. The examples are sketches from imagination insofar as Swinburne constructs in his mind the details of an affair. The examples are photographs insofar as the abstract truth that Swinburne learned came in some part from encounters—casual, tentative, or terrible; honorable, dishonorable, or neutral—with a host of women. The meaning of the word photograph shifts, and there is no clear line between photograph and sketch, either in Swinburne's experience or in our attempt to sort out his experience.

"Faustine" provides the plainest illustration of this ambiguity. In the "Notes" Swinburne says that the poem was inspired by "the sudden sight of a living face which recalled the wellknown likeness of ... Faustina, as seen in coin and bust. Out of that casual glimpse and sudden recollection these verses sprang and grew" (16). Unless this moment itself provided the terrible revelation of the evil god of love, we are likely to assume that Swinburne's current or earlier experience of the Dolores type was necessary background for the perception. The poem is both photograph and sketch. Admittedly Swinburne did not imply such hazards of distinction in his "Dedicatory Epistle," but his aim there was in part to discredit his critics, and in this respect he used the distinction as an amusing attack on prurient moralists.

It must be acknowledged too that the truth of the "Notes," "Thalassius," and the "play" is more broad than it is precise in its reference to Swinburne's life. It seems doubtful that he experienced a simple and straightforward descent from a great love into lust any more than he made a simple and straightforward escape from Dolores. We are not called upon to assume that the love affair preceded his very first perception of a flicker of evil on the god of love's face. To try to do so would perhaps take us back to his adolescence, for in a letter of 1863 he asserts that he began writing literature "totally unfit for publication" by 1854 (1:70). All the same, the truth has sufficient force that if we discovered certain details of an actual love affair, and those details contradicted or distorted the general truth or seemed irrelevant to it, we might want to say that the affair was a fortuitous outward drama that misrepresented the essential drama of love in Swinburne's life. And the fact is that the affair that Lang creates is almost without character, and the one that Fuller creates and F. A. C. Wilson supports is almost entirely tawdry.

"Thalassius" continues (ll. 421ff.) with a description of the deathlike state of "The Garden of Proserpine" and concludes with the redemption. The redemption is more complete than that described in "Hesperia," and the focus is on the final aspect of it. No beloved woman in the ordinary sexual sense is the agent, and the condition is not one of "innocuous desire" and fear of the huntress Dolores. The agents are father and mother (Apollo and Cymothoe), and the poet is restored to childhood grace and joy and to poetic power. It is worth remarking that the depiction of his childhood in the poem is quite in accord with Gosse's account and totally at variance with Fuller's.

V

The drama of Swinburne's love outlined in the "Notes," "Thalassius," and the letter to W. M. Rossetti seems to me to be powerfully supported by the general account of his life in Gosse's biography. There is first the ecstatic child of "fairy-like spriteliness and unearthly charm," whose nervous excitements of behavior are ascribed by a medical specialist to "an excess of electric vitality." He grew into a young boy who seemed extraordinarily different from other boys: "strangely tiny," "his features...small and delicate," walking with "that peculiar dancing step of his," and seeming like an "inspired elfin-something belonging to another sphere." At age fourteen he was an omnivorous reader with nearly total recall, and to his cousin at Eton "he would pour out in his unforgettable voice the treasures which he had gathered at his last sitting." Then came Oxford and London, where the excess of electric vitality began to manifest itself in epileptiform fits, marked by convulsions and unconsciousness and followed by miraculous recoveries. Of the underside of his life in these years—the drinking, the sado-masochism—Gosse indicates little, and gives us instead the developed ecstasies and enervations of poetry. He quotes Alice Bird on Swinburne reading the proofs of *Songs Before Sunrise* to her:

> dancing about the room convulsed with passion while he half-read half recited them.... In particular, those in which Napoleon III was denounced he repeated with such violence... that his voice sounded like the hissing of serpents, while he jigged round the room, his hair flying out behind him, and his arms flapping and fluttering at his sides. At these times, when he was transfigured by excitement, his wonderful head looked like that of a young god, if only the weak mouth and the receding chin could be ignored. Directly the storm of melody was over, and the poem put away, Algernon would sink down on a sofa with the gentleness of a child, and his voice would immediately resume its rich, soft cadences.[8]

After these years came Putney, informal and willing imprisonment, good health and poetic mediocrity. He became prematurely old as once he had seemed preternaturally youthful. He became entirely the child on the sofa after the frenzy of reading.

These images of Swinburne in Gosse's book suggest an altogether extraordinary figure—Blakean, Bacchic, absurd. In his very being he was unfitted for normal society and normal experience, and his life could hardly help being otherwise than isolated and extreme. His small stature and the fits and poetry expressive of his vitality doubtless made the social situation all the more difficult. Imagine such a man coming to love, seeing it, wanting it, wanting it as purely (let us say) as any of us normal people want it; and then in his isolation, intensity, physical beauty, and absurdity seeing it turn hollow. There must have come upon him in the course of growing up a realization that this woman, or any woman, would turn away from him, or already had, a realization that love would always betray him, laugh at him, and turn into the lust which alone he knew he could claim in the flesh. Was it not an evil laughing god who was lord of his birth?

It seems quite in accordance with such a state of affairs that so much of Swinburne's poetry should be preoccupied with love and lust, and that his life should offer so little objective evidence of his attachment to any woman. Gosse in the private essay suspects that Swinburne's generative instinct was weak, and I suspect that Gosse's phrase might be more apt—that the instinct was masked, hidden out of sight. Gosse says, again in the essay, that Swinburne did not seem to look at women sexually as other men did; but I think that unless the story of a loved woman is a fabrication, it must be believed that in society (away from the writing desk and perhaps the brothel) he would declare nothing, he would not leave himself open for laughter in this way, though he may have done so once, or twice, and with the unlikeliest of women. His characteristic phrase to express deep feeling for a woman was that of brother for sister. It is such an image of love that he arrives at poetically—resigns himself to, I would say—in "Hesperia." The poem itself has certain erotic traces; the intention is described in the "Notes": "Here, between moonrise and sunset, lives the love that is gentle and faithful, neither giving too much nor asking—a bride rather than a mistress, a sister rather than a bride" (13).

Surely this romantic agony led to an absurd conclusion in the Putney years, but it is hard to see that any other result was possible short of Swinburne's drowning himself like Shelley. We can be glad that he found some peace, and even be glad if he thought his poetic powers were restored (but we must not fail to take the assertion in "Thalassius" figuratively, just as in "A Leave-Taking"). Still we want our poets for our own sake, not theirs, and it is Swinburne in agony we want. In agony only one consummation of love was possible for him, a Shelleyan consummation:

> O fair green-girdled mother of mine,
> Sea, that art clothed with the sun and the rain,
> Thy sweet hard kisses are strong like wine,
> Thy large embraces are keen like pain.
> Save me and hide me with all thy waves,
> Find me one grave of thy thousand graves,
> Those pure cold populous graves of thine
> Wrought without hand in a world without stain.
>
> I shall sleep, and move with the moving ships,
> Change as the winds change, veer in the tide;
> My lips will feast on the foam of thy lips,
> I shall rise with thy rising, with thee subside.... [20]

VI

Of course it will not do merely to transform a possible love affair into a life problem or to say that the Jane Faulkner story was a metaphor. We have a legitimate interest in learning the facts of Swinburne's life and in conjecturing about other facts that lie beyond us. If he did have one special and conscious romantic encounter with a woman, we have a right to see his life and poetry with a somewhat different emphasis than if he did not. Suppose there lies buried somewhere a sworn affidavit in which Swinburne declares his affections. Who is the woman who is most likely to be named in it? The published case for Mary Gordon is certainly much weaker and more superficial than her advocates think it is, and yet Swinburne was intimate with her and loved her in some degree. She cannot be excluded as a possibility. Adah Menken? A lady with literary pretensions and owning physical attractions that might put Swinburne in mind of Dolores and of someone better. But the date of their liaison was 1867-68. Jane Faulkner? Surely she must be considered in the flesh if we think that in her ten-year-old laughter Swinburne heard the laughter of women he would not address. Mathilde Blind? My own candidate is Elizabeth Siddal.

The immediately relevant facts about Elizabeth Siddal are that she married D. G. Rossetti in 1860 and committed suicide in February 1862 after dining out with Rossetti and Swinburne, and that during the interval she and Swinburne were intimate with each other. Was it for Swinburne an innocent intimacy only on the surface? Swinburne denied that he loved her, and there is no direct evidence to the contrary, any more than there is in the Mary Gordon case; but he expressed an admiration for her that indicates far deeper feeling than anything he is known to have said of Mary Gordon:

> To one at least who knew her better than most of her husband's friends, the memory of all her marvellous charms of mind and person—her matchless grace, loveliness, courage, endurance, wit, humour, heroism, and sweetness—is too dear and sacred to be profaned by any attempt at expression.
> . . . .
>
> Except Lady Trevelyan, I never knew so brilliant and appreciative a woman.... I shall never forget her delight in Fletcher's magnificent comedy of *The Spanish Curate*.... I can hear the music of her laughter to this day. (6:49-50, 93)

There is also the opinion of F. M. Ford and Violet Hunt. Ford writes in *Mightier than the Sword*, "I suppose it to be generally known to the world interested in such matters that Swinburne entertained a passion for Mrs. D. G. Rossetti." He specifically connects Elizabeth Siddal with "Félise." In *The Wife of Rossetti*, Violet Hunt says that Elizabeth Siddal was the only woman Swinburne loved, and she likewise connects her to "Félise."[9] It is of course true that both Ford and Hunt have reputations for unreliability exceeding even Gosse's, but such reputations will not put them out of court here, and their Pre-Raphaelite background and associations give special weight to their view.

Aside from this, Elizabeth Siddal can be connected to certain poems and prose rather more suggestively than can Mary Gordon. With "The Triumph of Time" the case has approximately the same strength as Lang's for Mary Gordon: the probable time of composition of the poem that I suggest above accords with the time of intimacy; the possible songwriting talents of the woman of the poem are talents that Elizabeth Siddal claimed as readily as Mary Gordon; and the situation of the woman of the poem in belonging to another man was more clearly hers than Mary Gordon's. Of Elizabeth Siddal's possible musical abilities I will speak later, but it should be said here that the references to music in the poem are far from identifying a musically gifted woman. They are first and foremost metaphors to express the loveliness of life that the poet has lost. I should note incidentally that my interpretation of the first stanza of the poem fits Elizabeth Siddal somewhat better than it does Mary Gordon.

If "The Triumph of Time" concerns Elizabeth Siddal, presumably, though not necessarily, it would have been written before her death. And what would have come after? There is, of course, "Hesperia," in which the poet's beloved comes to him out of the past and out of death ("from the happy memorial places," "the fortunate islands"), and the "innocuous desire" for her resembles the playful affection between Swinburne and Lizzie that their friends observed and that Swinburne perhaps had resigned himself to. "Thy lips cannot laugh and thine eyes cannot weep," the poet says in the poem, but the beloved does there possess pity (as "The Triumph of Time" suggests the beloved in heaven might), and she will save him (whereas in "The Triumph of Time" he was not to be saved).

There is also "The Leper." This, I think, is one of Swinburne's finest poems, and if Elizabeth Siddal was the loved woman, its force becomes shocking. Here is the woman who belongs to another man, who laughs ("mere scorn God knows she had of me") but who is not diabolical like Dolores; here is a narrator who hardly deserves love ("A poor scribe, nowise great or fair"). More especially, here is a woman who sins sexually, as did Elizabeth Siddal in her relationship with Rossetti; here is a woman who is diseased, as Elizabeth Siddal was ill; here is a woman with golden hair, as Elizabeth Siddal's was sometimes described; here is the narrator serving the woman in another man's house, as Swinburne served Elizabeth Siddal. The poem cannot be a faithful photograph in a prosaic sense, but it could be the most exact sketch of Swinburne's desire:

> Yet am I glad to have her dead
> Here in this wretched wattled house
> Where I can kiss her eyes and head.

It is remarkable too that the poem has one of the most vividly sexual passages that Swinburne wrote:

> Yea, he inside whose grasp all night
> Her fervent body leapt or lay....

Violet Hunt connects the poem with Elizabeth Siddal, though not in the sense of its being inspired by her: "Algernon Swinburne would have nursed and tended her, as the poor serving man the leprous lady" (294).

There are certain hazards in linking "The Leper" to Elizabeth Siddal, mainly in that several of its details have parallels in medieval literature and the dating is uncertain. But the medieval element is no more of a problem, if a slightly different one, than is the Sapphic element in "Anactoria." The dating problem is double-edged. The poem exists in an earlier manuscript form under the title "A Vigil" with a watermark date of 1857. "A Vigil" is a much slighter, more conventional poem, concerned only to describe the mourning over a beloved woman. The woman's sin, her disease, the clerk's unworthiness, and the caressing of her dead body are absent from it. When "The Leper" itself was composed is unknown. It was published in *Poems and Ballads* in 1866, and the chief suggestions for more exact dating appear in Gosse's biography, where 1862 is offered as the terminus ad quem, and in an article by Robert A. Greenberg, where August 1862 is offered as the probable terminal date.[10] Also of some hazard in the matter is the fact that Swinburne wrote the somewhat similar story "Dead Love" by January 1861, but the quality of the story places it midway between the conventionality of "A Vigil" and the macabre and pure force of "The Leper," and in any event Elizabeth Siddal was ill most of the time that Swinburne knew her, and "The Leper" itself could well have been written before her death.

Before turning to the most intriguing document in the case for Elizabeth Siddal, I must say something about "Félise." Neither Ford nor Hunt mentions any reason for connecting the poem with her, but I suppose it to be that the poem is addressed to a loved woman whose physical appearance, specifically her eyes, calls Elizabeth Siddal to mind. The point is certainly very doubtful, and in any event Elizabeth Siddal's friends did not entirely agree about the color of her eyes. In *A Victorian Romantic* Oswald Doughty assembles several descriptions, including ones that he merely assumes are relevant: "greenish blue" (W.M. Rossetti), "a kind of golden brown—agate-color is the only word I can find to describe them—and wonderfully luminous" (Lady Burne Jones), "as of the sea and sky on a grey day" (D.G. Rossetti in "A Last Confession"), and "luminous grey-green...shot through with colors of sea-water in sunlight" (Swinburne in *Love's Cross Currents*)[11]. Félise has "bright bland eyes," "the greenest of things blue, | The bluest of things grey," "seagreen mirrors," "colored like a water-flower, | And deeper than the green sea's glass."

The most intriguing document is *Love's Cross Currents* itself. This novel is used briefly by Fuller in her case for Mary Gordon, in particular with regard to the youthful whippings received by Reginald Harewood and enjoyed by himself and his sister. The sister does not appear in the published novel, and Fuller suggests that her role was taken over by Reginald's cousin Clara. There is additional material in the novel relevant to Fuller's identifications. Reginald has been rusticated from Oxford, he writes verse, he knows of some unprintable family poetry, he loves the sea, he is preoccupied with Italian freedom, and he is a hero-worshiper. Swinburne himself in a letter to W.M. Rossetti of 21 August 1905 says that Reginald is "rather a colored photograph" of himself—though he does mention in the same letter that Reginald's sadistic father is totally unlike his own (6:195). Moreover, Reginald is infatuated with his cousin Clara, has loved her from childhood, writes verses about her, admires her riding ability, gallops over the sands with her, and is rejected by her without laughter. Mary Gordon seems a reasonable guess, even though Clara is older than Reginald instead of younger, does not play Handel for him, hears repeatedly his protestations of love, and is formally attached to another man. What casts the issue in rather more serious doubt is that the novel seems to have been written in 1862, well before Mary Gordon's marriage and almost two years before Lang's surmise of the date that she told Swinburne of her engagement. In a letter to W. M. Rossetti in March 1866 Swinburne said he wrote the novel in 1862 (1:158). Forty years later he expressed uncertainty whether it was written in 1861 or 1862 (6:194). Fuller suggests 1863, but with a very slender argument and apparently without knowledge of the 1866 letter to Rossetti. Of course it is not impossible that a romantic break with Mary Gordon took place in 1862, or that Swinburne had dim or clear forebodings then that it would take place, and the situation of Reginald's being rejected by a married woman may be merely the sort of translation of fact that any novelist undertakes. The only odd thing about this particular translation, if it is one, is that Reginald goes on at length about the horrors of Clara's being married to a dull husband.

On balance I am inclined to let the identification of Reginald Harewood and Clara with Swinburne and Mary Gordon pass, but only if it is viewed as an identification of inessentials used in the creation of figures of satire. For if one looks at the novel in the round, nothing is more absurd than to say that Reginald Harewood is Swinburne and that his affair with Clara is comparable to a supposed great passion in Swinburne's life. Reginald is a silly fool, and his love for Clara is calf-love, and Clara herself is a dull British matron with perhaps a taste for flirtation. Except for one passage, the part of the novel that concerns them is a satire against frivolity. Consider the exaggerated rhetoric that Reginald addresses to Clara. "What you are doing," he writes, referring to her marital fidelity, "insults God, and maddens men who see it. Think what it is to endure and to act as you do! I ask you what right have you to let him play husband with you?" He urges her to leave home and go to her brother Frank: "He is very young, I know, but he must see the greatness of what you do." He suggests that he himself can offer some personal compensation to her husband: "I would devote my whole life to Radworth—give up all I have in the world to him."[12] Clara replies to this letter with a sermon. Later he writes to her as though she is ready to run off with him, though he apparently has no grounds to think she will. She thereupon refuses to answer his letters. The affair seems then to collapse, and he is reported to be going through the customary youthful feeling that he will never be able to love again.

The other affair in the novel, that between Frank Cheyne and Amicia, stands in distinct and deliberate contrast to that between Reginald and Clara. In two or three superficial details Frank is similar to Reginald: he has been at Oxford and he is reported (by Reginald) to have been whipped at school for doing verses without a false quantity—having given them to another boy to pass off as his own (recalling Swinburne's letter on the same subject to Monckton Milnes). He too is in love with his cousin, Amicia, who is married; and like Reginald he has declared his love. At first blush it might seem that he is Reginald's double and that Swinburne is going to play "the game of cousins" (as one character puts it, 176) two ways. It should be noted that Swinburne often uses the names Reginald and Frank to denote characters with certain likenesses to himself. But Frank and Amicia are different from Reginald and Clara, and the expression of their passion is serious and moving.

In a certain respect they are more shadowy figures. There is less outward detail on their lives, and they do not have the two-dimensional vivacity that caricature gives to the other two. It is their feelings that are vivid. Compare Frank's letter of love to Amicia with Reginald's to Clara. It follows immediately upon Reginald's and the reply from Clara.

> I love nothing seriously that does not somehow belong to you; all that does not seems done in play, or to get the time through.... When I begin to write, I seem to hear you speaking. I believe at times I can tell, by the sensation, what you are doing at Lidcombe. I have heard you speak twice since I sat down, and I know the dress you have on. (113-14)

His is a genuine affair, and Amicia ultimately bears his child (Swinburne clarifies the matter in a letter to John Nichol of 2 January 1877); but her conventional sense of honor makes her break off with him just after the consummation of their love. Then her husband is drowned, and she suffers a collapse. She is reported to Frank to be very ill, and the fact of her pregnancy has perhaps been given to him. In a letter to Clara, who is his sister, Frank writes to deny any interest in a woman whom the family are urging upon him. Here if anywhere in the novel is the authentic note of love.

> There gets up between us [between him and the proposed woman] such an invincible exquisite memory of a face ten times more beautiful and lovable to have in sight of one; pale when I saw it last, as if drawn down by its hair, heavily weighted about the eyes with a presage of tears, sealed with sorrow, and piteous with an infinite unaccomplished desire. The old deep-gold hair and luminous grey-green eyes shot through with colors of seawater in sunlight, and threaded with faint keen lines of fire and light about the pupil.... Then that mouth of hers and the shadow made almost on the chin by the underlip—such sad perfect lips, full of tender power and faith, and her wonderful way of lifting and dropping her face imperceptibly, flower-fashion, when she begins or leaves off speaking; I shall never hear such a voice in the world, either. I cannot, and need not now, pretend to dissemble or soften down what I feel about her. I do love her with all my heart and might. And now that... she is fallen miserable and ill... it is not possible for me, sitting here in her house... to think very much of anything else, or to think at all of any woman in the way of liking. (153-54)

Is it not Elizabeth Siddal, with her golden hair and luminous eyes, and also the full underlip and general aspect of sadness that her husband painted? How often

Swinburne sat in the house where she lay ill and miserable, and now (if the novel was written in 1862) she was but a few months dead, and her stillborn child dead in May of the year before.

The case for Elizabeth Siddal in *Love's Cross Currents* is more serious than the case for Mary Gordon. If there is a case for Mary Gordon in the novel, it would seem to be (so far) that Swinburne had a youthful attachment to her that bore no resemblance to a great passion and that died well before 1862. But there are two more things to be said on her behalf, if rather ambiguously. The one passage in which Reginald speaks with creditable passion is in the letter in which he assumes that Clara is ready to run off with him, and for the moment Swinburne seems to be serious rather than satirical in describing the affair, and thus serious in the presumed allusion to Mary Gordon. The difficulty here is that the style of the letter is sufficiently out of character that one hardly believes Reginald is speaking, and the unrealism of his assumption convicts him of folly that is well beyond what he has previously shown. I am inclined to think that the letter began as a letter for Frank to write to Amicia, in a preliminary working out of the plot. There are incidental curiosities in the letter, including a reference to Clara's indifference a year ago (calling to mind "Félise" and somewhat contradicting the notion of childhood love) and an uneasy comparison between Clara's dark hair and the brilliant hair of his sister Amicia.

The other point for Mary Gordon is that one passage concerning Frank and Amicia can possibly be associated with Swinburne and her as well as with Swinburne and Elizabeth Siddal. In another eloquent letter Frank describes how Amicia played and sang to him.

> The voice and the sound of her dress come and go in my hearing. I see her face and all her hair glitter and vibrate as she keeps singing. Her hands and her throat go up and down, and her eyes turn and shine. Then she leaves off playing and comes to me, and I cannot see her near enough; but I feel her hands touch me, and hear her crying. (136)

The glittering hair and tears suggest Elizabeth Siddal, but did Elizabeth Siddal play and sing? Violet Hunt says that Elizabeth's parents played the violin and that her father was an organist and choir master, but she says nothing of musical talents on Elizabeth Siddal's part, except to mention once her singing to Rossetti (but she was possibly writing here more as novelist than as biographer), and she remarks elsewhere on Elizabeth's unpleasant reading voice. No one else seems to mention any musical gifts. Swinburne, though, thought her laughter was like music.

On Mary Gordon's side is the fact that she played the organ. The letter about her playing Handel for Swinburne does not mention her singing for him, nor do any of the letters between them or her memoir of his boyhood. Presumably she could sing. What is noteworthy about the Handel letter, though, is that in contrast to Frank's letter it is largely unconcerned with the woman who is performing. Swinburne is writing to his sister Alice from the Gordons, whom he is visiting after the death of his sister Edith.

> My greatest pleasure just now is when M—— practises Handel on the organ; I can hardly *behave* for delight at some of the choruses. I care hardly more than I ever did for any minor music; but *that* is an enjoyment which wants special language to describe it, being so unlike all others. It crams and crowds me with old and new verses, half-remembered and half-made, which new ones will hardly come straight afterwards; but under their influence I have done some more of my Atalanta which will be among my great doings if it keeps up with its own last scenes throughout.
>
> I repay M—— to the best of my ability but cheaply, by blundering over Greek verbs with her. She keeps her energy fresh by her versatility. I wish you were here, and as quiet as I have happily been all this time, thanks to their kindness. (1:93)

Is there even the faintest accent of love here, any suggestion that the kindness is more Mary's than the Gordons' generally, that the player has moved him by her person? If Elizabeth Siddal did not play and sing, one is inclined to think that Swinburne enabled her to out of love and esthetic licence. And if she was Amicia, was not W. M. Rossetti just the person to mislead about *Love's Cross Currents* by emphasizing his relation to Reginald instead of to Frank? In any event "rather a colored photograph" suggests at least as much difficulty for us as "photograph from life."

What is astonishing in the whole matter is that neither Lang's article nor Fuller's book reviews in any detail the claims of Elizabeth Siddal or of any other women aside from Mary Gordon and Jane Faulkner. Lang has studied Swinburne for more years than most of us have weeks, but his abrupt dismissal of Elizabeth Siddal is unpersuasive in view of the unsatisfactoriness of his general argument. My case for her may merely prove how easy it is to construct an argument out of bits of information and interpretation; and yet I am certain, if I think of Gosse's Swinburne, that Elizabeth Siddal with her great beauty and charm and tragedy could not have helped figuring importantly in Swinburne's thoughts about women and in his writing about them.

VII

How remote we are from Swinburne and his poetry! In one passage of his *Life* Gosse describes the frenzied poet reading "Dolores" to an audience enraptured and prostrate around him. Elsewhere Gosse says that Cambridge undergraduates stamped through the streets shouting stanzas of the poem, and he alludes to George Saintsbury's ecstasy at Oxford. It is hard to credit such scenes today. Fuller's account of the poem and of Swinburne is just the sort of misunderstanding that Gosse foresaw would occur if knowledge of Swinburne's interest in flagellation were let loose among people who did not know him. It would seem, indeed, that our serious emotions are reserved for scholarship rather than for Swinburne. "Far, far more culpable than... [Gosse's] hapless misidentification of an infant girlchild as the inaccessible Innominata is... his misreading of 'The Triumph of Time,'" says Lang; and Lang liked this censure so much that he repeated it in *PMLA* from his preliminary article on the subject in the *Yale University Library Gazette* in 1957. Ten years later Clyde K. Hyder felt the same way. His piece on Swinburne for the second edition of Frederic Faverty's *Victorian Poets* speaks of Gosse's "absurd misreading of the... poem" and of his "shockingly corrupt" and "grossly inaccurate" editorial work.[13] Were F.A.C. Wilson to consider this parallel language between Lang and Hyder as seriously as he does the parallels between Swinburne and the heroes of Mary Gordon's novels, he could not but conclude that Lang and Hyder were one and the same man. We are Victorian moralists, with merely a new morality.

Of course we cannot return to the casual arts of criticism and biography of Gosse, but luckily we can return to his book, where Swinburne occasionally glows into life unknown to Lang, Fuller, and Wilson. I close with one more quotation from it, in which Gosse describes his first meeting with the poet at D.G. Rossetti's home:

> He was not quite like a human being.... As he talked to me, he stood, perfectly rigid, with his arms shivering at his sides, and his little feet tight against each other, close to a low settee in the middle of the studio. Every now and then, without breaking off talking or bending his body, he hopped on to this sofa, and presently hopped down again.... The contrast between these sudden movements and the enthusiasm of his rich and flute-like voice was very strange. (200-01)

5 Tennyson the Sadist

IN 1952 ROBERT STANGE EXAMINED Tennyson's early poem "The Hesperides," and offered to show that beneath the surface it is concerned with "the conditions of poetic creation" and that it "affirms the value of an art which is withdrawn, introspective, and sensuous."[1] The details of his analysis involve a conscientious description of patterns of imagery, symbolism, and meaning within the poem and among related early poems. Stange is aware that other poems of the time such as "The Palace of Art" (like "The Hesperides" published in the 1832 volume) express or seem to express a different view, that the isolated and precious poet dies in isolation, however lovely his kingdom; and in this respect Stange is merely distinguishing what others have distinguished before him: the two Tennysons, the private and the public, the hermit and the laureate, the romantic and the Victorian. The common view for many years has been not only that in the course of life the public poet overtook the private but also that the public poet was inferior to the private. Stange notes that Tennyson suppressed "The Hesperides" in later volumes of his poetry, and he thinks Tennyson did so largely because he was uneasy about his fellow Victorians seeing this side of his artistic inclination.

Oddly enough, Stange remarks briefly upon another poem in the same volume, "The Poet's Mind," which transparently takes the same view that Stange claims for "The Hesperides," but he has nothing to say about the fact that "The Poet's Mind" was reprinted in the 1842 volume or that the 1842 volume concludes with another similar poem, "The Poet's Song." Strange that Tennyson should feel the need to suppress a poem that made its point (if it did) with recondite symbolism, and felt no need to suppress others that made the same point openly.

Providing additional difficulty are the close analyses that more recent critics have made of other early poems, among them "The Lady of Shalott." As the old joke goes, that was no lady, that was the poet. The poem, it seems to some critics, is about the poet requiring solitude and isolation in order to create. And this poem too appeared in the 1832 volume and reappeared with improvements in the 1842 volume. Apparently Tennyson could scarcely put pen to paper without writing about the poetic condition.

Of course criticism would not be criticism without disagreements, and other recent critics have decided that "The Lady of Shalott" shows that the poet finds recognition and fulfillment in society or reality. A discussion along these lines by Flavia Alaya appeared in 1970.[2] But the opposed critics do agree on the basic point, namely that the lady is the poet; and one rarely comes upon a reference to her among Victorian scholars today that does not allow this to be so. It should be only a matter of time before other Tennysonian ladies, and even gentlemen, are drawn into the case. There is Mariana isolated in her moated grange very much in the manner of the Lady of Shalott. There are the Lord and Lady of Burleigh who enter his palace of art where he paints and she dies. There is Elaine. Is each of them the poet? If we add them up, will we get the whole of the poet in the poems? Will we perhaps even get the whole of the poet in life?

I would like to cast the problem in another perspective, by identifying the voice of the poet in seven poems of his early career. First is "Mariana." The speaker of that poem speaks in slow, steady phrases: he circles about and dwells upon his subject. He seems like a conventional nineteenth century romantic poet, talking to himself, observing quietly, passively, in isolation. He seems very much like Mariana herself. He is, as it were, Tennyson in the moated grange. Part of the excellence of the poem is the harmony of the speaker's voice and Mariana's: his somewhat abstracted melancholy dies into Mariana's lament at the close of each stanza.

> Her tears fell with the dews at even;
> Her tears fell ere the dews were dried;
> She could not look on the sweet heaven,
> Either at morn or eventide.
> After the flitting of the bats,
> When thickest dark did trance the sky,
> She drew her casement-curtain by,
> And glanced athwart the glooming flats.
> She only said, "The night is dreary,
> He cometh not," she said;
> She said, "I am aweary, aweary,
> I would that I were dead!"[3]

In "The Poet's Song" there is the same voice, and the very account of the poet given in the poem supports the voice: the poet goes alone and sings alone, and the world stands still. But two words of the account do not apply:

> And he sat him down in a lonely place,
> And chanted a melody loud and sweet,
> . . . .
>
> And the nightingale thought, 'I have sung many songs,
> But never a one so gay.'

Loud and gay? Certainly not here, certainly not in "Mariana." The two words bring to mind similar language in the prologue of *In Memoriam*: "Forgive these wild and wandering cries." What wild cries?

The voice of the speaker of the poem in "The Lady of Shalott" is much the same as the voices in "Mariana" and "The Poet's Song," but it has more energy. If one compares the 1842 with the 1832 version of the poem, one can see Tennyson making the descriptive detail more simple and clarifying the narrative movement, and these increase the energy. Equally striking is the distinctness of voice of the two speaking characters in the poem. The Lady of Shalott and Lancelot possess independent dramatic existence. They are not the speaker of the poem, they are not Tennyson. Inferentially Tennyson has one foot out of the moated grange.

All three of these are satisfactory poems, though of course "The Poet's Song" is slight. "Mariana" was presumably written earliest, by 1830 and perhaps much earlier. "The Lady of Shalott" was written by 1832 and revised during the next ten years. They contrast with our other four poems: "A Character," written in 1829 or 1830, "Ulysses" and "The Two Voices," both written in 1833 with revisions of the latter some years later, and "Locksley Hall," written in 1837-38. "A Character" offers a new voice, a supercilious conversational voice. It is too brittle to seem a natural voice for the poet, and it also fails in the respect that it belongs equally to the satirized character and to the satirist-speaker. In "Mariana" the fusion of the two voices is harmonious; here it blurs the satire:

> With a half-glance upon the sky
> At night he said, 'The wanderings
> Of this most intricate Universe
> Teach me the nothingness of things.'
> Yet could not all creation pierce
> Beyond the bottom of his eye.

"Ulysses" offers a medley of voices purporting to be one. In just a few places Ulysses speaks with the sort of accent that seems broadly to be implied by the self-characterization:

> And drunk delight of battle with my peers,
> Far on the ringing plains of windy Troy.
> . . . .

> That ever with a frolic welcome took
> The thunder and the sunshine....

But whether Ulysses is meant to be a simple man of action or a complex one, whether he is sailing out to new adventure or to death, whether he is to be taken seriously or satirically, he has too many voices to be believable: a statesmanlike voice of the man rejecting kingship in the opening lines, Childe Harold leaving England in the next, then Polonius talking about his son Telemachus, and later Mariana moaning about the deep. Ulysses the man is merely a device in a poem that is essentially reflective, and as a device he manages to hold together a diversity of tones, a variety of voices, that might fall apart without him. The voices do not clash, they wash upon one another, and there are various beauties of rhythm and imagery that likewise sustain the poem. But the poet does not know quite what he is doing or what he wants.

In "The Two Voices" the speaker of the poem conducts an argument with the voice of despair within himself. Viewed dramatically, the voice of despair is disembodied. Tennyson has not dressed him like a character in a dramatic dialogue, with physical appearance and action; but he is nevertheless a voice, just as the disembodied speaker in "Mariana" is a voice, and his voice seems generally indistinguishable from that of the whole self. Together the two voices speak with a tedious orotund complacency that has little relation to the desperateness of their subject or to their antithetical views.

> A still small voice spake unto me,
> 'Thou art so full of misery,
> Were it not better not to be?'
>
> Then to the still small voice I said;
> 'Let me not cast in endless shade
> What is so wonderfully made.'

It is difficult to see how anyone could ever have imagined that the poem was composed in consequence of Arthur Hallam's death. It seems like the expression of someone who has been untouched by death or by active thoughts of suicide. Yet it was written not long after the death of Tennyson's father and some months after his brother Edward began a decline into insanity. In later years Tennyson said, "When I wrote 'The Two Voices' I was so utterly miserable, a burden to myself and to my family, that I said, 'Is life worth anything?'"[4] This discrepancy between actual mood and poetic voice will concern me again later, but what I want to emphasize here is the mutual complacency of the two supposedly opposed voices. The same thing can be seen in a small way in a pair of short poems of slightly earlier date that aim to express opposing views:

"Nothing Will Die" and "All Things Will Die." The voice of each is melancholic bravado.

It is easy enough to appreciate from a personal standpoint as well as from an artistic one why the two major voices of "The Two Voices" collapse into one—for it is indeed Tennyson talking to himself, and why should he attempt to fit his two voices out as independent characters? (In this respect the poem provides an ambiguous footnote to T.S. Eliot's view in *The Three Voices of Poetry* that a poet cannot speak in anyone's voice but his own unless he has two characters in conflict.) But observe that though Tennyson is talking to himself, the voice is not private but public, self-consciously conversational, almost addressed to a congregation. It is a voice entirely absent from "Mariana," "The Lady of Shalott," and "The Poet's Song," and present in less sustained and less convincing form in "Ulysses" and "A Character." "O dull, one-sided voice," the speaker of the poem protests at one point. Occasionally the voice rises in strength, and the end marks a softened rise, but overall it is a dull, complacent voice that not many people have especially cared to listen to.

Of "Locksley Hall" it need only be said that the voice is similar to that in "The Two Voices" but rather more disastrous—a voice in the grip of an inexorable and absurd rhythm. Generally speaking, then, the successful poems examined here are those of an elevated private voice—Tennyson in or almost in the moated grange; the poetic failures are in a public voice. This is not a startling conclusion, but it offers a particular perspective in which to consider certain questions. What would the future seem to hold for such a poet—taking the chronology of composition into account and assuming that these seven poems are fairly representative? What would we want the future to hold? Where would we expect to find failure and success?

In Memoriam, published in 1850, is the central poem around which to contemplate answers to our questions. It will be desirable to examine the poem fairly broadly.

One of the central problems of *In Memoriam* concerns its unity. Tennyson himself is customarily quoted on the point.

> The sections were written at many different places, and as the phases of our intercourse came to my memory and suggested them. I did not write them with any view of weaving them into a whole, or for publication, until I found that I had written so many.[5]

Earlier in 1850 there was a private issue of the poem, for which Tennyson contemplated using the title "Fragments of an Elegy." In the fourth edition, 1851, a new section, now 59, was added; and in 1870 another section, now 39, was added. There were other incidental published changes made by Tennyson; and the manuscript of the poem exists in several forms at several stages, as working draft and fair copy. At the time of Christopher Ricks's edition of the poems in 1969 the manuscripts at Trinity College, Cambridge, were under interdiction in perpetuity, but since then we have learned what in perpetuity means, and eventually there should be an edition of the poem in which the whole thing will be laid out from beginning to end.[6]

Until such an edition appears, one key to the problem of unity is unlikely to be thoroughly tested: that of chronology of composition. A.C. Bradley in his *Commentary* in 1901 reviewed the then known internal and external evidence for dating, and Eleanor B. Mattes in *In Memoriam: The Way of a Soul* in 1951 carried the investigation further.[7] But in fact we do not have much more than an outline. Arthur Hallam died on 15 September 1833, and Tennyson learned of his death on 1 October, and began writing stanzas soon thereafter. Presumably the stanzas describing the boat bringing Hallam's remains to England were among the first written. The stanzas on evolution were written wholly or in large part after Tennyson read Lyell's *Principles of Geology* in 1837 but before the appearance of *Vestiges of Creation* in the mid forties. The Prologue is dated 1849, but apparently most or all of the other stanzas were written by 1847. The marriage that the Epilogue refers to took place in 1842 and the Epilogue itself appears to have been written at the latest by 1845, and was possibly written in 1842, for in line 10 Tennyson speaks of "thrice three years" having passed since Hallam's death.

In a crude way the chronology of composition is similar to the chronology and course of the poem, for the poem tells of mourning and recovery of self in the passage of time; but Prologue and Epilogue apart, the internal chronology covers about three years after the death of Hallam, marked by the three Christmases, sections 28, 78, and 104, and the two anniversaries, 72 and 99, and seasonal changes. One might note incidentally that Hallam was not buried at Clevedon until January 1834, after the first Christmas, but the internal chronology implies that he was buried before.

Discussions of the poem usually assume that the internal chronology is mere artistic condensation of the actual chronology and that the course of thoughts and feelings recorded in the sequence of sections is in little—with fluctuations and reversions to earlier feelings—the actual course of Tennyson's thoughts and feelings; and analyses of the structure of the poem have relied upon this assumption. But the assumption is rash, and even the careful study of chronology that may one day be undertaken may tell us less than some people will want to know.

The structure has been looked at in several ways, somewhat dependent upon the general view taken of the merits of the poem. From the time of its publication there arose the question of whether it was a poem of faith or doubt, but in any event the poem had immense attraction to people in its day. Bradley is certain that multitudes took it to their hearts who cared nothing for poetry otherwise, and that they did so because it showed the great man Tennyson winning his way through grief and finding solace in thought, society, and love even as they themselves must, and his expression was a purgation for them. The structure of the poem was seen in this expressive movement out of grief, and Bradley himself offers what seems to him to be the fourfold structure of this movement. It is, he says, a structure he would not insist upon, for the poem is nothing if it is not fluid, but it coincides with the divisions at Christmas that Tennyson himself described. In summary:

I. The Poet absorbed in grief. Sections 1-27.
II. Semi-philosophical speculation, largely concerned with immortality and the possibility of reunion with Hallam. Sections 28-77.
III. Quiet retrospection and the beginning of a new life. Sections 78-103.
IV. Looking to the future and to the growth of love; Hallam as a type of future humanity. Sections 104-131.

On another occasion Tennyson gave a ninefold division of the poem to James Knowles, and a discussion in the *Journal of English and Germanic Philology* in 1962 attempts to support this division. What seems clear is that at least until the turn of the century the poem was often valued for this comforting progress and structure. Then, with Tennyson going out of favor and poetic tastes changing, there came a time when the poem was often read for isolated sections that did not offer comfort and a thought for the day but described a bleak, anguished, and psychological world. Two sections that make a powerful appeal in this way to modern critics are 7 and 95, the one describing Tennyson's visit before dawn to the dark house on Wimpole Street, the other describing the trance at night in which Hallam's soul was flashed upon his. T.S. Eliot is one of the admirers of section 7. At the same time Eliot is insistent that we must read the whole poem. He says that *In Memoriam* is "a series of poems, given form by the greatest lyrical resourcefulness that a poet has ever shown," but also that "the poem has to be comprehended as a whole"; "it is a diary of which we have to read every word."[8]

At any rate, modern criticism has tended to emphasize the poetic value of individual sections, but also in recent years Tennyson has been returned to the pantheon of great poets, and the modern analysis of structure has attempted to reassert the overall unity of the poem. The most conventional sort of approach can be seen in an essay by E. D. H. Johnson.[9] He describes a fourfold structure, like Bradley, but he has a modern critical preoccupation, namely the growth of the poet, and he shows that much of the poem is concerned with thoughts on poetry and that overall there is a fourfold progress in it from poetry as release from emotion, through poetry as escape from thought and poetry as self-realization, to poetry as mission. Broadly speaking the progress is from private to public poet. Johnson makes this analysis without questioning the relation between internal chronology and chronology of composition and also without reference to Tennyson's attitude toward poetry expressed in other poems of the same time or before. Other critics have similarly examined *In Memoriam* for the development of Tennyson's attitude toward religion, progress, love, and science.

But undoubtedly the main modern effort at seeing *In Memoriam* as a whole has been in the analysis of images and symbols, from the large images of Christmas-tide to the small images of individual objects and metaphors. Jerome Buckley isolates four main images: dark (or night), day (or light), rain (or water), and hand. According to him there are fifty references to water and thirty references to hands or to touching. (And it must be reckoned a matter of some curiosity that Monckton Milnes's lines on Hallam should use the hand image as well as other incidental imagery of Tennyson's poem: "I thought how should I see him first, | How should our hands first meet.") All of Buckley's four images can be seen in section 7, in the dark house, the drizzling rain, the hand that can be clasped no more, and the blank day breaking. And the section repeats itself with a difference in section 119, as do other sections. In 1963 another critic came forward to suggest that circle imagery is of prime importance to the poem.[10] Images of flowers, moon and stars, wind, heart, birds, eyes, remain to be explored. And one will conclude from all these structural analyses—spiritual, emotional, religious, aesthetic, imagistic, symbolic—that Tennyson's poem is well unified indeed.

I begin my own comments on the structure by saying that I have never read the poem through, either at one sitting or in several. I do not find it compulsive reading except in individual parts. I used to blame myself for this, thinking of my own preference for the short poem, and I also blamed modern times, which notoriously has no patience with the long poem. Then I read Bradley, who, writing in 1901 at the latest, said that "there are many readers of *In Memoriam* who have never read the poem through" (24). And now I am inclined to take Eliot's insistence that we read the whole poem as a piece of bluff: he was feeling uneasy about never having done so himself. This said, I will allow that I admire the poem immensely and that I think some of the merit of it lies in its having little more than rudimentary structure, and also that its merit rests upon its being rather bad as well as good. I will put this in terms of voice, but it will not be very different from some things Bradley says. He remarks that *In Memoriam* is unique among famous English elegies in its having been inspired by deep grief and in its showing the poet winning his way through his anguish in the course of time. Neither the anguish nor the transformation in such poems as *Lycidas* and *Adonais* has anything like the reality of the same in *In Memoriam*. We may thrill to "Peace, peace! he is not dead, he doth not sleep," but the thrill is literary and momentary and has nothing to do with the long passage of the actual transformation in *In Memoriam*, and indeed it has nothing to do with the sort of sudden union that section 95 of Tennyson's poem records—a true uncanny experience. "Thus much of *In Memoriam*," says Bradley, "is nearer to ordinary life than most elegies can be" (38).

If I listen to the voice of the first several sections of the poem, what do I hear, and what does it mean? In the Prologue itself, especially in the opening, the voice is strong, and has a measured confidence. It is the voice of a seer.

> Strong Son of God, immortal Love,
> Whom we, that have not seen thy face,
> By faith, and faith alone, embrace,
> Believing where we cannot prove;
>
> Thine are these orbs of light and shade;
> Thou madest Life in man and brute;
> Thou madest Death; and lo, thy foot
> Is on the skull which thou has made.

Here is a public Tennyson indeed, talking to God for the human race as it were, and very effectively. With section 1 there is a modulation to a more reflective personal voice, more tentative.

> I held it truth, with him who sings
> To one clear harp in divers tones,
> That men may rise on stepping stones
> Of their dead selves to higher things.
>
> But who shall so forecast the years
> And find in loss a gain to match?
> Or reach a hand through time to catch
> The far-off interest of tears?

Section 2 becomes direct address, rhetorical of course, with the tone deepening to melancholy.

> Old Yew, which graspest at the stones
> That name the under-lying dead,
> Thy fibres net the dreamless head,
> Thy roots are wrapt about the bones.

Section 3 becomes a melancholic, bitter cry.

> O Sorrow, cruel fellowship,
> O Priestess in the vaults of Death,

> O sweet and bitter in a breath,
> What whispers from thy lying lip?

Section 4 seems for a moment to lapse into impersonality, and then shifts.

> To Sleep I give my powers away;
> My will is bondsman to the dark;
> I sit within a helmless bark,
> And with my heart I muse and say:
>
> O heart, how fares it with thee now...?

This fifth line may be the most extraordinary line in the whole poem, with its sudden but soft descent into intimacy and despair. Not for a moment in "The Two Voices" does Tennyson succeed in talking to himself thus.

The opening of section 5 lightens the voice to one of almost calm reflection, and the opening of 6 loses the poet's voice in the impersonal cold sympathy of other voices. Section 7 brings us back to something like the melancholic voice which addresses the yew tree in 2, but with a different sort of intensity, ultimately with a kind of deadening restraint in the last line: "On the bald street breaks the blank day."

These comments give some idea of the variety of voice in the whole poem, though I have barely suggested the modulations within the sections themselves. These first sections are among the finest in the poem, but I do not want to emphasize their triumphs without noting also some of the absurd failures. The last stanza of section 9 descends to bathos, and the references to mother and brothers lack the substance for them to be anything but ludicrous. The voice falls apart. To me the worst failure of this sort comes in section 124 when Tennyson says that against the cold rational voice of a godless universe his heart stands up and says "I have felt." But these failures do not matter or they have a positive virtue in that they are part of the repeated reflection upon the subject, a reflection in all moods and manners as happens in life. They are part of the reality in which Tennyson keeps his vigil and in which the reader sees such a vigil is kept—sometimes passionately, sometimes coldly, sometimes bathetically, sometimes casually, sometimes ludicrously. To me the virtue of the poem lies in part in this inequality of lyrics and moods, and in the inexplicable shifting of them. I doubt that anyone will show that there is a detailed structure of mood and voice from verse to verse, or from section to section.

What the poem gives us is a circling about the subject, a repeated approach to the subject; and this circling repetition—with the slow, rudimentary structural advance in the course of the poem—is evident in some of the repeated phrasing. I would note especially section 11 with its calm morning to suit a calm grief, calm on the high wold, calm on the plain, calm in the wide air, and calm in the heart as a calm despair; and then calm on the seas that bring the bark, "And dead calm in that noble breast| Which heaves but with the heaving deep." The second stanza of the Prologue is also remarkable in this respect. If I think now of the other poems whose voices I have discussed, there is one poem that comes chiefly to mind: "Mariana," with its narrator who circles his subject and is one with Mariana herself who says, "He cometh not." If I looked at that poem and was satisfied with it, and asked what I wanted of the poet who wrote it, surely the answer would not be merely more of the same, even if the same were as perfect as "The Lady of Shalott." For their excellences are small and rigid. One could not add or take away many stanzas without disaster, and every little bit has to be perfect for the whole thing to stand. Who could have foretold that the poet of "Mariana" and "The Lady of Shalott" would find the same form, the same subject as it were, but without the rigidity, without the constricting small scale? Section 60 of *In Memoriam* itself describes Tennyson as a forsaken maiden in a lonely house—Tennyson the transvestite waiting in the moated grange for his Arthur. If Hallam had not died, someone would have had to kill him for the sake of poetry.

The view is absurd, of course, and the absurdity is measured in part by the voices of *In Memoriam* that have more in common with the voices of "Ulysses," "The Two Voices," and "Locksley Hall" than with those of "Mariana" and "The Lady of Shalott." Even when it is a yew or a house that is nominally addressed, the sense is of address rather than of the poet alone speaking in a trance. The poet describes trance, describes dream, but he is talking to someone, to Hallam, to the reader. He talks to himself—"O heart, how fares it with thee now"—and it is intimate conversation. If I wanted to link *In Memoriam* to one of the other poems, it ought more properly to be with "Ulysses" than with "Mariana." Like *In Memoriam*, "Ulysses" was inspired by the death of Hallam, and Tennyson said of it:

> [It] gave my feeling about the need of going forward, and braving the struggle of life perhaps more simply than anything in *In Memoriam*.
> . . . .
> There is more about myself in "Ulysses". . . . It was more written with the feeling of his loss upon me than many poems in *In Memoriam*.[11]

I heard a variety of mainly public voices in "Ulysses," strung together by an inadequate device of characterization. In *In Memoriam* Tennyson had his true subject instead of a device, and his voice could range with extraordinary freedom without any question of his cheating.

What I come to is this. When I looked at the other poems the voice I liked was the private voice, and I held no hope of the public voice. I could hardly have predicted *In Memoriam*. Moreover, I do not think *In Memoriam* represents a triumph of public voice over private. Nothing so simple as that. Rather I see that a conventional nineteenth century romantic voice—under exquisite control—yielded to something else rather more extraordinary, to which the term "public" does little justice. Surely the voice in *In Memoriam* is often public, oratorical, but it is as often private in the sense of being personal and intimate. It is in sum a flexible, human voice, not a conventional poet's voice either private or public. I do not mean that it is the voice of one's next door neighbor; it has too much range, and it is always mellifluous and controlled; but just as the form of the poem succeeds in coming close to the disorderly passage of grief, so the voice becomes a human poet's voice. I should not exaggerate, either, the distance between the voice in *In Memoriam* and the speaker's voice in "The Lady of Shalott," for certainly that voice has a plainness and directness that moves away from "Mariana" toward *In Memoriam*. Still, the distance is considerable, and it is astonishing to think that the two poems are by the same hand. The one is a perfect poem that strikes a single note, the other an imperfect poem that seems to me to surpass most other poems in the language in its sense of the complex and various man speaking it.

I would like now to turn to a few images of Tennyson the man. The first is a recollection by his younger brother Arthur.

> He ... had a powerful frame, a splendid physique, and we used to have gymnastics over the large beam in his attic den.... For our less active amusements we carved in wood and moulded with clay, and one of my earliest recollections of Alfred is watching him form with clay a Gothic archway in the bole of an old tree.

A friend from his Cambridge days wrote:

> Six feet high, broad-chested, strong-limbed, his face Shakespearian, with deep eyelids, his forehead ample, crowned with dark wavy hair, his head finely poised, his hand the admiration of sculptors, long fingers with square tips, soft as a child's but of great size and strength. What struck one most about him was the union of strength with refinement.

Edward FitzGerald described him to Bernard Barton in 1838:

> We have had Alfred Tennyson here; very droll, and very wayward: and much sitting up of nights till two and three in the morning with pipes in our mouths: at which good hour we would get Alfred to give us some of his magic music, which he does between growling and smoking.[12]

I hope that these images of Tennyson do not seem to support very adequately the character of the poet I have been describing, or the character seen by most modern commentators (including the morbid and neurotic person seen by Harold Nicolson and Christopher Ricks). Two things the images point to are the two words I rejected in "The Poet's Song": loud and gay. There is a difference between a man and his poetry, and I have been talking about the poetry as though it gave us the man, whereas it would seem that it gives us a distortion of part of the man. Though I hope that my discussion of the poems suggests more of the poetry-writing man than some of the other accounts of him, I am aware that my analysis is one more lie.

With Tennyson, it seems to me, the poet was less than the man. Just as "The Two Voices" could fail to reflect the actual anguish of the man, so it seems to me that his poetry generally, good and bad, is the man diminished—particularly the robust, hearty, witty, and often coarse man that some of his contemporaries described. Here he contrasts, I think, with T.S. Eliot, who was more of a poet than a human being. At any rate, to talk about the poetry as though it gives us the man seems a mistake, and Eliot's views on poetic voice seem rather more adequate when applied to him than when applied to Tennyson.

This matter has often preoccupied the study of Tennyson: to what extent as a poet did he labor under nineteenth century romantic notions of what a poet should be? To what extent did the laureateship force him into a particular poetic stance? And here is a broader question: to what extent is the art of poetry itself crippling to a man? Do we really want people writing poetry—unless they cannot help themselves? Let me quote Tennyson himself on his voice in *In Memoriam*, and it may seem that by modern standards of poetry he crippled himself, and it will seem also that he intended something different in part from what I myself hear.

> It must be remembered that this is a poem, *not* an actual biography.... The different moods of sorrow as in a drama are dramatically given, and my conviction that fear, doubts, and suffering will find answer and relief only through Faith in a God of Love. "I" is not always the author speaking of himself, but the voice of the human race speaking through him.[13]

Doubtless my discussion of *In Memoriam* suggests that Tennyson owed as much to Wordsworth as to Keats, and the fact that the poem struck the hearts of so many ordinary people of his time may prove that the forces making for industrial democracy were likewise altering the voices of poets. There is the fact that Victorian poetry never succeeded in dealing with the contemporary scene with the immediacy of Dickens, but many of the large issues of the day are certainly there in *In Memoriam*; and if one thinks that above all the Victorian age was a time-conscious age, a death-conscious age, one might want to say that *In Memoriam* was the most powerful expression of the age.

But these are larger issues. What I have mainly been interested to say was that the growth of the poet Tennyson could be predictable only in retrospect, and then only in ignorance. Tennyson the man was a sadist: he enjoyed very much putting a certain side of himself into the moated grange of poetry and listening to the groans, the solemnities, the intimate conversations.

6 A Shot at the Verbal Icon

WHEN W.K. WIMSATT published *The Verbal Icon* in 1954 the new criticism was triumphant, and his book must have appeared to some people to be the complete philosophical statement of the truth. Wimsatt is now dead, and his book is seen instead to have been one of the last flourishes of a school that had well-nigh run its course. What high-minded critic would think today of describing himself as a new critic? It was merely three years from *The Verbal Icon* to *The Anatomy of Criticism*, and both books seem to belong to a simpler age.

Where are the critics of yesteryear? Some people hope that past wisdom is incorporated in present, and in fact Wimsatt's views have not disappeared but remain solidly in place. Glance at the current range of academic journals and observe that new critical analysis is the staple item of most. The analyses may be enlivened by references to literary history, biography, and deep structures in a way that would have alarmed Wimsatt, but their aim will largely be to lay bare the verbal icon. "The dominion of Exegesis is great," said Geoffrey Hartman in 1971, "she is our Whore of Babylon, sitting robed in Academic black on the great dragon of Criticism, and dispensing a repetitious and soporific balm from her pedantic cup."[1]

Doubtless the main thing that new criticism offered to literary study was science, system, discipline. This ideal itself survives, sometimes transformed, improved if you will, raised to a higher power by the likes of Hartman himself. How many critics are there who do not believe that there are right methods for getting at the truth and who do not think that they themselves may have found them?

My attack on the verbal icon is meant to be a general attack on critical systems. But I acknowledge that I began my career as a kind of new critic and that I remain disposed to keep my eye on the verbal icon even as I look around and behind and in front of it.

I

In his book Wimsatt isolates the verbal icon—the true subject of the critic—with an argument that seems almost as undeniable as it is obvious. He distinguishes the poem from the creating poet on the one hand and from the attending reader on the other. What the poet did or thought he did, what he hoped to achieve in meaning and value, are subjects for biography and for theories of composition. How readers have responded, in the poet's own age or in classrooms, laboratories, and armchairs today, are subjects for history, morals, psychology, physiology. The critic may find all these things interesting or diverting (especially in the worst sense of the word), but his true task is to discover the meaning and value of the poem, and he will discover them only within the poem itself. What the poet intended may or may not be realised in the poem, and only the poem tells what is in the poem. How a reader responds may be irrelevant, and only an examination of the poem will display the meaning and value that make for relevant responses. Treating the poem as a verbal icon is "the only way by which criticism of a poem (rather than talk about its author and its audience or about its message) can be conducted."[2]

There are several incidental but significant points that Wimsatt scores against opposing views in the essays on the intentional and affective fallacies in *The Verbal Icon*. Firstly, knowing the intention of the poet is impossible as well as irrelevant; for poets often lie, or have bad memories, or change their minds five minutes before writing, or intend unconsciously. Secondly, affective theory is unfruitful as well as misguided. Aristotle's theory of catharsis says very little about tragedy and has mainly provided a puzzle of what he meant. As for I. A. Richards's theory of synaesthesia, "in applied criticism there would seem to be not much room for synaesthesia or for the touchy little attitudes of which it is composed" (32). Thirdly, the practice of both intentional and affective criticism often results in absurdities such as evaluation by goose pimples and shudders down the spine.

In my own argument I will be concerned with similar aspects of Wimsatt's position—the illogic of it first and foremost, and incidentally the impossibility, the unfruitfulness, and the absurdity of it.

II

The illogic can be seen in the issue of affective criticism. We may suppose for the moment that the poet does not matter to the critic—he can create and disappear like Shakespeare, and his works will stand without him, and who he was and what he thought may be subjects of inquiry mainly for the lunatic fringe. But can the critic do without the responses of readers—without his own responses especially, and perhaps also those of his fellow critics? To ask the questions is to suggest how untenable Wimsatt's position is, and we will not go far in reading him before we see concessions to affective criticism as well as stern denunciation of affective fallacy.

The first major break comes with the end of section 4 of "The Affective Fallacy." Wimsatt has talked about "dreary and antiseptic" (31) laboratory tests that aim to discover the physiological effects of poetry upon readers, he has shown up the semantic talk about emotive meanings for the nonsense it largely is, and he has ticked off Aristotle and Richards for their primitive and unhelpful theories of response. At this juncture it becomes clear that the incidental points have taken over from the logical point, that Wimsatt is talking less about the logical solidity of the objective critic's stance than about the practical advantages of it. The affective critic deals in the "psychologically vague" and "cognitively untranslatable," and the objective critic has a poem in his hand. The "insuperable advantage" of the latter is plain, and it extends to his role as a teacher; for talk of goose pimples and shudders may be agreeable, but the cognitive formulations of the objective critic are more likely to "enable readers to respond to the poem" (34). Wimsatt is not now shutting the door in the face of the affective critic; he simply prefers "the critic whose formulations *lean* to the cognitive" to "the critic whose formulations *lean* to the emotive" (34; emphasis supplied). But once the right of affective criticism is conceded, there is trouble ahead. For if the affective critic can display a more useful account of response than Aristotle or Richards, he will have to be granted that much more respect. And if the affective critic can show that shudders down the spine are sometimes less mind-numbing to students than analyses of irony and paradox, he must again be applauded.

Wimsatt's concession enlarges itself in a later essay in *The Verbal Icon*, "Explication as Criticism," in which he says he does not want the critic to lean too hard in the direction of neutral analysis, and does want him to lean somewhat—but not too hard—in the direction of affectivism: "the problem of explication ... puts before us in a compelling way both the desirability and the difficulty of finding an escape between the two extremes of sheer affectivism and of sheer scientific neutralism" (250). And thus Wimsatt becomes less than an unswerving advocate of objective criticism and something of a sensible mediator between extremes. This middle position is elaborated and modified in the opening essay of *Hateful Contraries*, in which Wimsatt displays literary theories in a neat diagram of extremes, and places himself firmly in the middle, with antennae reaching out in all directions, including the directions of intention and effect.[3] Such a position is a wise place to be, and perhaps every critic would put himself there if he thought about the matter long enough, but it is not the place that Wimsatt seemed to be in the early pages of *The Verbal Icon*, where he was preoccupied with the fallacy, the implausibility, the confusion, the irrelevance, of affective criticism.

The illogic can be seen in another way. Wimsatt is concerned in several essays in *The Verbal Icon* and *Hateful Contraries* to discuss poetry and religion, poetry and morals. He does not want to take the naive view that poetry must uphold the Ten Commandments in order to be good poetry, but he says, "there is a certain sense in which religion is the only theme of important poetry" (*H.C.* 39) and "the greatest poetry will be morally right" (*V.I.* 100). These assertions were made, I believe, from a specifically religious standpoint, but in the essays they are offered in such a way as to ask and claim assent from nominally unreligious persons. We live in a moral world, and the contradictions of moral attitudes from society to society, person to person, and time to time tell us only that contexts, knowledge, and means vary. Love, faithfulness, and charity are what we most require; and hatred, treachery, and selfishness are what we cannot do without. We live in an immoral world and perceive the moral reality. The poet, says Wimsatt, deals with this immoral-moral world not strictly as a moralist would but dramatically, and the greatest poetry displays profound moral insight and sympathy. "Characteristically, in its greatest instances, poetry has dealt with all the most intense, the hottest, human experiences and problems: with love and hate, sex, war, murder, youth and age, sickness and death, skepticism and faith—with religion" (*H.C.* 39). Such a play as *Antony and Cleopatra*, says Wimsatt, is immoral in the respect that it glorifies selfishness, sensuality, and suicide, but it is a great play because of its understanding of and sympathy for the human condition in which they occur. All the same, the glorification does in the end make the play a lesser play than *King Lear*. "The testimony of the critical tradition would seem to confirm this. The greatest poetry will be morally right, even though perhaps obscurely so" (*V.I.* 100).

The illogic here is that with such considerations the poem or play points to something outside itself. Its meaning and value are not self-contained and self-revealing, but they are to be seen and measured against a religious universe, and seen and measured most adequately—it would appear—by a critic with a sensitive perception of the religious universe as well as with skill in dealing with literature. Wimsatt heaps scorn upon the critic who sees himself as a great soul voyaging among great works, but he would hardly be prepared for the critic to be a great villain whose voyages might establish perverse canons of meaning and value. The great work, or evil work, can be seen properly only by a critic who possesses a moral sense and sees himself living in a moral universe, and its quality will be known to him by the extent to which his experience illuminates and is illuminated by his moral universe. Wimsatt's "verbal icon" implies the self-contained, isolated object, but his discussion of poetry and religion suggests a more elaborate and different metaphor in which the poem is a religious icon that the critic holds in his mind simultaneously with the vaguely shadowed great icon of his moral universe, seeing light flash forth from each upon the other. The critic's experience will matter to him, and he will not examine the immediate instrument, the poem, without his response being at the very center of his analysis.

This does not give us an affective theory either pure or simple. The critic is not likely to think that what goes on in his mind can be usefully measured in terms of electrical impulses; he may be chary of describing it directly at all—for reasons of strategy, modesty, or difficulty; he may suppose there is no point in talking about it without talking of the poem as well; but he may, in fact, and wisely, want to allude to it along with every objective thing he has to say about the poem. Wimsatt scoffs at judging poetry by goose pimples and shudders down the spine, and if anyone really did judge poetry by such means the scoffing might be deserved as well as unnecessary; but they seem instead to be useful shorthand expressions by which readers refer to their experience. "This great poem," says a critic, "made me sit up all night thinking." "This great poem," says another critic, "is dense with irony." Especially if we know the two critics, we may take the first as a meaningful statement and the second as a piece of nonsense—or vice versa.

It is indeed rather easy to show a respectable critic—and one admired by Wimsatt—using his response as a guide to his objective discussion. In an essay on Tennyson T. S. Eliot says of *In Memoriam* that "it gives me the shudder that I fail to get from anything in *Maud*." No one need suppose that his comments on the two poems will consist entirely of these fourteen words or that he approached all of Tennyson's poetry with body alert for an authentic shudder, but only that his sense of having been profoundly moved by one of the poems will be at the centre of his discussion. At the outset he talks of Tennyson's general merits of abundance, variety, and competence, and of the reader who will "appreciate" and "admire" and who will experience a "sense of confidence that is one of the major pleasures" of reading poetry. There follows some detailed illustration of the competence that is mainly responsible for the sense of confidence. Then he discusses *The Princess*, and he is "stirred" by the masterly lyrics, finds some of the ideas "exasperating," and thinks he might "swallow" the ideas if he could find the narrative "exciting." In general he is made to "recoil" from the poem—he would not like to read it again. And in like manner he proceeds to the objective analysis and shudder of *In Memoriam*.[4] No doubt the affective elements would be meaningless or useless without the objective analysis, and possibly the objective analysis would not seem to matter without the affective reference.

I do not suppose that the vocabulary of Eliot's response is a clear or elaborate expression of his experience, or gives much of a suggestion of an interplay between great and little icons (nor do I think his objective analysis covers very much of the poem). Presumably the adequacy of illustration of my point depends first upon the extent to which the critic himself is consciously concerned with response and sees poetry in terms suggested by the metaphor of the two icons, and secondly upon the extent to which response and the interplay between the two icons represent true critical concerns and the truth about poetry. As for the two icons, I have used the metaphor to describe what I think is implied by Wimsatt's views on poetry and religion, not to describe the truth about poetic experience. All the same I do think that Wimsatt's connection between poetry and religion is meaningful, more meaningful than his notion of the isolated verbal icon, without necessarily being true; and the metaphor of the two icons seems to me to be suggestive and somewhat useful, without telling us the truth either. All I would say is that I do believe response is of central importance to any critic whose criticism proceeds beyond rudimentary description, whether he thinks so or not, whether he visibly relies upon it or not.

Here, then, may be a more adequate illustration. Wimsatt's discussion of *Antony and Cleopatra* rests, I assume, upon fascination with and a measure of distaste for the play, and his discussion of *King Lear* upon virtually unqualified admiration, an emotion which in this instance may include a sense of catharsis. Whether my suppositions are right or wrong is of small importance; I use them to contrast with my own experience of the two plays. *Antony and Cleopatra* gives me a sense of the richness, variety, and beauty of life; it dazzles and creates joy; it suggests the grandness of human gesture. *King Lear*, on the other hand, seizes my universe and gives it a bad shake, and keeps on shaking. Catharsis? Not a bit of it; but a kind of unholy joy in the beauty with which the play delineates chaos. When I come to discuss the two plays, I can of course choose to hide my reactions, and my readers may prefer such restraint, but to do so will be dishonest—somewhat in the manner of one or another of our popular news magazines professing to give us just the facts. In any event, my objective comments will be different from Wimsatt's, for they will reflect a different experience. To speak of *Lear* only, I will argue that the order and justice that Albany brings at the end are a soft dramatic close to a vision of a malign universe in which the gods kill us for their sport. Gloucester with his eyes torn out, Lear on the heath, Cordelia hanged—these are the things that dominate the play in my analysis. I do not mean to imply that my view is right, and Wimsatt's wrong, or that we are both right, or both wrong, but only that my objective discussion is informed by my response and that there is material aplenty in the play for me to form.

It is not only in a general sense that I see response affecting objective analysis. I think such influence is sometimes visible in matters as small as vocabulary, especially when the vocabulary has religious implications. Wimsatt in his analysis of words emphasizes their public, shared, historical meanings, and he asserts that with negligible exception these are the meanings relevant to understanding and evaluating poetry. The poem is a complex of commonly understood symbols—the verbal icon—and its particular meaning and value are given and grasped through the interrelations of these commonly understood parts. But I think the wide variety of interpretations of even very short passages suggests the inadequacy of such a view and implies the importance of individual response. In two separate essays Wimsatt discusses Blake's poem "London," giving special attention to the phrase "marriage hearse" at the close. He refers to it as a "ghastly paradox" and speaks of the "explosive force of the two violently juxtaposed terms."[5] His description seems to me to be melodramatic. In an objective analysis I would say that the sure and certain rhythm of the poem, the unhesitating advance from image to image, give a status of revealed truth and ordinary fact to what otherwise might be ghastly, explosive, and paradoxical—and may have been in Blake's antecedent experience of life in London. But such objective comment would rest upon the assumption that Wimsatt and I had, or ought to have had, the same response to the poem and to the phrase; and this I do not believe. I suppose that Wimsatt's violent language may reflect a violent reaction. I suppose that to a conscientious Christian the individual words marriage and hearse may have so distinct a force and meaning that juxtaposition invariably spells violence. Who can quarrel with this? What I oppose to it is my own nominally unreligious background, in which marriage was not a sacrament and hearse was a black Cadillac whose insides I cleaned at seventy-five cents a time. Such a background contributes to a significantly different response to the phrase.

Aside from this, I think that the dryness of the new-critical approach to poetry is often disguised by dramatic language and even by a theoretical reliance upon the notion of poetry as drama ("the stage drama," says Wimsatt, "shows in a complicated way what holds also for the lyrical and meditative monologue"[V. I. xv]); and in this respect I am inclined to believe that Wimsatt's Christian response to "marriage hearse" may be badly represented by the sort of critical language he chooses to use.

I do not believe that we are mere passive respondents in a fixed universe to a fixed verbal assault. If we were, the critic might be able to follow either the objective or the affective course exclusively and describe the object or the effect completely in a way to satisfy his reader. Whether Wimsatt himself considered the universe to be fixed or nearly fixed, I do not know, and even if he did the decision to follow the objective course instead of the affective or a union of the two would be a matter of choice rather than logical necessity. But to the extent that the same held or seemed to hold for other people, he would have had to allow, I think, that the character of individual response is of central importance to criticism.

There are, of course, critics who live in rather nicely fixed intellectual universes—universes that seem to them to be so. In such good fortune are critics with firm understandings of myth, history, society, and mind—who if they are ever at a loss about anything know that it can and ought to be understood in terms familiar to or discoverable by them. The conscientious Freudian critic is luckiest of all (despite the low opinion in which he is held by his fellow scientists), for he owns a comprehensive account of human mentality from birth onwards, with ready explanations for desires, acts, gestures, and thoughts, and with a clear grasp of society and history that even mythologists, social anthropologists, and historians find themselves relying upon. As against Wimsatt's view that "the greatest poetry will be morally right," the critic who lives in a Freudian universe can say that "the greatest poetry will deal with the Oedipus complex and with other complexes central to human experience." He will likely accept Wimsatt's proposition as a corollary and point out that Wimsatt's "hottest human experiences" are exactly what poetry is concerned with—except that he has more precise knowledge of them than Wimsatt. It is entirely possible for the Freudian critic to analyse a poem in a consciously objective way for the psychological attitudes and relations that seem to be explicit or implicit therein, but it would seem absurd of him not to keep his Freudian universe by his side as he did so to guide his steps along a path that must by definition be tortuous. And though he could rest content with this guided objective analysis, it would seem equally absurd for him to do so; for Freudian objects and icons exist in relation to motives, acts, and responses. Response to poetic expression of the Oedipus complex must inevitably interest him. Wimsatt seems to classify Freudian criticism as purely or mainly affective, which surely it need not be; but the Freudian critic is always likely to see aesthetic response as a central part of his critical concern. And his situation seems only a more clearly defined or fixed one than Wimsatt's own—or than that of Frye or Hartman. I myself find intellectual universes the least believable kind, and the criticism associated with them especially unhelpful; but the question here is not who has the right universe but whether having a universe in mind implies the importance of affective criticism to the critic. I think it does, and does so rather obviously in Wimsatt's case, the Freudian's, and my own.

III

And yet it is agreeable to think that there lies the poem with its meaning and value waiting to be unraveled, and that the man with a truly disciplined mind may be fortunate enough to perform the task once and for all. Surely some of us do approach poems in this way, or believe we do; perhaps we all do some of the time. What are the results?

Wimsatt's view of poetry on this practical level is that of a new critic who is rather more rigorous than some of his fellows. The terms that he relies upon are irony, ambiguity, paradox, wit, symbol, complexity, and organic unity, and he is glad to use other familiar descriptive terms. A good poem is complex and organic, a bad poem is not. "Only poems which are worth something" will yield to serious explication (H.C. 240); "complexity of form is sophistication of content" (V.I. 82); and the good poem will throw out "ever widening concentric circles of meaning" (V.I. 81). Today, says Wimsatt, "Shakespeare has more meaning and value...than he had in his own day" (D.C. 225), for we have studied him harder in a sophisticated way; and if we apply ourselves well enough to a poem we may arrive at "total judgment" (V.I. 250).

This practical view of poetry seems to me to be visionary, and it produces a vision of the day when total judgment has been passed upon every known work, and there are armies of hungry cataloguers waiting to pass total judgment upon every new work as it issues from the press. The cataloguers are lean as well as hungry, and the rest of us are frozen to death—aside from the professional authors busy at their ironies, complexities, and unities. We know that such a day will not arrive, and we know that the situation today bears all too much resemblance to it, except that if we are very modern our favourite vocabulary is different. The characteristic tone in our academic journals is that of modest and serious self-righteousness, quite as though Wimsatt's total judgment has just been arrived at with the particular work under review.

Still we might ask a practical question. Is there general evidence that our careful study of literature is bringing us in the direction of total judgments that we did not possess before, or is it bringing instead a proliferation of contradictory meanings, many of them absurd, and a reassessment of values that is suspect? Wimsatt says that "our intuition of any complex whole will be improved by analysis" (V.I. 249), and no doubt most academic critics would agree in the abstract and for themselves. In this respect the answer is that we are moving toward total judgments, but I think the other answer is patent when we look hard at particular works that we ourselves have not announced final meanings for. Keats's "Ode on a Grecian Urn" has perhaps received more attention in recent years than any other poem in the language, and an analysis such as Earl Wasserman's is in line with Wimsatt's principles; yet there are Keatsians who laugh at Wasserman's analysis and others who take issue with it on grounds also in line with Wimsatt's principles. The range of opinion on the poem suggests—as I argue in my essay on the poem included here—that analysis often distorts the intuition of experience and that the more carefully we study anything the more nearly we may be brought to total confusion.

A more difficult case is that of Henry James, an author whom modern criticism has rescued from some neglect and installed as as central figure of the modern novel. He had his early admirers but they did not see him as we see him, and his elevation is widely accepted and understood in terms that accord with Wimsatt's principles. Thus we have a movement toward total judgment initiated and developed by modern analysis. Perhaps; but certain qualifications are in order. James has been rescued for only a few decades, and in a sense the favorable judgment on him remains a coterie judgment, with the academy taking over from part of Bloomsbury. And when one gets down to individual novels, the general agreement of modern analysis tends to disappear. Leon Edel says of *The Ambassadors* that "its peculiar greatness" lies "in the exquisiteness of its vision: a large, ironic, comic vision." F.R. Leavis says that it seems to him to be "not only *not* one of his great books, but to be a bad one"; it "produces an effect...of a technique the subtleties and elaborations of which are not sufficiently controlled." Ian Watt inclines in the direction of Edel, except that he thinks the book "is written with considerable sobriety." And I myself incline in the direction of Leavis: I think the book shows that complexity of form can be simplemindedness of content; it is thick with ambiguity and thin with substance—rather the reverse, say, of *Vanity Fair*, which I think of as one of the great novels of the language. (But here I part company with Leavis, who says that the notion that Thackeray is great "won't stand the touch of criticism.")[6]

Such disagreement is really what we expect when we get down to cases, and modern analysis seems to have multiplied the disagreements rather than lessened them. Perhaps in a broad way there is a consensus about James's merits that there did not use to be, but this does not seem to be an advance over the sort of consensus about Shakespeare or even Donne that was arrived at before modern analysis came to our aid. And in my own view, modern analysis seems inclined to gross misconceptions of general value when it is not guided by previously received opinion, and James is a prime instance.

Even if we assume the logical validity of Wimsatt's position, the practical task of scrutinizing the verbal icon and arriving at total judgment seems exceedingly difficult if not impossible, and the results are often plainly absurd. There is in Wimsatt himself a division between confidence in the notion of total judgment and puzzlement in the execution. Grandly widening circles of meaning become deplorably relentless analysis. He faces his predicament most philosophically in his essay on "The Concrete Universal" in a discussion of value, and he has to rest there with the hope that "approximate descriptions of poems, or multiple restatements of their meaning ... [will] aid ... readers to come to an intuitive and full realisation of poems themselves and hence to know good poems and distinguish them from bad ones" (V.I. 83). But his discussion is abstract, and it is similarly abstract in "Explication as Criticism." When he gets down to a case in *Hateful Contraries* he is less optimistic. He says that while he has been explaining, describing, and explicating "London" there, he has also been appreciating it. He means appreciation not in the sense of explicit affective statement or of response controlling a supposedly objective discussion but in the sense of a silent accompaniment. "We are engaged," he says, "with features of a poem which ... do tend to assert themselves as reasons for our pleasure in the poem and our admiration for it. We begin to talk about patterns of meaning, we encounter structures or forms which are radiant or resonant with meaning. Patterns and structures involve coherence ... , and coherence is an aspect of truth and significance" (240). But his discussion of "London" is lame, and largely ignores certain obvious things such as development of rhythm and imagery in the poem, and he seems to feel uneasy about what he has done, thinking he may have "said too much" and yet being reluctant to indulge in the sort of "relentless criticism" (238) that might uncover a good many more patterns, structures, meanings, and coherences. And he concludes: "I do not think that our evaluative intimations will often, if ever, advance to the firmness and completeness of a demonstration" (240). It is a far cry from total judgment.

IV

Whatever qualifications Wimsatt puts upon his views, and however contradictory they may seem all together, he keeps coming back to his original statements. Thus in 1968 in an essay in *The Disciplines of Criticism* we find him once again demolishing the intentional fallacy. He first performed the task in 1942, then again in 1944 and 1945, and in *The Verbal Icon* in 1954. In the new essay he expresses gloom about the situation. Why should the fallacy keep rising up? How could critics continue to be so obtuse? Imagine wanting "to throb in unison with the mind of the artist"! (194) And he has to admit a kind of defeat: "there is no way to keep the simpler kinds of intention-hunters from jumping on the vehicle of literary inquiry, and nobody I suppose really wishes the power to legislate against them" (196-97). Nobody serious as well as tolerant, nobody who has the truth in him, which Wimsatt then reexpounds for twenty-eight pages.

In this thirty years' war Wimsatt was the self-appointed champion of all good academics against a common enemy—frivolous academics, critics of the popular press, and old-fashioned critics. His attack is most pointed in the opening pages of *Hateful Contraries*, and we can see there that most of his targets are sitting ducks. Who ever took J. Donald Adams of the *New York Times Book Review* seriously? Who has taken Karl Shapiro seriously for the past fifteen years? Who takes David Daiches *very* seriously? Who bothers about old fuddy-duddies like Edmund Gosse, George Saintsbury, and Sir Arthur Quiller-Couch? Nobody again, and nobody means no self-respecting academic critic in America, perhaps even in England, whether he subscribes to Wimsatt's theory of criticism or not.

Once the shoe was on the other foot, and the new academic critics were the upstarts, outsiders, and fools. But it was not they who learned humility. In retrospect one sees that all they had to do was blow the trumpet for the walls to fall down. Science, professionalism, and education were all marching on their side, and the present high seriousness of academic criticism is the result. And the condescension? It is a return for the same, the complacency of the insider, the scorn of the just. Perhaps it also reflects some unease.

For academic criticism does not have things entirely its own way even within the walls. Who among us has not lamented the spiraling proliferation of books, articles, systems, and ingenuities? What English department lacks its dull and terrifying supercritic? Where is the learned journal that is a pleasure to read? Where in fact are the readers of the world—all those undergraduates we trained to approach poetry in correct ways? (Not those who became our graduate students, but all the rest.)

Set aside the issue of the logic or illogic of Wimsatt's theories. There remains a problem, human, practical, strategic. You are a teacher and you know the meaning and value of "London." How do you best convey the meaning and value to your students? You can require them to perform the sort of analysis you undertook and hope they come through it properly. Or you can disclose to them your acquired facts about charters, bans, and marks. But perhaps you choose to talk mainly about Blake himself, that absurd, direct, and honest man who sat in front of the fire with his wife and saw visions and wrote clumsy couplets about marriage.

> When a man has married a wife, he finds out whether
> Her knees and elbows are only glued together.

What was his vision of London? You realise that this third approach might fail, but you say that the door of perception is sometimes the back door—if you want to call this the back door.

You are a literary critic and you want to "tone the mind," as Wimsatt puts it (H.C. xvii). You ask yourself whether studying the tensions in *In Memoriam* as evidenced in the structure of the ten major images of the poem is likely to tone the mind better than reading Hallam Tennyson's memoir of his father. Having recently completed a mind-numbing analysis of *The Ring and the Book* you choose the softer task and excuse yourself by saying that criticizing poetry requires grace, flexibility, humanity, and that if there are true strategies for toning the critical mind it may be that to read about a human life, even a poet's life, or to go for a walk in the garden, are among the best.

It is not difficult to find Wimsatt himself making gestures in such directions. He says in the introduction to *Hateful Contraries* that there are times, perhaps especially in the classroom or on the front page of the *New York Times Book Review*, when critical impressionism or expressionism is the thing most needed; and at the close of his analysis of "London" in the same book he says, "Our aim I think should be to say certain selected, intelligible things about a poem, enough to establish the main lines of its technical achievement, of its symbolic shape. When we have done that much, we understand the poem" (238). But does he mean it? The concession to J. Donald Adams comes a page after the attack on him, and the concession is immediately withdrawn. What Adams practices is "not a very mature form of cognitive discourse" (xvii), and it is he who should tone his mind with "cogitation about the nature of literature" (xvii) and keep his eye on the verbal icon.

The concession is important, though, for it again suggests unease. The logician discovers the true function of the critic, and then he discovers that the true function has to be restrained. And who is going to do the restraining and by what as yet unrevealed logic? Wimsatt is pleased to draw a line in his own discussion of "London," and he is pleased to draw the line for you and me; but his position is insecure and admits large doubts about the whole high critical enterprise. It is the sort of unforeseen problem that revolutionaries are always stumbling upon. They rout the simple-minded exegetes—and all the while the throbbers keep coming back. They elevate literary criticism to a high plane and find themselves in a dense thicket—with throbbers peering at them from behind trees. Perhaps they even begin to imagine that there are only immature forms of cognitive discourse.

Think, then, of the critic of an earlier generation whom it is so easy to despise, who never had the discriminations of intentional and affective fallacy to light his way. Think, say, of Edmund Gosse, that prissy, effete, and snobbish literary man, careless of fact and carefree of logic, and with assistants of the same stamp. He wrote biographies of half a dozen English authors from Sir Thomas Browne to Coventry Patmore, edited works of another dozen, wrote histories or studies of seventeenth, eighteenth, and nineteenth century English literature, translated Ibsen and a French writer or two, and wrote several volumes of incidental essays on literature. He had, I should imagine, a range of interest and knowledge about English authors far exceeding that of any scholar in America today—and more especially exceeding that of any relentless critic. Call it superficial and confused interest and knowledge (from an absolutely secure vantage point); it was part and parcel of his being an intensely, inveterately literary person. He consorted with poets and throbbed in unison with some of them, and he himself wrote poetry quite naturally if not with immense success. He also owned a prose style that helps to make *Father and Son* a considerable work. Perhaps all told he was a better man at his job than his modern counterpart.

Or think of a living old-fashioned literary man like Sir John Betjeman, whose authority on literature I have yet to hear invoked by a serious academic critic. At a recent Christmas Sir John shared in a recital of poems, and one of the poems on the program was Thomas Hardy's "Beeny Cliff." He mentioned his love of Hardy and also his love of Cornish scenery, and then he declined to read the poem, because, he said, it always made him blubber. He left it to his partner in the recital, who then read it without blubbering. How simple the form of affective criticism! How lucky the man! I suppose that he may have been introduced to Hardy in the twenties. I suppose that in any event his English soul throbs more closely in unison with Hardy's than can an American—can hear Hardy's speech, read the lines in his face, share his sense of life more exactly. I suppose that his English eyes possess Beeny Cliff and Cornwall with a naturalness and to a depth that no devout pilgrim from across the ocean can acquire. And I suppose I could have told him that under the aspect of eternity "Beeny Cliff" will be stripped of the accidents of man and place; but instead I was jealous of him for the life and scene in which the poem exists for him. It seemed to me that the desire of the high-minded critic to abstract a poem from its source is a desire for death, and the aspect of eternity he gets is a living grave. Call the high-minded pose an unintentional mistake.

V

I think there is a sense in which almost anyone is likely to dismiss Wimsatt's views with a shrug of disbelief. Privately we know that our feelings about poetry may be feelings about a few poets in particular times and places; we realise that our critical taste is a ragbag of inclination, prejudice, sentimentality, ignorance, misinformation, and vision. To tell us that "poetry is characteristically a discourse about both emotions and objects" (V.I. 38) is to tell a lie. We do not read "I Remember, I Remember" that way, we do not read *Paradise Lost* that way, or "The Pobble Who Has No Toes." We like our fallacies, we live amid confusion, we see poets and their poems and ourselves in a world together and cannot and will not compartmentalize.

We speak differently in public before our inferiors, peers, and betters. We lean toward omniscience, we yearn toward science, we are grave and disciplined, we want to serve scholarship, culture, and posterity. The precisions of new criticism, certain grandiosities of history and myth, the solemnities of linguistic analysis are for us. The verbal icon is a reflection of our public and serious selves.

It may be relevant, then, to describe some part of the private world in which the public critic gets dressed. I will use my own experience because I know it, and I will hope to show that the act of new criticism and of related criticism and scholarship can be different from what they are supposed to be and can have different implications from those that Wimsatt sees.

1. Criticism as Revelation

I do not know anyone who has admitted that his own best criticism is revelation, though I believe it is often so. In my own case, some of my worst criticism has been revelation. But no one who sees God will deny him, and anyone who suddenly sees into the heart of a poem will know it. The denial comes later, in the cold light of another two or five years.

My own revelations have invariably sprung from close analysis, even though they follow only rarely upon analysis. The first one I had seems, in retrospect, to have been almost inevitable, but it was no less extraordinary for being so. For five years I read widely in psychoanalytical writings. I dare say that no one else ever read so much in so little space, or so uncritically, unless it was Otto Fenichel himself, author of the one-time bible for psychoanalysts in America. Then it happened that I was teaching Sherwood Anderson's story "Death in the Woods," and struggling with it in the ordinary new critical way. There was the story, lovely and with an aura of secret meaning, and there were the mechanical things I could seem to say about its structure, pattern, complexity. But I persisted. I contemplated the old woman of the story as she lay dead in the cold woods, her body exposed to the waist and seeming the body of a girl; I contemplated the dogs that circled her as in a ritual, and the people who came upon her. The images were a kind of music, or magic; there was something uncanny about them. Suddenly a critical shudder went up and down my spine. I saw that the unmentioned focus of the story was the female breast, and I saw resonances between the immediate scenes and the universal scene of infancy, of a child at its mother's breast. The story dealt in the uncanny, and I understood it in an uncanny moment of revelation. Moreover, I had read Freud's essay "The Uncanny" and was able to go back to it to bolster my revelation with the word of the master, and several years later I published an article on it that was all scholarly caution and critical rigor.[7]

Privately I was St. Paul on the road to Damascus, publicly I was a Jesuit; and now a good many years later both my revelation and my rigor dismay me, and my Freudian universe has been shrugged off. Was my original intuition of the story improved by analysis, as Wimsatt says it should have been? Or was my analysis improved by the revelatory intuition? Did the whole experience show that a critic can discover in a verbal icon whatever exists in his view of the universe?

The other revelation that I will mention came in two parts. I was reading Arnold Bennett's novels as examples of realism, and I was reading all his novels for a second time to see them in perspective better. I was settling down with a curious unrealistic one called *The Glimpse*, which tells in the first person of an aesthete's vision of previous existences. In the opening pages he attends a concert, and listens to Ravel's *Miroirs*, later he has a heart attack and calls for a mirror to look at himself dying; then come several images of himself in various incarnations. This mirror imagery struck me of a sudden, and half a dozen other images in the novel then struck me, and in a moment I saw the whole novel as a pattern of images. But *The Glimpse* was a sport among Bennett's novels. I turned almost without thought to a minor realistic novel about the Potteries, *The Price of Love*. There I was assailed by images again, in profusion and in a structure that the term realism did not account for; and underneath them, and far beneath the realism, I found the image and tale of Christ at Easter. Strange? Not if you think that Christ has stalked the thoughts of modern critics these last twenty-five years and more. Not if you think that a modern critic ought to see things that his predecessors have missed. But strange to me, who was at the time not only a naive critic but also a nonbeliever born and bred, with only the most rudimentary knowledge and interest in Christianity. I had to go to a Bible to learn about Christ's seven last words, and Mary's seven dolors, and what the soldiers did, and string these things upon my revelation, which continued for several days.

With my discovery about "Death in the Woods" I could see my Freudian universe prompting me. Here I had a blank—or rather here I had only my new critical technique prompting me. The experience seems to suggest that a new critic requires no universe but merely his technique. Possibly it suggests that technique is discovery (to transpose a new critical view of literature itself). And if my discovery was absurd—as I gradually came to think—it may even imply that the verbal icon does not exist, that discovery lies rather more in the technique than in the supposed object. Along with the intentional and affective fallacies should be listed a third, the objective. I filled some fifty pages, and could have filled many more, with a serious and systematic analysis of the religious imagery in *The Price of Love*. And in spite of all fallacies, I would have given much to have had a word from Arnold Bennett himself about the matter.[8]

2. Criticism as Deception

I will say nothing of the lower depths of deception, for they are familiar to everyone, and prove only that we are frail and need to cloak our ignorance, insecurity, and vanity in the complacencies of our learned styles. The two examples I will mention were puzzles to me. The first came at the end of my study of "Death in the Woods." My revelation covered only the central elements of the story, and Freud's essay fitted them; but there were incidental parts that I assumed could not be irrelevant—the material on Jake Grimes and the German, and the interpolated tale by the storyteller. But no further revelation came to light my way. In the end I had to apply Freudian theory to this material quite mechanically, and I fitted out two paragraphs on castration. I supposed they made sense, but I did not believe them, and I felt that criticism without revelation must be dust and ashes. At the same time I had to wonder whether the two paragraphs proved just the reverse—that criticism can get along very well without revelation, that I was just as good, or bad, in my science as in my revelation. Would the two paragraphs seem as reliable to Freudians as the rest of the analysis? To anti-Freudians would they seem more frivolous than anything else?

The other deception came when I undertook to conduct a seminar on the early poetry of E. A. Robinson, a subject that I knew only from reading Robinson's poetry in my adolescence. I proposed to do three things: (1) read his early poems in chronological order, giving special attention to his poetic voice, and trying to infer from it his theory of poetry, (2) read his early writings on poetry and derive his theory of poetry independently from them, and (3) read the critics of his early poetry in chronological order and infer their opinions of what his theory of poetry was and also infer their own assumptions about poetry. The exercise proved to be exacting, and it brought me to an unexpected result in the way of solving the riddles of certain poems. The essay on Robinson that I wrote (and that is reprinted here) recapitulates the investigation, but it conceals the fact that the interpretations I arrived at were the same as my adolescent understanding of the poems. As against Wimsatt's expectation that intuition will always be improved by analysis, this experience implies that intuition need not be destroyed by it—for in contrast to my own apparent good luck was the misfortune of certain other critics who saddled their intuitions with ludicrous interpretations.

3. Criticism and Scholarship as Illusion

I have tried to suggest that discoveries made through criticism and scholarship are often illusions generated by particular techniques and preconceptions, or that they are illusions in the sense of being constructions indistinguishable from prior intuitions. The two experiences I record here are perhaps notable only in showing how difficult, or impossible, it is to break out of the circle. In the first my preconception was that modern scholarship is a mistake. In both instances the details of my chosen illustrations filled themselves out with surprising ease. But I am not yet so sceptical as to disbelieve the evidence for my scepticism.

My first experience came at a time when I was becoming dissatisfied with my methods of criticism; I seemed to use them increasingly mechanically, and the result seemed increasingly unhelpful. I thought that this might be a common circumstance, that any given approach to literature provides insight at first and then hardens into system and sterility. And then I thought of Freud, of whom it was commonly said that his first work was his greatest, and in particular I thought of *The Moses of Michelangelo* and *Leonardo da Vinci*. Was it the case that the first, which seemed inspired, was the early work of genius, and the second, which seemed unconvincing, was the later work of the complacent scientist? So it proved to be, all too readily. Yet in a certain respect the essay that I wrote on the subject was very cautious ("Deeper Chaos and Larger Order," reprinted here); for the more thinking I did about it, the more thoroughly doubtful I became of systematic critics and their systems, but the essay argued merely that art is a mystery and that the systems by which we approach it should be managed gracefully.

My other experience came with my essay on Swinburne, printed here, and again sprang from dissatisfaction with earlier work of my own. Some years ago I read Reginald Pound's biography of Arnold Bennett, and I saw that it was riddled with error, misunderstanding, contradiction, and superficiality. It was the work of a journalist rather than of a scholar. And I thought that with due diligence and care for fact I might eventually write the standard definitive biography. And diligent and careful I was over the next several years, but I arrived at the wrong conclusion, namely that Pound's book was a better book than I could write; for Pound lived in Bennett's time, knew Bennett and some of his circle, and wrote out of an experience and knowledge that I could only dimly apprehend. I might get all those facts straight, but the whole thing would be scholarly wool.

It then began to seem to me that any biographer removed from his subject in time and culture as I was from Bennett would make a mess of it, and the more carefully factual the greater the mess. At the time I was toying with this notion, I became engaged in some work on Edmund Gosse and wanted to learn about his skill as a biographer. I had recently read a favorable review of Jean Overton Fuller's study of Swinburne, but it seemed to me probable that Gosse's biography of him would make more sense than anything written today. And so it did. But I was more than surprised to see the argument focusing itself perfectly upon a new fact turned up by modern investigation.

Doubtless it is well for Swinburne's reputation, and also for Bennett's, that biographies continue to be written, even if they reduce their subjects to abstractions; doubtless it is impossible for a man from another time and especially another culture to see his subject with the immediacy of a contemporary. I am talking only of the vanity, complacency, and simple-mindedness that make us prize our modern methods and results so highly. Our authors are not really served by such folly; they are buried in definitive graves.

VI

I do not know how to read. I stumble when I see. After four or five readings of a poem, some sort of poem lodges itself in my mind, more heard than seen. Sometimes it goes away and comes back seeming rather different. I do not understand the matter myself, and I will not trust someone else to tell me about it. Not that I believe in the mystery of mind and art, though once I did, but I do believe that the systematizers of both are among the more absurd people one meets, even when they are very clever. I have to rest with this as an assertion, but I believe it more firmly than I believed Gosse would do better by Swinburne than would the modern scholars. All my experience leads me to believe it, including the experiences recorded here. And what is recorded here is a shadow of whatever truth is in me. Said Yeats before he died, "When I try to put all into a phrase I say, 'Man can embody truth but he cannot know it.'" That seems good enough to stand by.

7 Mr. Pooter and the Little Tradition

F. R. LEAVIS'S GREAT TRADITION consists of those few novelists who are creative geniuses demanding our closest adult attention, through whom the novel takes a new direction and opens up to us new dimensions and perspectives of our moral, spiritual life. Those few novelists do write within a historical tradition, and the tradition is important to them—we would not have Jane Austen without Fanny Burney—but essentially the great creative genius is sui generis, or if he learns from anyone it is chiefly from the great creative genius before him. Thus Leavis says that George Eliot had Jane Austen to learn from, Henry James had George Eliot. And what they learned they of course transformed. So it is that Leavis describes a great tradition consisting of five novelists, the only novelists whom we can go to expecting our full intelligence to be wholly engaged and from whom we may learn something to change, ripen, deepen ourselves. They are not novelists whom we will fall asleep over; they are not content with thrills, melodrama, sentimental tears; they will not reinforce our prejudices, our cozy view of life. They are Jane Austen, George Eliot, Henry James, Joseph Conrad, D. H. Lawrence.[1]

Leavis markedly changed some of his views in the later years of his life. But in a fundamental way his views remained the same, and in a fundamental way his antagonists have always been Leavisites. Most of us believe in a great tradition, with a canon suitably enlarged to include Dickens and anyone else we can agree upon. Most of us distinguish between great authors who deserve our serious attention and minor ones like Mrs. Gaskell or Ebenezer Elliott who require apology or inflation if we give them very much of our time. What academic critic would not raise his eyebrows at someone who professed to like *Alton Locke* more than *The Ambassadors*? What attentive graduate student would think of ranking *Barchester Towers* with *Middlemarch*? Most of us are Leavisites. *Barchester Towers* is best only when we take a book to bed at night.

The claim of a great tradition is implicit in the phrase. What is great is better than what is not great, and though we cannot spend our lives thinking great thoughts and feeling great emotions along with the great artists, most of us would agree that the great authors deserve our great attention and reward us most greatly and that to abandon our awareness of this fact is to abandon our obligation to ourselves, to society, to culture, to history. We do want to know and preserve the best that has been thought and said, and Leavis was a self-conscious heir of Matthew Arnold. So it was that my fellow scholar raised his eyebrows when I spoke up for *Alton Locke*. He had his obligations, and though he admitted that Henry James might be overpraised, he was certain that we must make our discriminations. He accused me of not wanting to make judgments at all. But I do. It is merely my opinion that believers in a great tradition have their values wrong; and it is my aim with the notion of a little tradition to suggest values that I think are more helpful, more agreeable than the values we commonly associate with the great tradition—those values like profundity, complexity, subtlety, grandeur, and relevance. To put the matter rashly, I think that a book such as *The Diary of a Nobody* deserves more credit from us than Conrad's novels; I think that English music hall must have been more rewarding than Beethoven's quartets. In saying this I do not mean to play a game of musical chairs, the sort of thing we do when we say (as we did a few years ago) that the great poets among the Victorians are Hopkins, Hardy, and Meredith instead of Tennyson, Browning, and Arnold.

Let me distinguish three traditions: great, minor, and little. The great tradition is identified, and I need only add that the great artwork reaches its apotheosis when we say that it is universal—it speaks to all men, it is a world classic. Thus *Hamlet*, thus the *Iliad*. And we see it to some degree anomalous to admit that though universal, Beethoven's music is very German. The minor tradition is, in conventional parlance, all that fails to rise to greatness, not attempting greatness, failing in the attempt, or in too limited a mode for greatness to be possible. It includes all that accumulates historically and that is presumed to have some degree of importance. In speaking of a minor tradition we are conscious of two things: (1) absolute inferiority or smallness in the quality of the work—even though we admit we make mistakes in our absolute judgments, and (2) the local coloring, the eccentric cultural coloring that restricts appeal. Thus we say that the novels of Charlotte Yonge are inferior to the novels of Thackeray, or we say that the novels of Jane Austen are perfect of their kind or that *The Diary of a Nobody* is a minor classic, but what they attempt is so much smaller than *War and Peace* that we cannot speak of them in the same breath—though more and more is claimed for Jane Austen these days, so that some of us hardly recognize her. The essential point about the minor tradition is that it is defined in terms of the great tradition. It is the other side of the same coin, it is all the rest, it includes all the works on the rungs of the ladder (except the lowest) up to but not including the top. Where the work belongs on the ladder depends, of course, on whether you are talking nationally or internationally, about English, Western, or world literature.

Mr. Pooter and the Little Tradition

My third tradition, the little tradition, I would abstract from works commonly placed in both the great and minor traditions, and for reasons of necessity I will restrict myself to literature in England. I would define it as literature that is part of the natural and unique culture of the nation and whose existence is more significant to the ordinary life and the continuing ordinary life of the nation than other literature, whether that other literature is commonly reckoned to be great and is conscientiously studied within the society or whether it is minor literature of limited or wide appeal.

This brief definition is unsatisfactory. What is the natural culture of a nation? Who is so foolish that he will define the unique aspect of the ordinary life of England without a trace of suspicion that what he sees is not what someone else sees? My view is necessarily rather more personal than objective; it is my truth. But it draws on observations that others have made before me.

1. I think there is often a gap between what people profess to admire and what they like, between what they study and what they choose to read on their own, between what they acknowledge deserves their attention and what they want to give their attention to, between what is important in their conscientious thoughts and what is important in their lives. Over the years I have known people who have been consciously preoccupied with the poetry of Tennyson, Hopkins, Yeats, and Eliot, and who have admitted privately that the poetry that has always meant the most to them has been that of Thomas Hardy.

2. I think that the scientific criticism developed over the past forty years is radically deficient—not incomplete but deficient. Not long ago an eminent Dickens scholar looked into the future of Dickens studies, and what he conjured up was a vision of critics examining the myth, imagery, symbolism, and structure of *Bleak House* even harder in the next forty years than they had already. His future seemed indistinguishable from the present, and it seemed to have very little to do with literature and civilization.

3. I think that greatness, grandeur, complexity, subtlety, profundity, and like words often describe a narrow, limited experience; that what we choose to call the profound and complex interests of a great novel may be a thick disguise for interests very much the same as the compulsive interests of a motorcar race, a prize fight, a football match, a murder mystery. I think in contrast that a work that makes no attempt to seize or compel may have a wider range and more valuable quality.

4. I think that the forces that make for uniqueness in the ordinary life of England may have little to do with a great tradition in the arts or with a minor tradition. Over the past fifty years the chief influence in England in the way of a great tradition in music has been Germanic, and the chief influence in the way of a minor musical tradition has been American. I am inclined to think that on balance this is a bad thing rather than a good thing, that it may tear at the fabric of an individual culture; but what seems clear is that as yet Englishmen are in their

ordinary life quite unlike Germans and Americans, and are not even an odd mixture of the two; and I take it that what makes an Englishman may be largely something else than a great or minor tradition in music or in the arts generally.

As a corollary to this, I would say that I think a preoccupation with the notion of a great tradition may be evidence of cultural deficiency. It is observable that nations preoccupied with greatness, and even highly productive of what are usually reckoned to be great men, have sometimes been hideous civilizations. George Steiner has been concerned with this issue in recent years, and would like us to have greatness without hideousness; but I think the drive toward greatness may be a drive toward hideousness. Culture with a capital C may not be what we need.

The Diary of a Nobody was first published in 1892 after appearing in sketchier form in *Punch* in 1888-89. It has been highly praised, but the nature of some of the praise indicates a special character. Lord Rosebery said: "To write an appreciation of a book I esteem so highly is, I am afraid, beyond my power.... But I regard any bedroom I occupy as unfinished without a copy of it."[2] The bedroom, of course, is no place to study myth, imagery, symbol, and structure; it is where one falls asleep over light entertainment, and the praise automatically removes *The Diary of a Nobody* from the canon of great and serious books. Just as a confirmation of the obvious, I checked a standard American bibliography of English literary studies for a recent year and found not a single entry under Grossmith. No doubt someone somewhere will eventually write a Ph.D. dissertation on the Grossmiths, for as Walter Houghton says (expressing the common view) there is a "total picture" of Victorian life to arrive at.[3] Since the Grossmiths are part of Victorian life, and a bit beyond, we will not have the total picture until the Grossmiths are done. But turn to Conrad, Joseph, in the same bibliography for the same year, and you will find some forty articles and two and a third books on him, which are a fair measure of his greatness. The fact is that *The Diary of a Nobody* is barely known among American students of English literature, and where it is known I suspect it is not much liked, except as a useful tool for cultural history. I asked two respectable American scholars about it, one of them with pretensions to interest in Victorian literature. Neither had heard of it. I myself had it in mind for a long while as an obscure Russian work, Dostoievskian in character.

Not that it has official recognition in England either. The revised *Cambridge Bibliography of English Literature*, III, which has room for Mary Cholmonderley, Beatrice Harradan, and Lady Augusta Noel (including her book *The Life and Times of Conrad the Squirrel*), makes no mention of the Grossmiths and *The Diary of a Nobody*. Bonamy Dobrée and Edith Batho in *The Victorians and After* give the book a single sentence: "By some good judges considered a classic."[4] They provide the wrong date of publication, the same wrong date as does the *Dictionary of National Biography*. Nevertheless, the work is part of the English landscape. There has been a column in the *Times Saturday Review* conducted by Mr. Pooter's namesake, recently the poet laureate read favorite selections from it on the BBC, and the book often crops up in literary conversation. Most well-read Englishmen have read *The Diary of a Nobody* or know of it.

I myself have an English friend whose conscious cultural life is largely preoccupied with German music, but in his person he seems to me to be quintessentially English, and I assume his Englishness has been fed with things English. His bedside book, the book he alludes to most often, the book he dips into regularly, is *The Diary of a Nobody*. I asked him recently what thing he liked best in *The Diary of a Nobody* and he said: "Do you know where Mr. Pooter plants mustard and cress and next day writes in his diary, 'Mustard and cress not up yet', and then the next day, 'Mustard and cress not up yet'—that's the story of my life."

I asked him also what he thought of Conrad. "Very fine," he said. He had read Conrad just after the war; he ought to read him again. The judgment here was literary, the guilt cultural, the influence negligible. I do not forget the fact that he says he would be lost without Mozart; but picking my way among the subtleties of culture, I suspect that insofar as any art has had bearing upon his being an Englishman, Mozart and Conrad are nowhere, and *The Diary of a Nobody* everywhere.

A comparison between *The Diary of a Nobody* and *Lord Jim* is useful to make, for *Lord Jim* (despite Leavis's calling it one of Conrad's minor achievements) is reckoned by many American scholars to be one of the great novels in the English language, and it seems to me to exhibit the qualities of greatness in an extreme way. The novel was composed at the turn of the century, just a dozen years after *The Diary of a Nobody*. Notable first of all is the fact that Jim himself and Mr. Pooter are nobodies. Conrad emphasizes the ordinariness of Jim's background and his career, he sees many other such wanderers over the face of the earth, and various characters in the book ask themselves why such an ordinary luckless man should take his fate so seriously. Pooter, of course, is the most undistinguished inhabitant of suburbia. But there the comparison ends. Jim becomes Lord Jim, and Pooter remains Pooter. Marlowe in *Lord Jim* says of Jim: "I affirm that he achieved greatness"; and the philosophical and dramatic irony of the book is in its title. Jim penetrates terrors of self and psyche that forever distinguish him from the timid Pooter whom the cabman grabs by the beard. Both Jim and Pooter begin as anti-heroes, but Jim, like most anti-heroes studied at universities, rises above himself. We know the typical function of the anti-hero: to embody a certain nobility, wisdom, purity, and honesty that escape the normal hero. But Pooter remains Pooter.

Moreover, Pooter is English, and Jim is not. Nominally, Jim is English, comes from a pious English family; but so far as he is perceived in the novel he might as well be American or Australian. Marlowe says he is "one of us" and means only that he has a Western sensibility instead of an Eastern. Admittedly Conrad wants to avoid any finicking characteristic of a Frenchman in him, or the brutality of a German; but this said, he does not emerge as an English character. Pooter, though, you would recognize in a moment. He is a little Englander, pale, awkward, eccentric (in his choice of hats); he has no special interest in the arts, and his taste is generally deplorable. He is a creature of habit, polite, cautious, and deferential. He likes nothing better than a bad pun. His pleasures are small pleasures and he wants the same ones next year. His home is his castle, as he reminds Mrs. James of Sutton, and it is full of absurd bric-a-brac and a harmless pallid wife. One wonders how the two of them produced Lupin. Not an admirable Englishman, one may guess; a figure of fun. Arnold Bennett tells the story of going to see Pavlova in *Swan Lake*, and of sitting next to two fellow Englishmen who had almost nothing to say about the performance. In the middle of a dance a feather fell from Pavlova's costume, and the one Englishman said to the other: "Moulting!" That was all.[5] I had a German friend who described to me an altogether remarkable sunrise she saw on a plane flight from London to Munich. She was overcome with its splendor. An Englishman sitting next to her said to his companion: "Jolly good!" Pooters, all three men; and my English friend who dotes on *The Diary of a Nobody* sees himself as Pooter too.

Thirdly, Conrad's hero is an isolated person, away from society even when he is in it. Marlowe says that Jim had no dealings with anyone but himself, meaning that his life was lived out according to the most profound dictates of his soul. Pooter, on the other hand, is a social creature from first to last. His friends may be few, and they may be friends on a superficial level, and Pooter says that he and Carrie are quite capable of spending their evenings alone; but no private soul-searching goes on, and his friends are constantly around. He entertains and goes out of an evening. He belongs completely to a small ordered social world. He has no greater ambitions than to see his son in his own firm and to live in Brickfield Terrace forever. The first ambition is fulfilled in the conclusion as published in *Punch*, the second in the conclusion in book form.

Along with this contrast in heroes is a contrast in intentions in the two books. Conrad constructs his novel with some of the obvious apparatus of serious art—stylistic, narrative, structural, imagistic, symbolic. A critic can analyze the symbol of the leaps—Jim leaping from the sinking ship, one of the court assessors leaping to commit suicide, Jim leaping over the stockade, the narrator contemplating a leap from a balcony. Next year another critic can point out that the first critic has missed a half dozen leaps and half the significance. Next year new manuscript material is brought to bear on the issue. Take a simple matter like chronology, which can only go frontwards and backwards, and see how complexly Conrad handles it. But who will want to take the image of the red bathtub in *The Diary of a Nobody* and make anything of it? Examine the chronology—it proceeds in a straight line for a year and a quarter; it is not even tidy, and the Grossmiths are inconsistent in their matching of dates and days of the week. Think of the ending, a mere absurdity about promotion and reward tacked on in the last pages. Assuredly the book has merits of social observation, characterization, and humor, but a once-for-all analysis of them could be accomplished in fifty pages, could it not? And aside from *The Diary of a Nobody*, what did the Grossmiths show themselves capable of producing? George wrote comic songs and sketches, some of them slightly improper, and Weedon wrote a murder mystery and some inconsequential plays. It is clear that *The Diary of a Nobody* and the Grossmiths lack the artistic pretensions of *Lord Jim* and Conrad.

In sum, Conrad's aim is to make his reader think and feel powerfully, deeply, seriously. His book is written at high pressure, and there are great narrative, descriptive, and philosophical set pieces that the reader is meant to rise to. But the aim of the Grossmiths is to rouse a brief smile, a chuckle of recognition—of others, of self. The emotional and intellectual power are slight; you put the book down whenever you want, you fall asleep. Yet the book may remain with you—in your bedroom, in your mind. Amused affection is perhaps the keynote of it.

Here, then, arbitrarily drawn from a comparison of two books, are qualities I will associate with the little tradition—the English little tradition only. (1) The prerequisite: treating of English character in and of English society. (2) Unpretentiousness of subject and character, unpretentiousness of artistic method and aim. (3) Affection, sentiment, humor, and homeliness the keynotes. I will assume that a work may belong in the English little tradition even if its discernible influence is negligible or transitory; it can exist as an expression of English character as distinct from an influence upon it.

I need now to distinguish *The Diary of a Nobody* from work in the minor tradition, and my choice here is *Tom Brown's School Days*, produced in the middle of the century. The subject automatically puts the book in the minor tradition; for a novel about school days cannot aspire to greatness, cannot deal with great themes, great emotions—unless it transcends itself. Perhaps the American equivalent, or one equivalent, to *Tom Brown's School Days* is *Huckleberry Finn*, and the effort has been made by latter-day critics, if not by Mark Twain, to raise the boyhood novel to greatness. If the attempt succeeds, it is due to a transformation which makes Huck Finn an isolated figure like Lord Jim, standing outside civilization and judging it. Tom Brown, though, is rooted very realistically in his small English institution, and cannot be raised much above it.

We can see, though, that Thomas Hughes's book moves very much in the direction of *Lord Jim*. Hughes wants to make as much of his subject—given his manner—as he can, and in this respect he is minor to major and is to be judged by familiar standards of art. Thus though Hughes emphasizes that Tom Brown is a nobody (our hero...has nothing remarkable about him except excess of boyishness"), what he wants is to show that Tom is, or can be, the backbone of

England, and at the end Tom's dedication to Christ through Dr. Arnold is seen as the highest achievement of humble mortality. Tom wins through after much struggle, and our spines should tingle. He is a stay-at-home Lord Jim.

We can see in the novel, too, the same carefully plotted course of naive idealism, failure, and redemption that appear in *Lord Jim*; and if the skill and perception are not so remarkable as Conrad's, this is what also helps to make the novel minor. But it is skill not to be sneered at. Tom's arrival at Rugby and the Rugby game he immediately shares in and the virtuous talk by old Brooke he immediately hears are traps for himself and for the fond Victorian reader and old boy, and the rest of part 1 of the novel records in excellent detail Tom's gradual declension. The redemption in part 2 seems to display quite as good an understanding of the springs of character as Conrad displays. The structure is simpler but careful. And the novel has its set pieces of solemn emotion and drama. Today we may not be moved by the near death of Arthur, by the fight between Tom and Slogger Williams, by Tom in the chapel where Dr. Arnold lies buried; but there is no doubt that Hughes intended to move the reader powerfully within the limits of his subject. And he does to some degree invest his subject with symbolism. Rugby is war, and life is a fight. But Rugby as Rugby predominates.

It is in the respect that the novel treats of an ordinary English person in English society that it might belong with *The Diary of a Nobody* and the little tradition, and no doubt its influence in the shaping of ordinary English character must have been greater than most other books. I would not want wholly to dissociate it from the little tradition. But the seriousness of intent, the constant puffing up of episodes, the sense of the novel as moral example seem to me largely to smother those qualities of affection, humor, and homeliness that are essential to my tradition, which must surround the treatment of ordinary English character in English society. I do see them hovering on the edge of the novel, especially in the opening fifty pages or so before Tom grows up and goes to Rugby. There despite occasional jingoism is an image of rural England rendered in plain, affectionate, and sometimes humorous terms, worthy of the Grossmiths' treatment of suburbia— especially the account of the "veast" in Tom's village when he is a child, a simple description of village revels, with the contests, shows, amusements, pleasures of country people. Hughes comes closer to the mark in another novel of his, *The Scouring of the White Horse*, which describes country life in Berkshire, though it too suffers from self-conscious art.

There are, I suppose, two ways in which academic people are likely to approach *The Diary of a Nobody*—as social history and as literature. For the social historian the book may seem unusual among literary works in the reliability of its details. No conscious demands of art, no wilful distortions by the authors, seem to stand in the way of its accuracy in describing English suburbia of the 1880s. But literary scholars, who rightly take a jaundiced view of the raids of social historians upon their realm, will want to insist that literary questions be answered first. To what extent is the work satirical, describing a life that the Grossmiths abhor or condescend to and that presumably contrasts with the life of their own sort of people? And hence to what extent are they liable to exaggerate and distort? Were there really red enamel bathtubs in Holloway in the 1880s? Or what is to be made of the fact that the foolish Mr. Burwin-Fosselton, Lupin's friend who does the Henry Irving imitations and who writes the absurd letter on my-art-the-stage, must have been drawn in some part from Weedon Grossmith, who made his stage name with an imitation of Irving that he had been doing for some while informally?

On June 4th the Pooters enjoy a convivial evening at the Cummings', and Mrs. Cummings sings several songs. Mr. Pooter especially likes "The Garden of Sleep," which was in fact a popular song of the day, apparently first published in 1886 and reissued at least three times in the next three years. It must be a good index of suburban taste. The words will have to suffice here, and I will quote them in full. They are by Clement Scott. The music we can well imagine; it was by Isidore de Lara.

> On the grass of the cliff at the edge of the steep,
> God planted a garden, a garden of sleep!
> "Neath the blue of the sky in the green of the corn,
> It is there that the regal red poppies are born.
>
> Brief days of desire and long dreams of delight,
> They are mine when my poppy land cometh in sight.
> O! heart of my heart! Where the poppies are born
> I am waiting for thee in the hush of the corn.
> O! heart of my heart! etc.
>
> In my garden of sleep, where red poppies are spread
> I wait for the living, along with the dead!
> For a tower in ruins stands guard o'er the deep
> At whose feet are green graves of women asleep!
>
> Did they love as I love, when they lived by the sea?
> Did they wait as I wait for the days that may be?
> O! Life of my life! on the cliffs by the sea,
> By the graves in the grass, I am waiting for thee!
> O! Life of my life! etc.[6]

Shall we image Clement Scott—and who is he?—composing these maudlin sentiments out of thin Victorian air? And shall we imagine (because the Grossmiths do not tell us) Mr. Pooter and Carrie glancing shyly at each other as they listen? Of course there are lighter moments in the evening, notably when

Mr. Stillbrook sings the comic song "We Don't Want the Old Men Now," the words to which I do not know; but we will not suppose it was lewd or low, for it makes Mr. Pooter "shriek with laughter."[7]

Now George Grossmith was a composer of songs, and perhaps the closest he came to maudlin sentiment was in his love song "Thou of My Thou" written by him (both words and music) around 1889. The song has an introduction to be spoken: "There is a tendency, Ladies and Gentlemen, in modern ballad poetry, to repeat a word frequently and fervently, such as 'Heart of my Heart,' 'Love of my love,' 'Soul of my Soul,' and if necessary 'Heel of my Heel.' As I have no desire to be behind the times, my song is entitled: 'Thou of my Thou.' You may be able to fathom the depths of its poetical meaning. *I* can't." Some selected verses from the song:

> Only once did we meet, only once did we part,
> But I loved thee, Oh! whole of my heart of my heart.
> I've waited for thee on the brow of the hill,
> My heart it was aching, and breaking at will.
>
> I saw thee but once, and I heaved but a sigh,
> 'Twas a Heave of a Heave, and for thee I would die.
> I knew thou would'st come, and we never shall part,
> Thou hast come, oh! whole of my heart of my heart.
>
> 'Tis thou, thou, thou,
> It is thou, thou of my thou.
> I have waited for thee on the brow of the hill,
> On the brow, brow, brow....
>
> Thy spirit and pride I shall ever admire:
> Thy cheeks were ablaze—thine eyes were on fire;
> The kiss that I gave thee thou did'st not give back,
> But thou gavest a smack! 'Twas a smack of a smack....

So we know what George Grossmith thought of "The Garden of Sleep."

Another song by Gee-Gee, as he was commonly known, was the familiar one "See Me Dance the Polka":

> You should see me dance the polka
> You should see me cover the ground,
> You should see my coat-tails flying
> As I jump my partner round....

On November 2nd Lupin comes in at night and goes directly to his room, where as Pooter writes, "For a quarter of an hour afterwards he was positively dancing in his room, and shouting out, 'See me dance the polka,' or some such nonsense" (89). Surely this places Grossmith on the side of Lupin, but for how long?

Another of Gee-Gee's songs:

Do Not Spoil Your Children

> When talking to your friends be sure your children interrupt,
> When questioned, let their answers be both noisy and abrupt;
> Let them burst into your boudoir when you seek a little nap,
> And play with people's spectacles until you hear them snap,
> And jump up upon your piano and smash a note or two.
> But do not spoil your children whatever you may do.

Grossmith accompanied himself on the piano when he sang his songs, and one of his books of reminiscences is entitled *Piano and I*. We can readily infer where he stands on the subject of spoiling children, and it is precisely where Mr. Pooter stands on May 26th:

> We went to Sutton after dinner to have meat-tea with Mr. and Mrs. James. I had no appetite, having dined well at two, and the entire evening was spoiled by little Percy—their only son—who seems to me to be an utterly spoiled child.
> Two or three times he came up to me and deliberately kicked my shins. He hurt me once so much that the tears came into my eyes. I gently remonstrated with him, and Mrs. James said: "Please don't scold him; I do not believe in being too severe with young children. You spoil their character." (211)

Then there were the Grossmith songs that would have made Pooter blush but that his friends in suburbia would have enjoyed.

A Little Bit of Rope

> If a girl desires to marry
> And has got a bit of brain,
> And would make her husband happy,
> She must not hold tight the rein.
> Her darling may resent it—
> He was once a bachelor!
> She must let him have a latch-key—
> He has had a few before!...

And there were others that Pooter would have let pass.

Oh! That Today Were Tomorrow

Oh! that the days were weeks, love,
Oh! that the months were years,
The bloom will remain on your cheeks, love,
That bloom which at night disappears.
Oh! that the years were in thousands—
No poet my love can pen,
I shall love you for ever and ever,
And ever so long after then!...

I think what is clear is that there is no simple satirical relationship between the Grossmiths and Mr. Pooter. Their pleasures and opinions were in some respects of a piece—the brothers who lived in Bohemia and Mr. Pooter who lives in suburbia. Max Beerbohm said that at the turn of the century suburban life was a disagreeable joke to most of his friends, but it is not a disagreeable joke in *The Diary of a Nobody*. In a memoir of the Grossmith brothers, a friend wrote of Weedon (Wee-Gee): "In his art, as in his life, he was clean and comely, and in the twilight of reflection one had never to blush for the laugh he had raised."[8] Pooters all of them!

At any rate, with due discretion the social historian could use *The Diary of a Nobody* with reasonable confidence to describe life in the London suburbs in the 1880s—the domestic architecture, the domestic decor, business activity, evening amusements, manners, morals. He could doubtless drain the blood out of the book in so doing, but he need not, and I think that at best he might round off his account by saying something to the effect that the life portrayed in *The Diary of a Nobody* had much gaiety and affection in it, and was viewed with gaiety and affection, so that in large part the distance between authors and their characters dissolved—they shared a common, ordinary English life in which the differences must have been differences of detail.

I am even inclined to think that *The Diary of a Nobody* invites the approach of the social historian more readily than it does that of the conventional literary critic. One of the common defects of literary criticism is that it does not connect literature to life, and in my little tradition the relationship of literature to life is central. To me the most valuable aspect of Leavis's book is that it insists on the connection between literature and life, but its terms are grandiose and life becomes Life. (Thus I think that the Max Beerbohm cartoon of Henry James looking through a keyhole at life is the final criticism of him as a novelist.) In *The Diary of a Nobody* literature points to life, and does so without pretensions. And taking a social historian's view of it—using some human and literary tact withal—seems reasonable enough.

I have no doubt, though, that one can play the usual tricks of literary criticism upon the book. Take that red enamel bathtub, and see it as the emblematic object of the book—Pooter defining himself as a nobody in comparison with Marat who was somebody, Pooter defining himself as the sort of man who would paint his bathtub red, as the incompetent but would-be-competent domesticated English male in his home-castle. Think then that the bathtub is the central image of cleanliness in the book, the meaning of which radiates from a multitude of such references, beginning with the scraper at the front door and with Horwin the butcher's "nice clean shop" (21), and you have the foundation for an analysis of the complex satiric imagery and symbolism of the book. But though the pursuit might be ingenious, it might be unrewarding as well. Likewise in other areas that immediately suggest themselves—the range of means by which Pooter's character is delineated, the range of humor, point of view—what might be said might be useless. The book does not invite literary scrutiny. I come back to my friend's comment on the book. I asked him to tell me what he liked most about *The Diary of a Nobody* because I wanted some unexpected, striking illumination from the horse's mouth, from an Englishman. In telling me that he liked the bit about the mustard and cress he gave me what I deserved, and, as it turned out—as it always does turn out—just what I wanted. For he refused to think of the book in high literary terms. It was not the funniest episode, or the most damning satirically, or the most complex and subtle that he offered, but something entirely insignificant, a mere detail. Moreover, he immediately connected it with life, with his own life. Certainly he was not thinking as a social historian; it was an intimate personal connection he made, and had nothing to do with life in the 1880s except insofar as it suggested that we are Victorians still (surely a heretical notion to those of us who are consciously trying to penetrate the Victorian mind).

It would not be in the service of the little tradition to set up a canon of major works. The little tradition must take care of itself. Not that it necessarily will; not that there is inevitably a little tradition everywhere to take care of itself. The reason I have restricted my comments to the little tradition in England is that I am not sure I could find my examples elsewhere. Matthew Arnold may seem the wrong man to quote in this context, but in one of his essays on America he remarks that the landscape of America is not interesting, "the inhabitant does not strike his roots lovingly down into the soil, as in rural England."[9] The observation seems to me to be as applicable in the 1970s as I imagine it to have been in the 1880s, and I take it to reflect Arnold's sense of the homely and unpretentious affection that invests the little tradition of the English landscape (including the cottage garden) as well as of English literature. I do not know that there is an appreciable little tradition in American life. There have been people like Mark Twain who have contributed to it (and whose works have been seized and glorified); but the urge to pull up roots, to write the great American novel, to win all the Nobel prizes, even to know the best that has been thought and said (via Harvard Classics, great books, college education, and buying the *Encyclopaedia Britannica*) has worked powerfully against the little tradition in America.

Perhaps every person should have his own canon of works in the little tradition. My own would include much of Thomas Hood's poetry ("I Remember, I Remember" and "The Song of the Shirt," and for humor "Our Village" and "Ode to Mr. Malthus"), Christina Rossetti's "In the Bleak Mid-Winter," with "Winter: My Secret" for leaven, and Ebenezer Elliott's lines:

> The people, Lord, the people,
> Not thrones, and crowns, but men!
> Flowers of thy heart, O God, are they;
> Let them not pass, like weeds, away—
> Their heritage a sunless day.
> God save the people![10]

I would have much of Thomas Hardy, but not the Thomas Hardy of plot machinations, immanent wills, and presidents of the immortals, but rather Tess in the countryside milking her cows, Marty at Giles's grave, the Reddleman, Gabriel Oak, Tranter Dewy, and the lyric poems. I would have some of D. H. Lawrence, the Lawrence whose mother comes home from the hospital in *Sons and Lovers* and says, "There are my sunflowers," but not the Lawrence of much of *The Rainbow* and *Women in Love*. Jessie Chambers said of Lawrence that when he wrote of the things he loved, the small and intimate life of his youth, he was at his best, and when he turned philosophical, psychological, moral, and satirical, she thought he was mad. There is much in her judgment, I think.

I must conclude by identifying Clement Scott. He was dramatic critic for the *Daily Telegraph* and adaptor of French comedies for the London stage. He also wrote sentimental verse and light travel literature, and "The Garden of Sleep" appeared in slightly different form as the epigraph of a book, *Poppy-Land Papers, Descriptive of Scenery of the East Coast*, published in 1886. The maudlin sentiment of the poem had quite specific reference, which Scott elaborated upon in a tale published in a collection of *Travellers' Tales* in 1892. The tale, "In the Garden of Sleep," describes how the narrator and friends discovered an isolated village on the east coast on a holiday trip and how he and the woman he loved returned there for many years. He and the woman sometimes met in the ruins of a church on the cliffs, a church whose yard full of poppies was known locally as "the garden of sleep"; and he and the woman enjoyed there for brief spells an idyllic rural life. Readers of Scott's poem might condemn its vague sentiments; readers of the tale might find it a touching memorial of days spent on the east coast with his wife, who died in 1890. In its sentimental, melancholic strain, the tale is rather in my little tradition, and I suspect that the Grossmith brothers would have enjoyed it as much as Mr. Pooter enjoyed the song. I imagine that if I looked harder I could find something of Scott's that was humorous as well as homely and affectionate; for along with his work on French comedies he was an intimate friend of W.S. Gilbert and F.C. Burnand. Burnand was editor of *Punch*, and *The Diary of a Nobody* was dedicated to him. He and the Grossmiths were intimate friends too, and I take it on faith that the Grossmiths were thus intimate friends of Scott. *The Diary of a Nobody* and *Travellers' Tales* were both published by J.W. Arrowsmith of Bristol.

8 Ottoline the Terrible

OTTOLINE MORRELL (1873-1938) WAS A superficial and flamboyant aristocrat with a taste for literature and the arts, and she now has a biography and two volumes of *Memoirs* to document her career. D.H. Lawrence summed her up, and in so doing summed up womankind and himself as well: "Ottoline has moved men's imagination, deeply, and that's perhaps the most a woman can do." Lawrence doubtless had Bertrand Russell in mind, who was Ottoline's lover for a few intense years. Perhaps he also thought of himself writing to Ottoline that "the feeling that comes out of your letter is like the scent of flowers, so generous and reassuring."[1] He may even have thought of all the other bright people—Aldous Huxley, Katherine Mansfield, John Middleton Murry, and many others—who came to Garsington Manor for solace, conversation, and the redemption of their powers. The count of such people is altogether impressive; and if some of them went away and said nasty things about their hostess and her world, that was merely the other way in which Ottoline moved them.

Ottoline was not entirely content to be such a mover. She had yearnings of her own. In the first volume of her *Memoirs* she asks why she is writing them, why she "should burden this world with the ashes of my past." She answers: "The inspiring desire of Immortality" (1:61). And so the reader comes in both volumes upon passages that are pure Ottoline—sensitivities and perceptions of her immortal soul. She describes the hollowness of conventional aristocratic life, she is profoundly moved by Italian and Spanish culture, she analyzes the English female character, she dilates upon her need for solitude and her hatred of war. And it is all pale purple, save for one extraordinary passage dated 1 December 1915. This passage, purple though it is, describes Garsington with considerable power; and the dubious reader must grant Ottoline a small personal immortality for it, except that when he comes to the end of the passage he sees it was written by Lawrence. A few pages further on appears the reflective Ottoline herself, talking about the fire and flame of natural life versus the mechanical tick-tick of intellectuality, and one sees that Lawrence moved her—not very deeply. Never was there woman less capable of being either natural or intellectual than Ottoline.

So she was better at being useful to others. Because she was rich and idle, she often lamented being not useful, and she thought of giving away every penny to young artists or of becoming a nun; but mainly she got on with her torrent of visitors. One of them in the 1915-18 years was Siegfried Sassoon, and she reflects that what is best in her cannot give itself to a woman (for women "don't really feel the fundamental things as strongly as a man does" [2:151]). She had of course already given herself to her husband (to say nothing of Russell, Augustus John, Henry Lamb, Roger Fry, and others), but she knows that she has more to give than Morrell wants. "I tell myself to put it into my writing, but then I know that what I want to give needs another soul to mingle with" (2:151). She thinks Sassoon might be that soul, and she has intimate conversations with him, and makes some kind of advance to him; but he remains aloof, and later tells her that he too likes men better than women. It is the same thing with Lytton Strachey, who is the one other person she feels most intimate with. They never get any further than Strachey's reading poetry to her and prancing around her private rooms in her high-heeled shoes.

In fact Ottoline seems not to have given much in the intimate mingling way. She remarks at one point that marriage is a humiliation for a woman, at another that she lacks the instinct for motherhood, at another that she is too fastidious to enjoy the passions; and the great love of her life, with Russell, is apparently a sacrifice of her person at the altar of the great man, who repels her physically—an "awful responsibility" (2:269) as she calls it. That it was an intense affair, that it meant much to both of them, there is no denying; but it seems equally true that many another woman would have served Russell quite as well, and many another famous man could as easily have flattered Ottoline's ego. Although the first volume treats of the Russell years, the details of the affair are cloaked therein, and the nastiness of it is revealed only in an appendix to the second volume. In the first volume the courtship and marriage with Philip Morrell occupy very few lines, and there is hardly a hint that Ottoline has any feeling for the man until several years later (1911) when she becomes involved with Russell. Then suddenly she finds herself loving Morrell "more and more"; he is "the only human being I crave for"; he is her "darling" (1:206, 209). Perhaps it was a case of not knowing how much she loved him until she deserted him wholeheartedly, but it seems more likely that he was her darling for being so complaisant. In the account of her liaison with Russell published in the second volume, she says feelingly of Morrell's complaisance: "He *is* generous" (2:275). Elsewhere in about the same year she describes going to look at a cottage that Morrell owns, with a view to their living in it. Morrell has agreeable memories of the cottage, and Ottoline, who does not want to live there, "shrank from hurting Philip" (1:221) in saying no. Not a glimmer anywhere that she shrinks from hurting him with her affair with Russell. One sees a totally self-indulgent woman, a faceless husband, and Russell grinning in the bushes.

What, then, can be said for Ottoline? That she existed for clever people to write interesting letters to? Certainly the best parts of the second volume of *Memoirs* are the letters from Lawrence, Huxley, the Murrys, and others. Some of these letters are readily available elsewhere; others are not. Occasionally Ottoline's characterizations of and anecdotes about these people are interesting, but to this reader the interest seems to be in inverse proportion to the amount known otherwise about them. Ottoline is more interesting on Frieda Lawrence than on Lawrence, more interesting on Huxley than on Arnold Bennett. The second volume is much more given over to such portraits and correspondence than the first, and may be reckoned as that much better.

The virtues of the *Memoirs* should be put more positively. Here are some good glimpses of the English aristocracy from 1873 to 1918; here is a self-portrait of an eccentric aristocrat who yearned for the artistic and literary life; here are any number of artistic and literary lions wandering in the gardens of Garsington, fighting and frolicking among themselves, fawning upon and rebelling against their keeper, going off into gloomy corners. In spite of all defects the *Memoirs* give a far more vivid and genuine picture of this scene than can be had from a work such as Martin Green's *Children of the Sun*. No doubt it is the aristocratic side that is most fascinating to Americans—most fascinating because most alien. In the first volume there is a photograph of Ottoline in the gardens of Mells Manor with Edward Horner. Horner she describes as a young man with the "dazzling beauty of a Greek athlete" (I:147), and we see that beauty even though it lies beneath a suit of exquisite cut. He moves behind Ottoline with the assurance, poise, and strength of the best of the aristocracy; and we may assume that he is intelligent, witty, charming, masculine withal. He went off to war and got killed. There in the foreground is Ottoline herself in a long brocade gown with sleeves to the wrist, a scarf in one hand, and a great floppy hat on her head (shadowing the face that in some photographs looks strong and brooding and in Augustus John's portrait reproduced on the dust jacket of the second volume looks ugly and corrupt). All that birth, breeding, and civilization in her step, in her poise, in her elegance! Though we may laugh at her literary maunderings, though we may scorn her self-deceptions and immorality, still she was a woman such as American men never meet at home.

Quite a lot to see in a photograph! Turn, then, from the photograph and from the self-portrait of the *Memoirs* to Sandra Jobson Darroch's biography. We see less there. First, though, it must be said that Darroch has done a careful piece of work. The years are laid end to end from 1873 to 1938 with a certain skill; people are introduced and complex relationships explained with a certain competence. Anyone who has attempted a similar task will commend the result. Furthermore, the biography covers years that the *Memoirs* do not, it is more explicit about many matters (Ottoline's relationships with Russell, John, Fry, Lamb, etc.), and it introduces unpublished letters by a good many notable people. It must be acknowledged too that the faceless husband of the *Memoirs* is given a face: like "a grey bowler hat" says Huxley (240). Morrell's complaisance is made explicit, and he is shown participating uneasily at the parties. There is a photograph of him in the garden at Garsington looking like an obsequious butler, servant to his mistress's every wish. Surely the most interesting passage in the biography is that which describes Ottoline's collapse in 1917 upon discovering he has been unfaithful to her. Darroch says that she was "reduced to a state of partial sanity..., totally distraught" (202). What extreme form must the man's infidelity have taken to have moved Ottoline to anything more than contempt? Unfortunately, Darroch cannot provide details, for people involved are still alive.

Perhaps the general interest of the biography lies in this direction—as a record of the sexual to-ings and fro-ings of Ottoline and the people who surround her. Dora Carrington, for example: first pursued by Mark Gertler, who himself has been pursued by Strachey; then falling for Strachey himself and going to live with him; then falling in love with Ralph Partridge, who has come to live with her and Strachey, Partridge himself more interested in Carrington than in Strachey and Strachey interested in Partridge and not at all in Carrington; then marrying Partridge and the three of them continuing their menage; then falling in love with Partridge's best friend, with Partridge attaching himself to another woman, for whom Carrington then develops desire. Unfortunately, again, there is not much detail, and the recital of such matters for three hundred pages is tedious.

The biography is in fact made up of bald detail: where Ottoline went, what she wore, who came to visit, who was sleeping with whom, who hated whom. One has to have unflagging interest in the superficial to want to read on. Yet willy-nilly the book brings one to serious reflection. If Ottoline was the vulgar, silly, outrageous, puffed up, and repulsive person that both *Memoirs* and biography show her to be, why did a procession of gifted, handsome, brilliant men become her intimate friends and lovers? The answer that emerges is that insofar as these men themselves appear in an extended way in these pages they show themselves to be vulgar, silly, outrageous, puffed up, and repulsive. Russell is merely the easiest example. When Russell took up with Ottoline he was at the end of nine years of spartan living with a wife he no longer loved. One day in 1902 he had confessed the fact, and all that night he worked on *Principia Mathematica* while his wife sobbed in the next room. "Oh the pity of it!" he noted in his journal. But pity was not the tone to take. He must instead be cold, "in the deliberate hope of destroying her affection"; and some while later he was pleased to record that he had "certainly effected a great moral reformation in her, and that depends upon keeping her hopes alive but unfulfilled" (88). He was good at this. He later adopted the strategem of never looking at her. So it was that in 1911 after he had told his wife of his new love, he could write to Ottoline, "I do not think she is suffering much. All the real pain was nine years ago." He was slightly wrong. The next day his wife spoke to him "in a most harrowing way" (94). He and his wife soon parted, and then she threatened scandal over his liaison with Ottoline; in turn he threatened to throw himself under a bus, and that shut her up. When Ottoline later talked of a separation from him, he thought he might throw himself under a motor car. Perhaps in all this there is nothing either vulgar or silly, but Russell himself in his *Autobiography* calls some of his behavior to his wife "repulsive."[2]

For the lighter side we go to his opinion expressed to Ottoline that "no woman's intellect is really good enough to give me pleasure as intellect" (91); but he was not troubled about Ottoline's intellect because with her he could be poetical: "The flames of our inmost fires meet and mingle. I know your springs of living water, and my spirit drinks at them" (121). We imagine Ottoline so moved by the language of the future Nobel laureate of literature that she remembers to want to mingle with Siegfried Sassoon.

Russell was a terrible creature, and his mind, which he described to Ottoline as "a sort of logic machine warranted to destroy any ideal that is not very robust" (90), was a confused mind. Anyone who traces his thinking about such an ideal as free love from the time that his affair with Ottoline began, through several other affairs, to his second marriage (of four), and to his book *Marriage and Morals*, will find the logic machine shaking itself apart. A destructive machine it was, surely, as D. H. Lawrence saw. He and Russell were pacifists together in the war, and friends for a while, until Lawrence wrote the letter that Darroch quotes in part: "What you want is to jab and strike, like a soldier with the bayonet, only you are sublimated into words. ... It is *not* the hatred of falsehood which inspires you. It is the hatred of people."[3] Who, though, was Lawrence to speak? We see him fawning upon Ottoline and then making the spiteful portrait of her in *Women in Love*. We see the aggrieved, petulant, and smug tone that he takes about her to others. We recall (not from Darroch) his writing to Katherine Mansfield some years later in the same vein he wrote to Russell: "I loathe you. You revolt me stewing in your consumption." In *Portraits from Memory* Russell says of Lawrence. "He had...a hatred for mankind."[4]

One comes away from Ottoline's *Memoirs* and biography thinking what a scurvy lot all these people are. We think we want to read about Ottoline Morrell because she was a friend of the great. We would not read about her otherwise. But are the great worth reading about? Would we want to read about them if they were not great? Should we want to read about them because they are? Could the twentieth century have got along without Russell, Lawrence, and, say, T. S. Eliot? Very nicely. Why are we all such obsequious butlers to these masters? Where does civilization lie—with Russell, Lawrence, Eliot, whose private lives by any sane standard were a mess? (Ottoline had at least the good sense to say of Eliot that he was "dull, dull, dull."[2:101]) Does it lie with their works? Or does it lie with sensitivities and perceptions of more ordinarily mortal souls?

The virtue of Ottoline's *Memoirs* and biography is that one learns to ask questions of her and of her famous associates: If you're so rich, why aren't you smart? If you're so great, why aren't you smart? The actual butler at Garsington must have had more sense than most of these people. Just like the admirable Crichton, and like Hudson in *Upstairs Downstairs*.

9 Leda and the Dumbledore

TWO POETS AT THE HEIGHT of their powers, in their late fifties:

Leda and the Swan

A sudden blow: the great wings beating still
Above the staggering girl, her thighs caressed
By the dark webs, her nape caught in his bill,
He holds her helpless breast upon his breast.

How can those terrified vague fingers push
The feathered glory from her loosening thighs?
And how can body, laid in that white rush,
But feel the strange heart beating where it lies?

A shudder in the loins engenders there
The broken wall, the burning roof and tower
And Agamemnon dead.
                      Being so caught up,
So mastered by the brute blood of the air,
Did she put on his knowledge with his power
Before the indifferent beak could let her drop?

An August Midnight

A shaded lamp and a waving blind,
And the beat of a clock from a distant floor:
On this scene enter—winged, horned, and spined—
A longlegs, a moth, and a dumbledore;
While 'mid my page there idly stands
A sleepy fly, that rubs its hands....

> Thus meet we five, in this still place,
> At this point of time, at this point in space.
> —My guests besmear my new-penned line,
> Or bang at the lamp and fall supine.
> "God's humblest, they!" I muse. Yet why?
> They know Earth-secrets that know not I.[1]

Yeats's poem is one of the great and glamorous poems of the language. He has gone upstairs for his sword, and he has given a display worthy of Montashigi or Sergeant Troy. He has produced a sonnet that is more dazzling than an English sonnet ever was before, with a more brilliant image, a more grandiose thought, a richer sensuality; and he has wrapped it all up with a question instead of a Shakespearian answer. Who else but the chief poet of the twentieth century could have written the poem? Turn then to Thomas Hardy's poem and ask what comparable things might be said. One thing: no one but Thomas Hardy could have written it.

The problem of Thomas Hardy has long been with us. From the first there has been praise for his honesty, directness, sincerity, simplicity, homeliness, and profundity, and from the first there has been doubt about his skill, taste, intelligence, and originality. In critical argument, the second opinion has overweighed the first; for the first reflects the old-fashioned view of poetry and the second the modern view. Hardy's poems, that is to say, have not been able to withstand the sort of scrutiny that modern criticism can bring to bear on them. Sincerity and profundity are for readers who imagine that the poem is the poet and the poet a philosopher; skill and intelligence are for critics who know that the poem is an artifact. Nothing written by Hardy's admirers has been nearly so persuasive as the attacks by R.P. Blackmur and F.R. Leavis in the *Southern Review* in 1940. Old as these attacks are, they represent the modern view (pre-structuralist-deconstructionist), and they have never been answered. Donald Davie in his book on Hardy in 1974 wants to provide an answer; but sensitive though he is to Hardy, his comments on individual poems fall into the vein of old-fashioned appreciation ("the grimness of this poem is quite extraordinary") or else make inadequate gestures toward rigorous scrutiny ("elaborately and exactly tooled"). The failure of the old-fashioned defenders of Hardy is that their terms of criticism have been discounted, the failure of the modern defenders is that they find bits and pieces of the artifact to praise but never enough to outweigh the devastating critiques of Blackmur and Leavis. Here is the problem of Thomas Hardy: everyone knows that his poetry is better than our criticism can make it out to be, but no one knows how to open up the critical ground without letting the place be flooded with vague rhetoric. After completing his demonstration of Hardy's defects—his "bad or inadequate practice"—Blackmur expresses the hope that we may now be better able to grasp "the extraordinary poetry which was produced despite and aside from the practice." Blackmur himself never undertook to write the complementary essay on Hardy's extraordinary virtues, and his first essay was not a necessary preliminary. Hardy's virtues have always been apparent. The problem is merely to find words that will satisfy a modern critic.[2]

The present essay offers to try, mainly through certain comparisons and contrasts with Yeats. For a start it will be useful to take note of Hardy's development as a poet. This subject has drawn little attention, apparently because the answer has seemed obvious: Hardy developed very little. The early poems are like the late ones. Compare "Postponement," which is dated 1866, with "Voices from Things Growing in a Churchyard," which was written in 1921. Compare "Neutral Tones," which is dated 1867, with the poems of 1912-13 on the death of his first wife. Early and late, the poems are of similar character and maturity. The most striking—if most uncertain—example is "In Time of 'The Breaking of Nations,'" written in 1915 but conceived during the Franco-Prussian War in 1870. The poem is so simple, so timeless, so anachronistic, so Hardyesque, that it invites one to believe that Hardy would have found virtually the same words for it had he written it out all those years before. Such a risk of inference is easy to run with Hardy: one has the sense of a man who was the same from first to last, who never went searching for or was swept away by new ideas, new attitudes, new modes, and whose poetry therefore—reflecting the man—remained essentially the same. The craft of it might improve, but the craft was surface. Had his wife died twenty years before she did die, he would—it seems—have written the same poems about her, with the same terrible sadness, strength, and strange simple perception.

These things may be admitted or allowed. One might argue similarly, though less easily, of Yeats that had Maud Gonne died in 1908 or had the Easter Uprising happened then or had Germany won the First World War, the later poetry might have happened earlier. It is nevertheless the fact that both Hardy and Yeats wrote their best poems late. Unlike Yeats, Hardy did not make a revolutionary progress. He began at a more mature and less pretty level. He began nearer to what he became, or remained closer to what he was. If "Neutral Tones" as it exists is the same poem that was written at age twenty-six, it shows merits surpassing anything that Yeats wrote at the same age. Not until the 1893 volume is there a line in Yeats ("I spit into the face of Time") that has the original force of the whole of "Neutral Tones," and not until the 1904 volume is there a whole poem of equal or superior merit ("The Folly of Being Comforted," "Adam's Curse").

Yeats grew up as a poet in part by abandoning the poetic idiom of the 1890s, or by transforming and enlarging it. Hardy's task was more straightforward, and his progress was less flashy: to master the idiom that he already possessed in some measure. One has only to look at the "She to Him" poems to see the young poet uncertain of himself, yielding to Elizabethan or Jacobean rhetoric. What is often praised in these poems is merely successful imitation, as in the third sonnet: "Numb as a vane that cankers on its point, | True to the wind that kissed ere canker came." Other poems from later years (the "Poems of Pilgrimage" of the 1880s) show Hardy still occasionally caught in the grip of a high rhetorical mode. His strength was in the ordinary subdued language of "Neutral Tones" ("We stood by a pond that winter day") and in the modulations from it that the same poem shows ("And the sun was white, as though chidden of God"). The later successful poems are sometimes wholly in ordinary language ("The Self Unseeing," from the 1890s, and "The Walk," 1912-13) or rise slightly from it ("Your Last Drive," 1912), or mingle ordinary language and modulation in a manner similar to the last stanza of "Neutral Tones" ("In Tenebris—I," from the 1890s, and "The Going," 1912):

> Since then, keen lessons that love deceives,
> And wrings with wrong, have shaped to me
> Your face, and the God-curst sun, and a tree,
> And a pond edged with grayish leaves.

It is also the case that the rhythm and melody into which Hardy cast his idiom developed over the years. The rhythmic force of "The Trampwoman's Tragedy," 1902, and the extraordinary lilt of "The Voice," 1912, are not to be matched among early poems. It might be noted in passing that on at least one occasion in his lyric poetry Hardy mastered a high rhetorical mode. "The Convergence of the Twain," 1912, is a dazzling poem, rather like "The Second Coming" in grandness of image and vocabulary, but Hardy subdues it with his rhythms and with humble ironical perspectives.

It was implicit in Hardy's development that he did not become a poet of great lines or great poems. His poems are one poem—rather more so than Yeats's—and the defects of individual poems so visible to modern criticism reflect the hazards of his course: to find success in plainness, to hold to the clumsy, familiar, and obvious rather than search for the smooth, artful, and original. For dazzling lines and dazzling poems, one goes to Yeats, to the end of "Among School Children" and to "Sailing to Byzantium." Yet Yeats had his greatness in plain lines too, and so did Hardy after all, and it is useful to compare them. In Yeats, "You are more beautiful than any one"—that broken-hearted line in "Broken Dreams," or "Old kettles, old bottles, and a broken can"—that harsh acceptance of himself in "The Circus Animals' Desertion." Insofar as Yeats's greatness encompassed plainness as well as extravagance, he may be said in this respect to be a greater poet, and "Among School Children" shows his range in its rise from first stanza to last. But one sees in "Old kettles..." and to a lesser extent in "You are more beautiful..." the tendency to excess that "Among School Children" gives movement to—a striking plainness, a passionate assertion—whereas one sees in Hardy's great plain lines the plainest statement of the plain man: "Goodbye is not worth while!"—that wry and sad perception of individual character and of life in death and death in life at the end of "Without Ceremony," and "You are past love, praise, indifference, blame"—that helpless pain at the end of "Your Last Drive."

The course of Hardy's development was, one might say, a process of becoming what he was, of revealing himself, of creating himself poetically, rather than of hiding or transforming himself. Aside from reticences of a certain kind, he intended to speak with his own voice as that voice could find expression in verse. He rid himself of Elizabethan-Jacobean rhetoric as he might rid himself of flashy clothes that did not suit him, but he did not rid himself of archaisms, inversions, dialectal words that did suit him (picked up from his region, his past, his reading), and he mused upon curious rhythms and melodies that might suit him. Most especially he brought to his poems the ordinary language of home and street, and ordinary thought and feeling thereof. He was content at his writing desk to be what he was otherwise. Luckily for him and for us he was an unusual man in his ordinariness: he was able to reveal himself in words, and he was worth knowing. He said that there was more autobiography in a hundred lines of his poetry than in all of his novels, and he made his finest poems directly out of personal anguish. There he stands in his poems, the lonely, humble, wise, compassionate, and sardonic man, and this creation of himself is the chief object of admiration of his readers, old and new. "I cannot speak objectively of Thomas Hardy," said W.H. Auden, "because I once was in love with him."[3]

It is, however, to speak objectively that modern criticism has wanted to do. But in the rejection of naive equation of poet and poem, modern criticism has itself been naive. The notion of mask, exhibited so splendidly by Yeats, has been regarded too simply, perhaps because the word itself is too simple. Suppose that all one has in Hardy's poems are masks. Suppose additionally that Hardy was a supreme artificer (or even allow that he was a naive and unconscious one). His peculiar success was then to have created masks that seem least masklike, that seem transparent, that seem to show an ordinary man standing behind them. One may suggest that such masks are the most deceptive masks of all masks (in contrast to Yeats's obvious masks), and the task of Hardy criticism is thence to scrutinize their painstaking or unconscious construction in nine hundred lyrics. Or suppose instead that Hardy saw mask as one of the hazards of poetry, in the way that another poet might see rhyme as hazard. He could not avoid mask as that other poet might avoid rhyme, but he would not make it the chief object of his attention to play upon in virtuoso performance—he might even try to see to what extent he could subvert mask. His peculiar success would then provide a different focus for critical analysis.

Both of these views of mask take us into areas where mask nearly dissolves or seems to dissolve. Their virtue is that they provide a basis for laudatory scrutiny of Hardy's work—for the second essay that Blackmur might have written. But at the same time they seem inaccurate accounts of Hardy's poetry-making; and insofar as they nearly ramify mask out of existence, they seem to suggest the inadequacy of the term itself. Naive appreciation has already seen the result—the man in the poems—that diligent and suspect scrutiny might arrive at. Perhaps something is wrong with modern tools and conceptions when they cannot cope with Thomas Hardy. It is understandable that modern critics have chosen to blame Hardy instead of themselves.

Yeats has fared better with modern critics, and there are many critical displays of his virtuosity. But it is permissible to ask whether such displays have always got closer to the heart of the matter than have the demonstrations of Hardy's defects. One of the ways in which modern criticism has generally been seen to fail is that it can show a bad poem to possess all the virtues of a good one—to contain mask, myth, irony, and organic wholeness in rich complexity. The criticism that can fail with the bad poem perhaps sometimes fails as well with the good poem with which it seems to succeed. If it demonstrably fails with one sort of good poem (Hardy's), might it not occasionally fail with another sort (Yeats's)? Suppose that preoccupation with the Yeatsian artifact, the Yeatsian mask, ought rather to be attention to the man in the poems. That yearning young lover of the first three volumes is merely an inadequate, too partial, and uninteresting glimpse of the man. The later dancing man is rather more attractive if partial too. The whole man comes to us in bits and pieces, early and late, and yet we get the true sense of him, say, in "The Circus Animals' Desertion," in his amusement over the early poems, his attenuated anguish over Maud Gonne, his rueful acknowledgment of disorderly beginnings. Is it not Yeats the man rather than Yeats the craftsman that we go to in the poems? We talk about the craft because craft is easier to talk about—we being shy and embarrassed in our emotions. It is so at least for some of us. Of course the man is a poseur—so self-conscious, so carefully dressed, so flamboyant in a civilized way, and thus so laughable to imagine as a wild old wicked man. The image is quite as vivid as that of Hardy the plain, unpretentious, solid man. And how similar the two men are in spite of all difference: as men, in their loneliness, isolation, and preoccupation with love and loss; as poets, in that (for some readers) their chief success is their creation of themselves in their poems.

One is inclined to say that Hardy is the more personal and more revealing of the two, especially insofar as his poetry shows little playacting. It seems equally true to say that Hardy is the more objective poet. He is able to create characters in his poems distinct from himself, and Yeats is not. Yeats's poems on Crazy Jane and the Woman Old and Young are lively, amusing, and sometimes beautiful, but the masks take on little independent life. Crazy Jane speaks with the formality of a bishop, her ideas are sophisticated, and the foul sty she inhabits does not exist. As a dramatic monologue (with a little dialogue) "Crazy Jane Talks with the Bishop" is less than inconsequential. It interests the reader as a minor example of the humor of the poet who is playing a game. Likewise "Before the World Was

Made" is in the main a tidy little abstraction with an ironical twist at the end of each stanza, making a familiar point about the gap between the real and the ideal in fleshly beauty and in love. The small ingenuity of the poem lies in the perspective from which judgment is made. What gives the poem dignity is Yeats's presence: his compassion for the yearning, the weakness, the coldness of "woman."

By way of contrast consider "Julie-Jane," where with a few touches Hardy creates a real girl in a real world with a real passion and a real death. Another poet might have smoothed out a rough spot or two in the poem, but not many other poets could have created Julie-Jane so surely and swiftly with the rhythms and images of the opening stanzas:

> Sing; how 'a would sing!
> How 'a would raise the tune
> When we rode in the waggon from harvesting
> By the light o' the moon!
>
> Dance; how' a would dance!
> If a fiddlestring did but sound
> She would hold out her coats, give a slanting glance,
> And go round and round.
>
> Laugh; how 'a would laugh!
> Her peony lips would part
> As if none such a place for a lover to quaff
> At the deeps of a heart.

Of course Hardy is present in the vivid life he portrays, just at Yeats is present in his pale mask. "O never again!" Hardy cries, in admiration and compassion, seeing Julie-Jane brightsome-eyed and dying. It is a substantial aspect of Hardy's greatness that he could create character in a way that few other lyric, personal poets could. Among the most notable in his gallery is the trampwoman in the short narrative that bears her name, who walks the world alone, with Hardy beside her:

> Thereaft I walked the world alone,
> Alone, alone!

It is time to return to "Leda and the Swan" and "An August Midnight" and to say that despite differences they possess similar qualities of greatness. Hardy is to be elevated to the level of Yeats, and Yeats is to be reduced to the level of Hardy.

What has seemed valuable in Yeats is to be discounted; what is valuable in Hardy remains.

The surface of "Leda" is its glamor. Here is Yeats encompassing the whole of Greek myth and history in fourteen lines. Masterful poet! Well of course one knows that his ideas about history (if not of myth) are actually rubbish, and old familiar rubbish at that—fit for fourteen-liners and German tomes. The thrill of the sweeping perspective is a cheap thrill, and the good sense of it comes down to the point that civilizations come and go. And how do they come and go? Did she put on his knowledge with his power? It is well that Yeats leaves the matter as a question. He has already implied such rigidity in the course of history that positive assertion would render his viewpoint doubly absurd. Even if the Trojan War was inevitable—in the way that the Second World War might be said to have followed inevitably from the conditions of the peace after the First World War—foreknowledge is something else again. Yeats is playing games with the problem of history and understanding, and not many admirers can contemplate his thought with any seriousness.

Say instead, then, that the poem is a superb vision of a particular myth and a particular past. Who has told the tale of Leda so succinctly and brilliantly, and linked it so swiftly and intimately to a splendid image of the Trojan War? No one. All the same, many readers have to go to a footnote every time they read the poem in order to appreciate its finery—to remember who Leda's children are and the rest of it; and though Yeats is not to be blamed for their persistent ignorance, it may be the case that they return to the poem for another quality.

"Leda" is about sex, not Godlike sex or bestial sex but ordinary human sex. God and beast are mere metaphors for the character of it. Man is in love, says Yeats (in another of his great plain lines that tends to excess), and loves what vanishes; and he himself loved what he could not have. Much of his poetry concerns the yearning, unfulfilled man; but the yearning man imagined conquest, and a few of the poems express it as best they can. Yeats was not good at literal scene and character: he had to climb the ladder, fetch the sword, and come downstairs if he could. "Leda" portrays the ordinary ecstasy of male conquest. The object of conquest is a woman of loosening thighs and thighs caressed (the latter phrase revised from the less humanly sensual "thighs are pressed" of the draft), and the male attitude exhibits a variety of familiar sensations: mastery, omnipotence, knowledge, animality, beauty, satiety—expressed in suitable metaphor. The real glamor of the poem is the glamor men want or possess in the ordinary act of love.

"An August Midnight" offers another familiar scene and experience, but instead of Hardy dressing himself up as Zeus or even as a subtle poet, he is there with paper and pen as you or I might be. The effect is of the most common of common occurrences. If we think that "fall supine" might be improved, we think as subtle poets who want the scene to be enhanced and artful. For Hardy, surface and essence must be as one: ordinary man, ordinary scene, ordinary point, ordinary poem. God and animal are in the poem, nevertheless, and the man is related to both. He sits at his desk, detached and kind, superior and indifferent, while the insects perform their blind, helpless, self-destructive acts. Hardy does not say that the man is a God who might kill the insects for his sport, for that is not the sort of poem he wants; nor does he say that the man is a kindly God who treats his insects like guests. The man has the power of reflection and self-conscious action that separate him radically from the insects, and at the same time he sits alone inactive and unthoughtful except in a rudimentary sense. Stillness dominates the poem, human stillness, the setting aside of active and thinking man and the listening to the insect world. The insects are guests and he is a guest, and what he learns is not exactly what the last line says. For in the perception of a world alien to the human world, he is drawn down into that still aspect of the human world where he hears his own earth-secrets, where human and animal are kin.

There is no other poet in the language who can do this sort of thing the way Hardy does it. Lawrence can do it, but he has to do it with snakes and elephants and tortoise shouts—with razzle-dazzle. Yeats does it in "Leda," but he has to choose that most extreme aspect of ordinary human experience to write about, and he does it with razzle-dazzle too. Hardy is unique: he makes the reader listen carefully to the voices of animal life, he uses the most real, the most ordinary occasion, he adds no shine. It is tempting to say that "An August Midnight" makes "Leda and the Swan" seem like a cheap bauble, but that would be to exaggerate.

It was in the same issue of the *Southern Review* that Auden said that he loved Hardy and that Leavis said that he hated him. If we think that Auden was really talking about the man and Leavis clearly talking about the poetry, there may seem to be no clash; but if we believe that the man is in the poems, then perhaps Leavis was talking about the man as much as Auden about the poetry. It is in any event a comment upon modern attitudes that we have been inclined to trust the judgment of the critic Leavis instead of that of the poet Auden. It is also a comment upon modern attitudes that the recent biography of Hardy by Robert Gittings has found so much that is unlovable in the man—the impotent young man, the heartless old one. What else should we have expected? What has our knowledge told us except to expect revelations of the risible, the unsavory, the despicable, and the mean? Even if we are not inclined to accept it all, we cannot deny the absurdity of the loveless marriage and of the remorse that followed. Likewise with Yeats, we cannot deny the ridiculousness of the proposals to Maud Gonne and her daughter and the yearnings after magic.

It is possible to love Thomas Hardy and Yeats in spite of their failings, just as we love other people and ourselves in spite of failings. Love takes place in a real world, not a fantastical one, and though love of a poet in his poems may be a bit rarefied, it is Hardy the ordinary man leaning against his coppice gate or taking the cat in that we love, and it is Yeats the preposterous seer who does not take his act entirely seriously whom we love. Life is not here, and art there, but art is part of life. What is lovable in life may be lovable in a poem, what is ordinary may be loved as well as what is extraordinary. We do not have always to choose and exclude.

How lovely Yeats's swans are, but we would not want to be without Hardy's darkling thrush. How impressive Yeats's winding stair is, but no less impressive is the stair that Hardy's father descends and ascends in "On One Who Lived and Died Where He Was Born." Yeats's "Black Tower" is very black, but it is no more black and perhaps only slightly better than the hammerings and quakes and shoots of "A Wasted Illness." That moon of Yeats's is a compelling moon, and sometimes obscure, and in "The Black Tower" itself the reader may want to commit the intentional fallacy of asking Yeats what he meant by it; but Hardy's moon is quite as memorable and troubling in "Shut Out That Moon": "Close up the casement, draw the blind, | Shut out that stealing moon...." Yeats in his tower calling upon the supernatural may seem no more dignified than Hardy in his high room watching a fly besmear a line of (say) "An August Midnight" or *Tess* or a letter to a publisher. Yeats's natural visions of Maud Gonne in "Among School Children" are no more intense than those by Hardy of Emma in the poems on her death. Yeats's anguish is no more anguished than Hardy's.

How many images and attitudes Hardy and Yeats share! If we say one poet is greater than the other, it may be because the one poet has treated his material so brilliantly or because the other has drawn it so close to our ordinary lives; or it may be because the one has dressed himself up so eloquently, or because the other looks like an old and loved acquaintance who speaks with merely a slightly affected idiosyncrasy.

II Other Essays

10 The Notebook for *Riceyman Steps*

I

THE CONVENTIONAL IMAGE OF Arnold Bennett as a novelist-at-work has three or four sources: general notions about realistic novelists, inferences from Bennett's completed novels, glimpses of Bennett at his task, and fragmentary remarks by Bennett himself. The image of Zola, notebook in hand, going down into the mines to gather material for *Germinal* is the image of Bennett interviewing an elderly couple to gather material on the Siege of Paris for *The Old Wives' Tale*. The ninety volumes of Zola's notebooks in the Bibliothèque Nationale are matched by dozens of notebooks that Bennett kept. J.B. Atkins asserts that Bennett "would divide his scheme [for a novel] into parts which he numbered and divide each part into sections. He knew in advance what he would put into each part and each section." And George Doran recollects that on one of many silent walks in the forest at Fontainebleau he interrupted Bennett's thoughts to say, "I suppose in these silences you are actually phrasing your thousand words for tomorrow" and got "yes" for an answer. Some of Bennett's voluntary remarks about his writing support the image. In his preface to *The Old Wives' Tale* he comments upon the tedious but necessary research that he undertook for the novel. And in his *Journal of Things New and Old* he says about *Imperial Palace*, then being written: "I have the whole of the material for the novel; and it is indexed, in a notebook. I would sooner lose fifty pages of the manuscript than that notebook."[1]

If one accepts the conventional image, three things follow: preparatory notebooks will deal primarily with observations of the external social scene (somewhat in the manner of George Eliot's notations on economic matters for *Felix Holt*); preparatory notebooks for social scenes with which Bennett was unfamiliar will be longer than others; and the notebooks will display careful and orderly organization of material. A close examination of the notebook for *Riceyman Steps* affords little support for such views. It is worth observing incidentally that although the notebooks for *Imperial Palace* are extensive, there appears to be no index for them.

II

The notebook for *Riceyman Steps* consists of thirty-six small pages of material, amounting to perhaps four thousand words. According to a letter from Bennett to Richmond Temple, to whom he gave the notebook, it contains all the preliminary notes for the novel.[2] There is no reason not to believe this is so. The first striking fact about these notes is that they are approximately two-fifths as long as the notes for *The Price of Love*. The latter novel is Bennett's next-to-last Five Towns novel. It was written with the experience of eight other Five Towns novels behind him as well as the personal experience of twenty-one years in the district and another twenty-five years of occasional visits. In contrast, *Riceyman Steps* concerns scenes and situations with which he was unfamiliar—more so than with any other subject that he ever wrote about. Why should *The Price of Love*, which is only slightly longer than *Riceyman Steps*, require so many more notes? One answer is that neither set of notes gives more than a small fraction of its space to the external scene. Virtually all the material in both sets could have been produced in the isolation of Bennett's writing room.

Bennett did do some prosaic research for *Riceyman Steps*. He read some of William J. Pink's *History of Clerkenwell*, and he made several excursions into Clerkenwell District. No historical material appears in the notebook, and one assumes that Bennett either absorbed the material as he read the book or kept the book at his writing desk. The information that he obtained from his walks through the district amounts to fifty words in the notebook. The following excerpt represents half of it.

K C Rd [King's Cross Road]
gingerbeer=everything indigestible
Police Station
one shop all soap
free library
forage shop
whips and dog within
fried fish

Fifty words do not constitute a novel, and half of those here recorded do not appear in *Riceyman Steps*. Bennett does, of course, use material on Clerkenwell other than that which appears in the notebook; but the paucity of material in the notebook makes one realize how slight is Bennett's interest in the external scene within the novel: he makes formal acknowledgment of the district by having his hero, Henry Earlforward, walk through it once, but he preoccupies himself with an action that takes place inside the Earlforward home. The only other material in the notebook that concerns the external scene is a page of about one hundred words on Madame Tussaud's Waxworks, which Earlforward and his wife Violet visit on their wedding day. Again the material is a list of things seen—the signing of the Magna Carta, the execution of Mary, Queen of Scots—and again the material is only half used in the novel.

The rest of the notebook patently concerns aspects of the novel as an isolated artwork, presenting problems of plot, scene, character, and theme. This material is similarly fragmentary and disorganized; it consists of notations of new ideas, reminders of old ones, and questions. According to Bennett in his letter to Temple, he developed the notebook both before and during the time he was writing the novel. It is impossible to distinguish the material on such a basis, although it seems probable that the first twelve pages come beforehand. It is also impossible to infer the novel from the notebook.

The very first note in the notebook consists of four phrases on a page that otherwise is given over to friends' addresses:

more intimate psychology
grand passion
heroic plane
spiritual grandeur of all 3

The last remark indicates that the third main character, Elsie, the servant, is already in Bennett's mind, an advance upon his original conception of the novel as a story of two misers. (Bennett first definitely conceived the novel in the summer of 1922; he began writing it on 10 October 1922.) The term "grand passion" refers to Earlforward's miserliness; it appears at several points in the novel, notably in the chapter entitled "The Passion," in which Earlforward, who is walking along the street with Violet, refuses to spend money on a taxi or a tramcar, despite the fact that one of his legs is paining him severely. As the last three phrases of the notation suggest, Bennett does not regard his main character simply as a curious or monstrous miser—one more realistic portrait from life. However ludicrous and grotesque Bennett intends Earlforward to seem as he debates with himself whether or not to spend twopence to ease his pain ("with death in his very stomach"), he means him to seem heroic in his adherence to his passion.[3] The term "more intimate psychology" suggests Bennett's lesser interest in the social scene.

Many of the entries in the notebook consist of key phrases, such as "double saucepan" and "sawed off wedding ring," that refer to material that Bennett was developing in his mind or was adapting from other sources. "Double saucepan" identifies an occasion in part 2 when Elsie damages a new saucepan that Violet has bought. The occasion provides an opportunity for Bennett to suggest Violet's increasing hysteria. Thirty-five pages later Violet refuses to accept money for the saucepan from Elsie. The incident here serves to disclose Violet's changing attitude toward Earlforward, for whom the saucepan was to have provided more nourishing food. The sawed-off wedding ring is the ring from Violet's previous marriage. Earlforward saws it from her hand in order to have it re-made—at a saving—for their own wedding.

The most interesting of the key phrases is "neighbours over wall," which occurs seven times in the notebook. In the novel, the bare fact that Earlforward's house is separated by a wall from neighboring houses is mentioned twice. Then toward the end of the novel, when Violet has been taken away to die at the hospital, when Earlforward lies dying at home, and when Elsie's lover lies ill in her bedroom, Elsie looks out of her window late at night and sees across "a pattern of dark walls" (316) an unknown woman come out into a yard and beat a dog. The scene is extraneous to the action of the novel: the woman has not appeared previously, and she appears only once again, equally briefly and unnecessarily. The link to the rest of the novel is imagistic, thematic. When Elsie sees the woman and the dog again, it is in the daytime, and she cannot connect the woman who now inquires sympathetically about Earlforward's health with the woman who coldly threw the dog against the kennel, and cannot connect the affectionate and proud dog with the groveling and beaten dog. Elsie is sentimental; she does not believe that sympathetic people are capable of beating dogs; she thinks that beating dogs is unnecessary and unusual. But she has a lover who attacks her with a knife and strikes her a blow on the shoulder. At the end of the novel "she even desired to suffer at his hands as a penance for the harshness of her earlier treatment of him" (382). In the novel as a whole, Bennett presents a grotesque action that at the same time is ordinary and even humorous. To the public, Earlforward presents "an appearance of quiet, intelligent, refined and kindly prosperity" (11); to Violet, when she knows him at first, he seems "self-reliant without being self-confident. He was grave, but his little eyes had occasionally a humorous gleam.... In brief, Mr. Earlforward... was nearly faultless" (59). Then he proceeds to starve himself and her to death, incidentally starving her sexually. Once in a bitter rage she says to him: "And you're always so polite! As if that made any difference! I wish to God often you weren't so polite. My first husband wasn't very polite. And I've known the time when he's laid his hand on me, knocked me about, yes, and more than once.... There's worse things than a blow, and every woman knows it" (273).

Like most of the other phrases in the notebook, "neighbours over wall" is bare of psychological, thematic meaning, and the linking of the scene to other material in the novel has to be inferred. A few phrases, though, do indicate some of the broad connections among these and other scenes, and they are worth recording.

Remember that he inspired love & dread

. . . .

She makes him eat for sexual intercourse sake.

. . . .

She must accustom herself to her love and dread of him

. . . .

Elsie on cancer and Violets death due to stomach
. . . .

He had pretended to be dying when he was dying
. . . .

Killing yourself. Killing me. Nursing you will kill me.
. . . .

Death feeling
Vi[olet] Just as well Elsie should think he's very ill

Aside from the fragmentary and seemingly disorganized material such as that which has been quoted, the notebook contains a few outlines for whole scenes. There appears to be no significant reason for the particular scenes selected. The most carefully developed scene, an occasion on which Violet does business with an American book dealer during Earlforward's absence, is of small importance to the novel. In the notebook it is given four or five times as much space, relative to the rest of the material, as it occupies in the novel. Presumably Bennett diverted himself with outlining it during an idle moment.

The most interesting feature of the notebook is, indeed, not the material it treats most fully but the material it lacks. There is, of course, a certain amount of superficial detail in the novel that Bennett must have been utterly familiar with, such as the newspaper placards described in the fourth chapter of part 1. But although in the immediate context his description is merely one more element of a realistic scene, the later news story of the fight at the Communist Club, which forms a central episode in the novel, and the subsequent newspaper headlines describing Earlforward's macabre death, give the original description a thematic function. There would have been reason for Bennett to have written a reminder about the motif into the notebook. Likewise, there are no notations on matters that are more complex: the division of the book into five major parts and actions, the time structure, the parallel plotting, the dominant imagery. It is true that *Riceyman Steps* is, in these respects, one of Bennett's simpler novels; but it is also true that the surviving notes and information on his other novels betray no need for outlining such matters. The time scheme for *The Old Wives' Tale* is sufficiently complex and subtle so that the two published attempts to describe it contain many errors.

III

The notebook to *Riceyman Steps*, then, tells some important things about the composition of Bennett's novels. The notations rarely deal with the external setting; they reveal a clear interest in psychology; they focus upon the novel as an isolated work, with its own internal demands. At the same time, the fragmentary and unsystematic quality of the material, the disproportionate development of minor scenes, the perfunctory notation of major points, and the omission of significant and complex material suggest that the notebook was not a necessary prologue to the novel. Given Bennett's apparent compulsiveness as a writer (of which his notorious preoccupation with the number of words he produced and his actual production of an immense body of fiction, drama, journalism, letters, and private records are the obvious evidence), it may be inferred that the notebooks for all the novels may mainly have served a writing compulsion. The few that have survived are mainly very much alike.

There may, then, be a measure of truth in the accounts by J.B. Atkins and George Doran of Bennett's writing habits; that is, that Bennett was capable of complex and systematic development of his novels in his mind. H.G. Wells remarks that Bennett could assimilate information "with extraordinary rapidity and precision," and he once wrote to Bennett himself, "You have the best mind in Europe (in many respects)."[4] Whatever allowance must be made for friendship and for Wells's limited perspective, the opinion does come from a man who himself possessed extraordinary mental capacities.

Some other comments by Bennett on his writing habits may now seem more impressive than they might hitherto have seemed. Three entries in his *Journal* on *Clayhanger* are particularly interesting. At Fontainebleau, a month and a half before he began writing the novel, he notes that "in the forest I practically arranged most of the construction of the first part of the novel." (The whole novel, which is Bennett's third longest, consists of four parts, of about equal length, amounting to one hundred and sixty thousand words.) Three weeks later, after having spent an evening at a theatre in order to obtain some material, he writes, "I had got into an extraordinary vein of 'second sight.' I perceived whole chapters." And a few days before he began writing the novel, he "schemed out the first nine chapters." The same sort of thinking seems to have preceded the writing of his lighter novels. Dorothy Cheston Bennett says of *Dream of Destiny* that the whole construction and characterization were fixed in his mind before he began writing. Bennett himself wrote to his adopted son two months before beginning the book, "My next novel is all in my head."[6]

The final evidence of Bennett's mental grasp is the manuscript of any novel of his mature years. Shortly before he began writing *The Old Wives' Tale* he developed an interest in calligraphy, and he decided to write the novel in a fine calligraphic hand. In his prefatory note to the facsimile edition of the novel, he describes the implications of his decision:

> Of course if your manuscript is to have even the most modest pretensions to calligraphic decency, you must know all the time exactly what you are about to do; otherwise a regular mess will ensue. It will be noticed that now and then in the writing of *The Old Wives' Tale* something rather like a regular mess did ensue, consequence of not having absolutely decided in advance just what I wanted to write,

The Notebook for Riceyman Steps 133

and in what order, and how. The reader, however, sees the worst of these messes; no page, so far as I remember, was destroyed and rewritten.

Anyone who has seen the manuscript of *The Old Wives' Tale* and who himself has had much experience in writing must be astonished by its decency. There are no abandoned chapters or pages, no observable structural dilemmas. The corrections consist of occasional rephrasings of paragraphs and sentences. Whether or not one believes that *The Old Wives' Tale* is a great novel, and whether or not one believes that a novel ought to be composed rather more along Laurentian principles, Bennett's conceptual grasp, both in its scope and in its precision, is impressive. He wrote his later novels in the same fine calligraphic hand. The manuscript of *Riceyman Steps* is as neat and clean as the notebook for it is disorderly.[7]

11 Some Curious Realism in *Riceyman Steps*

I

AS A REALIST, Arnold Bennett is most readily identified by his faithful delineation of the visible world. When a reader enters Pemberley in *Pride and Prejudice*, he merely enters a stately home; when he enters the Baines Shop in *The Old Wives' Tale*, he has to be careful not to trip over the step that joins two rooms on the ground floor (caused by the fact that originally the rooms belonged to two separate dwellings), and he perforce notices in the parlor the corner cupboard of oak (inlaid with maple) that hangs to the right of the fireplace and above a shelf on which sits a copper tea urn, etc. If he wants to be absolutely convinced of the unique reality of the shop, he can go to Burslem in Staffordshire (Bursley in the novel) to find it—standing to this day, now in part occupied by a Woolworth store (1960). Bennett's maternal grandfather owned the shop, and Bennett as a boy visited it frequently.

No critic has examined the description of the Baines shop to see if it is anything but the most prosaic realism. There has seemed to be no need. Similarly, Earlforward's bookshop in *Riceyman Steps* may seem to be the very image of some reality. It is situated in the Clerkenwell district of London, below Granville Square (Riceyman Square in the novel), with its front on the areaway that leads to the Square. One side of the shop is on King's Cross Road; the other looks toward the Steps that go up to the Square. The shop has three floors; a couple of its windows are bricked up; the blind on one window is broken; and so forth. What is the reality?

At the time Bennett writes of in the novel, 1919-20, there was no bookshop at or near the spot where he places Earlforward's shop. One writer has suggested that the model for the shop was a bookshop in Red Lion Passage, Holborn, and another writer has suggested that Bennett simply transformed a watchmaker's

"Some Curious Realism in *Riceyman Steps*" appeared in *Modern Fiction Studies*, c 1962 by Purdue Research Foundation, West Lafayette, Indiana 47907.

shop that stood on the same spot. In the absence of more than the slightest supporting argument for either suggestion, they must be rejected. The watchmaker's shop, in any event, has been destroyed and cannot be examined. Besides, Bennett himself says (his remarks were apparently unknown to the writers suggesting the other shops) that he transposed the shop from Southampton to the Clerkenwell site. Reginald Pound in his biography twice quotes him to that effect: Bennett writing in his journal (in an unpublished portion of it) of buying "two books at James' (original shop of *Riceyman Steps*)" and writing in an *Evening Standard* article in the late twenties of "a feat of transport surpassing anything ever done in that line in the U.S.A.—the moving of an entire bookseller's shop with all its books and dust from a South Coast port to... [Clerkenwell]."[1] The question is whether Bennett himself is to be believed. The shop in Southampton has been destroyed too.

What is the reality of the shop in the novel? The more closely one examines the shop, the less substantial it becomes. Despite many details, despite the consistency of these details (and despite the fact that most of the action of the novel takes place inside the house), there are three rooms that one cannot locate even by inference, except with respect to the floor they are on. Moreover, the piecemeal fashion in which Bennett offers his details suggests that he built the house as he wrote the novel, keeping his plan open to meet the exigencies of both his narrative and his theme. Thirdly, most of the description of the interior is metaphorical rather than literal, suggestive rather than visual.

Consider Bennett's description of the shoproom that he transported so carefully from Southampton: "The first bay was well-lighted and tidy; but the others, as they receded into the gloomy backward of the shop, were darker and darker and untidier and untidier. The effect was of mysterious and vast populations of books imprisoned for ever in everlasting shade, chained, deprived of air and sun and movement, hopeless, resigned, martyrized."[2] One day during Earlforward's absence, Violet Arb, who is contemplating marrying him, persuades the servant Elsie to show her through the house. She hopes to obtain from it some impression of the man. Earlforward has won her favor: "His pointed short beard, so well trimmed, seemed to give him the status of a pillar of society. She... liked his full red lips and his fresh complexion. And he was exceedingly neat" (58). The shoproom belies his appearance. "She peered... into the dark spaces between the bays, and descried the heaps of books on the floor. The dirt and the immense disorder almost frightened her" (90). Then she goes into his office and is even more appalled by the sight there. She and Elsie agree "that the contrast between the master and his home was... tragic" (91). They go upstairs, and in addition to more dirt and disorder, Violet sees a bathtub—the only bathtub—filled with books, and she sees fireplaces that have not been used for years. She begins to understand: "The character of the man was displayed beyond any misunderstanding by the house with its revelations of his daily life; but there was no clue to it in his appearance and deportment. She was more than intimidated—she was frightened. Withal, the terror—for it amounted to terror—fascinated her" (94).

Looking back to the description of the shoproom, one sees in the room itself Earlforward's public self (the first bay) and his private self (the farther bays). Moreover, Bennett's description of the farther bays suggests the qualities of Earlforward's mind that Violet dimly apprehends when she sees the literal scene. In the course of the novel Violet learns enough about the man behind the mask to be afraid to be in the house alone with him. The reader sees all. In his miserliness, in his fear of life, in his reaction against Violet's intrusion into his existence, he starves himself and her to death. The neighbor who discovers his body sees what the description of the farther bays of the shop had suggested: imprisonment, withheld motion, torture, martyrdom. "Mr Earlforward... [was] moveless in a peculiar posture in his office-chair... [whose] left arm had caught under the ledge of the desk.... He was leaning over the right arm of the chair, his body at half a right angle to the perpendicular and his face towards the floor.... What a dreadful face! White, blotched, hairy skin drawn tightly over bones and muscles—very tightly. An expression of torment in the tiny, unseeing eyes" (370-71).

In other ways, too, the shop suggests the man—ways that sometimes only the author can control, not the owner. Bennett mentions that originally the house faced onto King's Cross Road but that the front entrance was bricked up at a time "lost in antiquity" (215)—presumably more distant than when Earlforward came to the shop about 1900, that the two front windows on the first floor of the King's Cross Road side are also bricked up, that the front window on the second floor will not open, that the window in Elsie's room has to be propped open, that the sole window in Earlforward's office remains shut against King's Cross Road by a blind whose cord breaks in the opening pages of the novel, and that the electric lights in the house are giving out one by one and are not being replaced. It is a house that, like the man inside of it, is turning away from the city, protecting itself against the city, shutting itself up in darkness. On her wedding day, Violet enters the house and realizes that she is passing under her husband's dominion: "It was as if she had entered a fortress and heard the self-locking gates thereof clang behind her. No escape! But in the fortress she was sheltered; she was safe" (129). On the next day: "Inside the sealed house London did not exist" (148). The chief images by which Bennett describes Earlforward's mentality are "fortress" and "safe" (202, 273, and elsewhere). One is led to believe that when Bennett wrote (in a light tone) in his *Evening Standard* article of "the moving of an entire bookseller's shop from a South Coast port" he was playing at being the photographic realist that the public, including Virginia Woolf, assumed him to be. How amusing becomes Virginia Woolf's criticism that Bennett and the other Edwardians try to create character by offering the reader external facts: "They have given us a house in the hope that we may be able to deduce the human beings who live there."[3]

II

Just as curious as the fact that Bennett did not transport T. James's shop is the fact that he transported it to Clerkenwell. In his early and later years in the city Bennett occasionally walked through the district, and in preparing his novel he made expeditions into it; but otherwise he did not know it. Frank Swinnerton, who spent his childhood near Granville Square, says that he thought upon reading *Riceyman Steps*: "It isn't Clerkenwell; he doesn't know it as he knows the Five Towns." In view of the fact that there are several other districts of London that Bennett knew quite well, his selection of Clerkenwell seems—on realistic grounds—unaccountable. In his preface to *The Old Wives' Tale* Bennett remarks: "I hated, and still hate, the awful business of research"; yet his choice of Clerkenwell involved him not only in visits to the district but also in some historical research.[4]

And then the odd thing is that having chosen the district, he failed to use it in the way that a realist should. Almost all of the action takes place within the shop or on the Steps or outside the district altogether (at Madame Tussaud's Waxworks). He describes the house as "sealed up from the world" (145) and he makes hardly an effort to present the district. His historical material is indicative. It is slight, and it is given over almost entirely to a description of Clerkenwell in the twelfth century and a description of the building of the underground railway in the nineteenth. None of the material is sociological or cultural background for any of the characters or any of the actions.

In William J. Pink's *The History of Clerkenwell*, which was the source for all of Bennett's historical material, the description of the building of the underground railway is a lengthy, clumsy, and sometimes unintentionally humorous account of a great public enterprise that was attended by catastrophe; it is full of information about costs, faulty engineering, and quarrels over the project. Bennett reduces the account by three-fourths and concentrates upon the catastrophe. So far as the narrative is concerned, he offers it as an indirect cause of Earlforward's acquiring his shop and his limp: one night the uncle who owns the shop tells Earlforward about this episode in the history of his beloved Clerkenwell, and becomes so excited that he has a stroke; Earlforward in helping him slips and hurts his knee; the uncle then decides to leave the shop to Earlforward. Imagine the realist who hated research ferreting out a historical incident (beginning on page 573 of the *History*) with which to explain an inheritance and a limp![5] Had Earlforward's uncle died peacefully, his will could have read the same. A quotation from the end of Bennett's description—an account of the collapse of the Fleet sewer—suggests instead a thematic, imagistic purpose.

> The populace screamed at the thought of workmen entombed and massacred. A silence! Then the great brick piers, fifty feet in height, moved bodily. The whole bottom of the excavation moved in one mass. A dark and fetid liquid appeared, oozing, rolling, surging, smashing everything in its resistless track, and rushed into

the mouth of the new tunnel. The crown of the arch of the mighty Fleet Sewer had broken. Men wept at the enormity and completeness of the disaster.... But the Underground Railway was begun afresh and finished and grandly inaugurated, and at first the public fought for seats in its trains, and then could not be persuaded to enter its trains because they were uninhabitable, and so on and so on....

Old fat Riceyman told his tale with such force and fire that he had a stroke. (24-25; ellipses are Bennett's)

The substance of the scene as well as the touch of grotesque comedy that Bennett lends to it relates to two major images in the novel that concern horrible burial: the subterranean Chamber of Horrors at Tussaud's that Earlforward and Violet visit on their wedding day and the sealed house where Earlforward starves himself and his wife to death. The railway disaster is a prefiguration of the Earlforward disaster; the Chamber of Horrors is a distorted image of the Earlforward home. The sewerage in the railway disaster that engulfs everything "in its resistless track" suggests the "accumulation of dirt in the shop, very gradual, but resistless" (156). The end of the railway episode and the end of the novel are similar. The horror of the Fleet sewer collapse is forgotten, and the railway is built anew. The "Midnight Tragedy in King's Cross Road" (newspaper headlines by which semi-literate Clerkenwell obtains from Earlforward's shop something akin to a bloody murder) shocks the populace for only a few days, and the buyer of the shop "discussed with the experts what he should do, and at what cost, to annihilate the very memory of T.T. Riceyman's by means of improvements, fresh dispositions, and paint" (377).

III

According to Edward Knoblock, Bennett derived Earlforward in part from T. James himself and in part from a book that he picked up at James's shop, F. Somner Merryweather's *Lives and Anecdotes of Misers*. Knoblock says nothing more about James than that he was "an eccentric, kindly, elderly man," and Bennett in a journal notation at the time of his first visit to the shop says only that he conceived there "a short story about two old misers."[6] The extent to which Bennett used James cannot be known. But the extent to which he used Merryweather's book can.

What must have struck Bennett first about the book was Merryweather's fascination with his subject. The complete title of the work concludes "with a Few Words on Frugality and Savings," and Merryweather devoted chapter 2 to these words to assure the reader that in displaying the unhappy lives of misers for their edification he is by no means recommending prodigality. His chief illustration of proper frugality concerns a dirt contractor, who promises his daughter's fiancé a wedding present, which the young man assumes will be a few hundred guineas but which to his consternation proves to be a large pile of dirt.

From the sale of the dirt, though, the young man receives two thousand guineas. The anecdote proves, says Merryweather, that "there is nothing without its use and nothing that will not produce a price" (48). In *Riceyman Steps* Earlforward receives as an unexpected wedding present from his wife not a pile of dirt but a removal of the dirt that has been accumulating in his house for twenty years. Violet hires a company to do the job while she and Earlforward take their wedding breakfast and go to Tussaud's; but the couple return before the job is finished. Because this is his wedding day, Earlforward accepts the loss of his dirt with some grace. Nevertheless, "he had been robbed of something," and he says to the workmen who are operating the huge vacuum-cleaner, "Do you sell it? Do you get anything for it?" (127, 128) The subject is the same, the occasion for the gift is the same, but in his transformation of the gift into a loss, Bennett transforms the story: the unconsciously ludicrous example of proper frugality becomes a consciously ludicrous one of miserliness. Why did Merryweather write his book on misers? As one of the endpapers tells the reader, he also wrote a book entitled *Bibliomania in the Middle Ages*. He himself may have sat for Earlforward's portrait.

There are misers in his book, dozens of them, and Bennett must have been impressed by the uniformity of the type. They are characteristically thin; they deprive themselves of food, light, and heat to an extreme degree; they sometimes have piles of new clothes that they never wear; one or two of them hate doctors and die rather than obey their doctors' orders; one of them happens to be a bookseller. All of these things apply to Earlforward. They do so in a rudimentary sense. They are the thin substance of anecdotes, brief accounts, that with one or two notable exceptions consist of imperceptive and undramatic recitals of curious facts. Thus Earlforward's refusal to eat the steak that Violet one day offers him for tea may have its origin in the miser Ostervald's refusal near death to accept proper nourishment: "I have no appetite for the meat" (79); but the particular ludicrous drama and subtlety of Earlforward's situation are Bennett's own, without a trace in Merryweather. Violet has a tantrum in consequence. She calls Earlforward miserly, tyrannical, cold, and destructive. Earlforward maintains his composure but decides that his wife is a sinister woman. He defeats her, and she retreats to her bed conscious of a peculiar pleasure in having yielded to him. Elsie clears the table and is attracted to the steak. In the absence of her lover she has taken up gluttony. She devours the steak and then runs to Violet to confess. "Violet laughed in the dark: an unusual laugh, not vivacious nor hearty, but a laugh. 'I'm glad, Elsie,' she said" (190). Earlforward decides that he must plot against Violet. He performs two unmiserly acts: he lights a fire and sends Elsie for the newspaper. Then he draws Violet from the bed, and after he has frightened her with the newspaper story about the fight at the nearby Communist club, he shows her the secret compartment in his safe where he keeps his gold.

The fact is that it hardly took Merryweather to inform Bennett that misers are very often thin, deprive themselves of food, and so forth. What is more interesting is the use that Bennett did not make of Merryweather. For there are some other important characteristics of most of the misers in Merryweather: their faces are pinched and bloodless; their clothes are ragged, patched, and filthy; and they have extraordinary hiding places, such as piles of manure, for their money. None of these things applies to Earlforward. It is true that at the end of the novel his face is thin and grey from starvation (which stems from both self-denial and cancer of the stomach); but as he appears in the first third of the novel, he is in some respects the very reverse of Merryweather's misers. Not only is his dress neat and presentable but "his complexion [for a middle-aged man] was still fairly good, and the rich, very red lips, under a small greyish moustache and over a short, pointed beard, were quite remarkable in their suggestion of vitality" (11). Whether Bennett violates probability or possibility in so describing Earlforward need not be answered here. It is clear that he did not rely upon Merryweather. Furthermore, Earlforward would have continued to thrive upon his miserliness except for the intrusion of Violet into his life. The novel records a crisis in his existence, when his sexual needs override his psychological predisposition. In the battle between his needs he destroys himself. The novel is not a life, with anecdotes, of a miser; it is specifically a crisis in a miser's life when his miserliness fails him. The integrity of his miserliness is violated when he shares himself with Violet. The violation is formally undertaken with the vacuum cleaning on his wedding day. At the end of the novel his integrity is violated by Elsie's robbing his safe. His marriage precipitates his cancer and starvation; Elsie's robbery produces the shock from which he dies. The necessary conclusion is that Bennett either had another prime source for Earlforward than Merryweather's book (and one cannot seriously believe it to be the formally known T. James) or created the man out of his own imagination and according to the needs of his novel. Perhaps by exceedingly good fortune he knew intimately a miser such as Earlforward. Surely he makes effective use of the good fortune by developing the ironical contrast between the exterior of Earlforward's appearance, behavior, and shop and the interior of his soul. What would have been lost had Bennett taken careful notes from Merryweather's book? Merely such irony, merely the grotesque humor of the situation, merely the dramatic penetration from appearance to reality, merely the substance of the novel.

Apart from the episode of the dirt-collector (along with a fragment of another episode that Bennett probably combined with it), there is only one portion of Merryweather's book that Bennett clearly used. It describes Foscue, a French miser, who builds a cave under his cellar in which to hide his gold. The cave has a secret door, which can be locked from the inside. One day Foscue disappears. He is not found until his house is torn down and the cave discovered. He has accidentally locked himself in.

> They [the workmen] threw back the door and descended with a light. The first object upon which the lamp reflected was the ghastly body of Foscue the miser, and scattered around him were heavy bags of gold, and ponderous chests of untold treasure; a candlestick lay beside him on the floor. This worshipper of mammon had gone into his cave to pay his devoirs to his golden god, and became a sacrifice to his devotion...! How hated, when the gnawing pangs of starvation came slowly upon him, must have been that yellow vision. (69)

In *Riceyman Steps* Earlforward comes down in the night to his office from his sickbed after hearing that Violet has died. He intends to recreate his existence. He opens his safe and discovers that Elsie has stolen some money. The shock kills him, but he is ready to die of starvation too. He is discovered by his neighbor, who has suspected that something is wrong by the fact that a light is burning in the house in the middle of the night. "[Mr. Belrose]...advanced firmly into the office. A faint glow of red showed in the ashstrewn grate. The electric light descended in almost palpable rays on Mr. Earlforward's grizzled head. The safe was open and there was a bag of money on the floor.... [Mr. Belrose] bent down in order to look into Mr. Earlforward's...face. What a dreadful face!...An expression of torment in the tiny, unseeing eyes" (370-71).

If major elements of the scene come from Merryweather's book, the irony is Bennett's own. Not that the electric light is burning so uselessly nor that the safe lies exposed. These are ironies of the occasion comparable to Merryweather's irony of the worshipper sacrificing himself. They are Bennett's ironies by virtue of three hundred and seventy pages that give them special meaning. Earlforward hides his tormented soul in darkness; he cannot live in light; he survives only as long as he can remain the way Violet describes him once in anger: "a locked-up cast-iron safe" (273).

IV

In *The Author's Craft* Bennett describes the preliminary process of making a novel:

> The novelist may take notes of phenomena likely to be of use to him. And he may acquire the skill to invent very apposite illustrative incident. But he cannot invent psychology. Upon occasion some human being may entrust him with confidences extremely precious for his craft. But such windfalls are so rare as to be negligible. From outward symptoms he can guess something of the psychology of others. He can use a real person as the unrecognizable but helpful basis for each of his characters.... And all that is nothing. And all special research is nothing. When the real intimate work of creation has to be done—and it has to be done on every page—the novelist can only look within for effective aid.[7]

At least for *Riceyman Steps* Bennett looked within more than he looked without, not only for the character of Earlforward but also for Earlforward's house and Earlforward's Clerkenwell.

12 E. A. Robinson's System of Opposites

IN A LETTER TO Harry de Forest Smith of 3 June 1894, E. A. Robinson says of his poem "The Night Before":

> The story is unpleasant, founded upon my system of "opposites" that is, creating a fictitious life in direct opposition to a real life which I know. My recent mental disturbances have rendered some kind of more or less literary expression an absolute necessity; and this story, which, by the way, comes dangerously near to being what the world calls "hot stuff" is doing me a good service in working off my general discontent. It reflects, in a measure, my present mood in the narration of things of which I know nothing except by instinctive fancy.[1]

The phrase "system of opposites" does not occur elsewhere in Robinson's published writings; and the absence of critical comment upon it is perhaps tribute to Robinson's general indifference to poetic theory. But this passage itself and a few remarks in other letters throw adequate light upon the term, and the term itself provides an interesting starting point for examining the development of Robinson's poetic voice and vision.

When *The Torrent and the Night Before* was printed, Robinson wrote again to Smith:

> I don't exactly understand what you mean when you say I have put too much of myself into my work. With the exception of an occasional sonnet and the obviously didactic—"damned didactic," if you prefer it so—pieces, I intended the book to be entirely impersonal. I fear you are inclined to make too much of my frequent use of the first person singular. (269)

In a letter of 3 February of the same year, 1897, he remarks that "'The Night Before' is purely objective, and may be called anything from pessimism to rot" (273). On 4 April he says that "Zola is the greatest worker in the objective that the world has ever seen" (282). Later in the year he remarks:

> If anything is worthy of a man's best and hardest effort, that thing is the utterance of what he believes to be the truth. Of course I like a joke, and I like art for its own sake; but those things in themselves are not enough. Just as deliberate pathos in literature ... is almost always a mistake, so, I think, is mere objectivity ... at the best

unsatisfactory. So I hope you will like my "Octaves," "Calvary," "L'Envoi," etc. better than "The Night Before." (289)

In sum, then, Robinson associates his poetry of opposites with objectivity and realism; he sees such poetry to be divorced from his own voice and vision; and he seems generally to regard it as lesser work.

Difficulties begin when one examines the chief exhibition of the system of opposites. To be sure, the situation of "The Night Before"—a man about to be hanged for the murder of his wife reviews his crime—is far removed from anything the celibate and mild-mannered Robinson ever experienced; but the fact that the poem followed as "an absolute necessity" upon Robinson's "recent mental disturbances" suggests that the removal is mere disguise. In presenting a brief account of Robinson's life, Louis Coxe remarks somewhat ironically: "To a Freudian, all things are Oedipal and there is indeed a case for seeing in Robinson's life the familiar pattern of the unwanted third son, rejected... by the father and kept at a distance by a too beloved mother."[2] Thus to a Freudian, "The Night Before" is Oedipal, especially in view of the fact that the poem was composed during the interval between the death of Robinson's father and the final illness of his mother. But the case need hardly be conducted in such fashion. If one thinks of Victor Hugo's observation that we are all condemned to death, and thinks then of Robinson's reiterated opinion that he would die early ("there is not enough of me... to last a great many years," he wrote to Arthur Gledhill), one equally sees a personal poem.[3]

Perhaps, though, Robinson means "a fictitious life in direct opposition to a real life which I know" to apply more to the views of the condemned man than to his situation. Thus one might point to the fact that the man observes that "after| The last loved thing in the world has left us,| We know the triumph of hate."[4] And one would note in contrast that Robinson himself says in a letter to Smith of 13 May 1896, "I am inclined to be a trifle solemn in my verses, but I intend that there shall always be at least a suggestion of something wiser than hatred and something better than despair" (247). The difference, however, is superficial. The condemned man is himself nothing if not solemn in his speech, and he also suggests something wiser than hatred; for in fact he has moved beyond that attitude: "So I foster| Even tonight for the woman who wronged me,| Nothing of hate..." and "for all who have fallen —| Even for him (the lover)—I hold no malice...." He does not know the opposing triumph of love, but he is moving in the direction of such wisdom rather than against it.

The similarity of vision of Robinson and his condemned man can be inferred from other evidence. In his letter to Smith of 3 June 1894, Robinson remarks of the poem, "Here is a little observation that will come in towards the end:

> I tell you, Domine,
> There are times in the lives of us poor devils
> When heaven and hell get mixed." (162)

The phrase "poor devils" is echoed in a letter to Smith of 13 May 1896, just at the time the poem was printed: "if some poor devil of a man or woman feels any better or any stronger for anything I have said, I shall have no fault to find" (247). In his letter to Smith of 3 February 1897, Robinson uses the phrase "despairing devil" similarly (273). One infers that the catharsis which he offers the reader is just what he says he himself experienced in writing the poem. He sees himself, the reader, and the condemned man as all poor devils in the world.

It is apparent that "The Night Before" partly expresses rather than opposes Robinson's own voice and vision. Its position can be seen more clearly by examining another early poem, *Captain Craig*. Although Robinson does not speak of his system of opposites with regard to this work, his comments on it are similar to those on "The Night Before." He writes to Smith on 2 June 1900: "There is not very much of myself [in the poem], but there are pages of what certain people take to be myself.... I should never have written it, as it stands, if I had not passed through those six months of hell in the College Office [as private secretary to Charles Eliot Norton]" (306). Again the acknowledgment that other people do find him in the poem and the admission that the poem sprang from personal distress suggest that the assumed objectivity is unreal. Also, the material circumstance of Craig's life, and his character, are similar to Robinson's. Craig is poor and an outcast, as was Robinson at the time; and aside from Craig's garrulity, he fits rather well the description of Robinson given by Daniel Gregory Mason in 1937: "Admirable, all through this time [when he was "distressingly poor"], was his half-serene, half-humorous detachment from his surroundings."[5] (This is not to deny, of course, that Craig was also drawn from Robinson's acquaintance Alfred Louis, or even that he bears resemblance to Jesus.) In contrast to "The Night Before," in which the similarity of voice and vision to Robinson's needs to be argued, the similarity in *Captain Craig* seems obvious. From the time of publication to the present day, most critics have taken for granted that the eponymous hero of the poem speaks entirely for Robinson.

A glance at a few details of the poem may nevertheless be useful to clarify the ways in which Robinson and his hero seem similar. The poem comes close to being a monologue like "The Night Before." A narrator introduces himself and then introduces Captain Craig, who by line seventy takes over and who in monologue, letters, and testament speaks the vast bulk of the poem's two thousand lines and virtually all its philosophy. The narrator presents himself as a skeptic who listens to and is won over by Craig; but his opposition to Craig's views amounts to no more than a brief tossing and turning in bed one night, and he is thereupon the Captain's champion. His friends such as Killigrew and Plunkett have little to say, and nothing directly. The other characters who do speak to some purpose in the poem are mere instruments of Craig's viewpoint. In the Captain's first letter are described a man and a girl, the one "the child in absence" and the other the child "in excess." These are the extremes whose union produces the true visionary such as Craig: "The Child that is the Man, the

Mystery, | The Phoenix of the World." In the second letter the Captain describes Count Pretzel von Wurzburger, who is a mendicant like the Captain and who is child enough to play cradle songs on the piano. Elsewhere Craig has spoken of "God's music of the soul"; because to the idealist death is a triumph, Craig will have a triumphal brass band at his funeral; and Craig's last word at his death, "trombones," implies that he hears "the golden tone | Of that far-singing call you all have heard." The incarnation of his philosophical outlook is properly a musician such as Count Pretzel. Other figures such as the soldier and Carmichael are comparable.

The views that Craig and his doubles express in the poem seem transparently the same as those expressed by Robinson in his own person in such poems as the "Octaves," "The Children of the Night," and "Credo," and in his letters. Frequently the imagery is the same. A few illustrations may be appropriate:

> Then shall at last come ringing through the sun,
> Through time, through flesh, God's music of the soul.
> For wisdom is that music, and all joy
> That wisdom. *(Captain Craig)*

> For through it all,—above, beyond it all,—
> I know the far-sent message of the years,
> I feel the coming glory of the Light! ("Credo")

> Through dusk that hindered it,
> I found the truth, and for the first whole time
> ...as a man, a scarred man among men,
> I knew it...
> The light that burned above me and within me. *(Captain Craig)*

> Let us, the Children of the Night,
> Put off the cloak that hides the scar!
> Let us be Children of the Light,
> And tell the ages what we are! ("The Children of the Night")

These things [the present age, scientific progress, materialistic philosophy] ... are damned uninteresting to one who can get a glimpse of the real light through the clouds of time.... [Christian Science] is only a stepping stone to the truth....

The great scholars of the world are for the most part spiritual imbeciles, and there is where the trouble lies. The willingness "to be a child again" comes hard. (Letter to Smith of 15 March 1897)

You see I have come to look on death as a deliverance and an advancement (vide "Kosmos," "Two Sonnets," etc.) and I am very glad to be able to stand up and say that I am an idealist. (Letter to Smith of 7 December 1896)

It is hard to believe that had Robinson written *Captain Craig* by 1897 he would not have included it among such poems as the "Octaves" and "Calvary" (and presumably "The Children of the Night" and "Credo") as the higher personal poetry that he contrasts to "The Night Before" in his letter to Smith of 1 November 1897. And it would seem, then, that he describes this poem as well as "The Night Before" inaccurately. Neither presents a vision opposed to his own. That in "The Night Before" is partial; that in *Captain Craig* is truly his.

But to make such a judgment upon *Captain Craig*—to infer that it wholly expresses Robinson's voice and vision—is equally to rely upon Robinson's word. For although there can be no doubt that Robinson means himself when he uses the first person singular in such poems as the "Octaves" and "Credo," the vision in these poems and in *Captain Craig* is as exaggeratedly exalted as the vision in "The Night Before" is anguished. "The Night Before" and *Captain Craig* present, in fact, the two poles of Robinson's experience. The circumstances of their heroes are identical in the respect that they are men who have been scarred by life and who are now at the point of death; but Craig has won his way to love, truth, and light, whereas the condemned man has sunk too deeply into passion and darkness to attain more than a liberating glimpse of what Craig sees. As man and poet, Robinson had ideas about what he wanted to see and what he ought to see; but actuality—what he did see—was something else again. In the letter of 15 March 1897, in which he speaks of the glimpse of light through the clouds, he adds:

> It is that glimpse that makes me wish to live and see it out. If it were not for that glimpse, I should be tempted, as Tennyson used to be, to stick my nose into a rag soaked with chloroform and be done with it—that is, if I could screw up the courage. But now, thank God, that is not the kind of courage I am praying for; what I am after is the courage to see. (279)

Remembering too that the exalted vision of *Captain Craig* followed upon the "six months of hell" in Cambridge, one is brought after due reflection to the opinion that the poem is not one whit more wholly Robinson's voice and vision than "The Night Before." Indeed, it seems less.

It must be concluded that although Robinson was aware that the voice and vision of some of his early poems were only more or less his own, he had an imperfect and inconsistent notion of what in them was "opposite." The situation is fascinating because his best and most personal poetry is often that poetry which he regarded as alien and inferior. At the same time, one of his best poems, "Luke Havergal," is not to be understood without invoking the system of opposites in a significant way.

II

Among the early poems, probably the least successful are those such as the "Octaves" in which Robinson the moralist and seer speaks directly and publicly to his audience without a trace of irony. If anything makes *Captain Craig* a better poem, it is the nominal disguise of person and the occasional irony with which Craig regards himself and is regarded by the narrator's friends. But these things apart, the voice of Craig has the same high moral tone as that of Robinson in his own person in the "Octaves." The voice is pitched slightly less moralistically in such poems as "The Torrent" and "Supremacy," in which Robinson mainly presents an image which contains the moral point. At a still lower pitch are some of the portraits: "Reuben Bright," "Cliff Klingenhagen," and "Richard Cory." How different the voice is can be seen by comparing the ending of "Richard Cory" ("And Richard Cory, one calm summer night,| Went home and put a bullet through his head") with the typical ending of one of the "Octaves" ("That record of All-Soul whereon God writes| In everlasting runes the truth of Him"). But the difference should not obscure the fact that the moral intention in both sorts of poems is the same. Characteristically in the poems of an explicitly high moral tone, the last line or lines provide the final uplift and vision: it is here that we get "untriangulated stars," "the coming glory of the Light!" and "dead men singing in the sun." In the portraits the last lines are no less indispensable, but they leave to the reader a task of interpretation. Uplift and vision follow only upon the reader's success. The obvious irony of "Richard Cory," that the envied and happy man is unenviable and unhappy, is intended to bring the reader to an awareness of the light that both Richard Cory and the people on the pavement fail to see. The greater irony of the poem, then, is its irony of voice: the moralist and seer forswears his characteristic tones and assumes the manner of one of the unenlightened.

In what are probably the two best early poems, "The House on the Hill" and "Luke Havergal," Robinson completes the descent from a high moral tone. The special interest of "The House on the Hill" is that two versions of it show him eliminating the moralistic voice. The poem as it originally appeared in a letter to Smith of 25 February 1894 is as follows.

> They are all gone away,
> The house is shut and still:
> There is nothing more to say.
>
> Malign them as we may,
> We cannot do them ill:
> They are all gone away.

> Are we more fit than they
> To meet the Master's will?—
> There is nothing more to say.
>
> What matters it who stray
> Around the sunken sill?—
> They are all gone away,
>
> And our poor fancy-play
> For them is wasted skill:
> There is nothing more to say.
>
> There is ruin and decay
> In the House on the Hill:
>
> They are all gone away,
> There is nothing more to say... (132).

In the letter, Robinson describes the poem as "a little mystical perhaps" and also as "poetry of the commonplace" (132). Although he does not suggest so, the terms are presumably contradictory, the mystical element pointing to a meeting with the Master in the next world and the commonplace keeping the focus upon the present plain world. The failure of the poem in this first version is that the contradiction does not become a poetic irony comparable to that which sustains "Richard Cory." Instead of commonplace language and imagery whose reverberations are mystical, there is merely a clash of tones. The formal, moralistic diction of the third stanza jars against the plain language of the first stanza, and the return to plain language in the final stanza jars again. Unlike other early poems with a moralistic voice, though, this one does not provide the rising note at the end, and even the voice in the third stanza is softened by the interrogative form.

Robinson's revision of the poem for the volume *The Children of the Night* eliminates the moralistic strain altogether, so that the mystical meaning is entirely to be inferred. Nor does he replace the moralistic strain with the slightly ironical tone of the speaker in "Richard Cory." He gives nothing away: his voice is somber and detached; he relies upon the general simplicity and repetitiveness of his diction to yield the overtone of meaning. In the revision, the second, third, and fourth stanzas read thus:

> Through broken walls and gray
> The winds blow bleak and shrill:
> They are all gone away.

> Nor is there one to-day
> To speak them good or ill:
> There is nothing more to say.
>
> Why is it then we stray
> Around that sunken sill?
> They are all gone away.

One might describe the revised poem as an attempt to set voice and vision at a far remove from each other, not through verbal irony (in which distance dissolves as soon as the irony is grasped), but through a neutralization of the resonant voice that is ordinarily to be associated with a moralistic vision.

The question is whether readers of the poem in its new form understand it in the way that Robinson presumably intends it to be understood. The reverberations seem to this reader to be less lightening than darkening, less mystical than materialistic. Robinson seems to have put an almost impossible burden of interpretation and illumination upon his audience, to have defeated his announced intention of always leaving his audience with "at least a suggestion of ... something better than despair." One is inclined to say that of all the poems thus far examined, "The House on the Hill" comes closest to being a poem of opposites (though not exactly in the sense that Robinson himself meant); it presents a powerful case for despair by a man who professed to have hope. The ramifications of the situation can best be explored by looking at "Luke Havergal," upon which there exists more comment by both Robinson and the critics.

Not least among the critics of that poem is Theodore Roosevelt, who in his review of *The Children of the Night* confessed that although he liked it he could not understand it. Robert David Stevick came to the same conclusion in writing a dissertation on Robinson in 1956. Reviewing several interpretations of the poem, he took their irreconcilability to be "good evidence for its lack of intelligibility"; but he also asserted that the poem "is a rare example in Robinson's verse in which unintelligibility is not damaging." The paradox is perhaps less difficult than Stevick sees it to be, since not all the interpretations are equally legitimate; but the fact remains that most critics have liked the poem in spite of being puzzled by it. The chief problems of the poem are the following: (1) is the speaker ("Out of a grave I come to tell you this") to be identified with Luke's presumably dead lover ("Yes, there is yet one way to where she is")? (2) does the speaker recommend death? life? life after death? and is his counsel to be regarded by the reader as wise? and (3) what specific interpretations are to be put upon "western gate," "eastern skies," "night," "dawn," and other symbols? Perhaps the main stumbling block for the critics has been the fact that the imagery of the poem is Robinson's familiar imagery of light and darkness, and the temptation has been to read the poem as one more expression of his quasi-religious outlook. Thus one critic identifies the western gate with Christianity, the eastern skies with Eastern religions, and explains the poem as an exhortation to Luke to choose the former. Other critics connect the western gate merely with faith or the future. But most of them are also uneasily aware of a contrasting implication. Yvor Winters states the dilemma succinctly in his book on Robinson: "It might be said, I presume, that the poem seems to display a faith in life after death; but if one considers the intense desolation of the tone, it becomes rather an expression of longing for death, of inability to endure more."[6] The way out of the impasse has been pointed to by a few critics, but they do little more than note the comments by Robinson that imply an unusual intention.

The first of the comments appears in a letter to Smith of 14 December 1895: "I also have a piece of deliberate degeneration called 'Luke Havergal,' which is not at all funny" (238). The second is in a letter of 18 May 1900, to Daniel Gregory Mason, in which he refers to the poem as "my uncomfortable abstraction" (30). Both references suggest the unpleasant and alien qualities that are associated with his poetry of opposites in his letter of 3 June 1894; and the first makes an illuminating allusion to Max Nordau. There is no doubt that in some respects Robinson was sympathetic to Nordau's onslaught upon modern art in *Degeneration*. In one of his letters to Smith he remarks that the *Yellow Book* was "an elegantly got up fake" (168); in another to Smith he gives reserved approval to Nordau's attack upon Zola (229); and in *Captain Craig* he has Craig condemn Swinburnian poetry. Nordau's general theory of art requires that it be expressive but not unhealthily so, and expressive rather than objective. Robinson's remarks about the "morally debilitated" art of Gautier (in a letter to Smith of 20 May 1894, [156]) and his relegation of his poetry of opposites to an inferior status indicate broad agreement. In the very same years, though, Robinson wrote in praise of Zola, and in the late nineties he was being swept off his feet by Wagner, who for Nordau was a prime example of degeneration. What perhaps was most likely to put Robinson off was that Nordau's general description of the degenerate man must have struck home at several points. Despondency, an inclination toward reverie, intellectual doubt, and an inability to share in normal human labor are some of the terms of Nordau's indictment, and Robinson could hardly have avoided recognizing their applicability to his own case. But he must have had too much egotism, Puritanism, and good sense in him merely to have pleaded guilty. At any rate, as early as 1894 he wrote "A Poem for Max Nordau," which mocks Nordau's attack on Swinburne by being Swinburnian. The poem is negligible, no more than an exercise. But its very existence, along with Killigrew's fin de siècle poem in *Captain Craig*, shows Robinson to have written poetry in a mode that he himself opposed and labeled "mere mellifluous rhyme" in the "Octaves."[7] Here is a poetry of opposites. And "Luke Havergal," by being a piece of deliberate degeneration, presumably belongs in the same category. The poems differ, though; for "Luke Havergal" is Robinson at his best, and its presentation of a degenerate attitude is in truth an expression of profound personal feeling.

To regard the poem as a piece of deliberate degeneration, one must assume that the speaker voices despair in his meaning as well as in his accent. He is addressing Havergal, whose beloved has died, and he is counseling suicide. He is a projection, an objectification, of the voice of despair in Havergal himself. In the first stanza he tells Havergal to pursue death: go to the western gate where the sun dies, where the autumn leaves die, where the wind moans. In the second he denies the possibility of any human recovery from despair: no dawn can lift the fiery night of Havergal's anguish; only the darkness of death can end his darkness. The speaker then presents an image of the whole universe dying ("God slays Himself with every leaf that flies"). In the third stanza he acknowledges that his is the voice of death ("out of a grave I come"), and admits that the enemy to his own counsel is love. He must quench the kiss—the memory of love and the desire for life—that still prevents Havergal from committing suicide and following his beloved into death. The final stanza largely repeats the first, with the speaker emphasizing that Havergal should not try to find an explanation for death: he should abandon all feeling and die.

The difficulties with this interpretation are first of all problems in irony. In the first and fourth stanzas the speaker says, "if you trust her she will call"; in the third he says that the way to where she is is "one that faith can never miss." In order for the interpretation to stand, these lines must be understood ironically; but since the speaker of the poem is not being ironical, the reader may be misled. Only from the pervasive gloom of the poem is the reader enabled to see that what the speaker calls trust and faith must be distortions of conventional Christian notions. (In editions of the *Collected Poems* Robinson made a few revisions of the poem, among them a change from "trust her" in the first stanza to "listen." However, he retained "trust her" in the final stanza.) The other difficulty concerns Robinson's imagery. In a certain respect it merely repeats the imagery of other poems. Darkness is spiritual and literal death, and light is truth. But when the speaker of the poem says, "No, there is not a dawn in eastern skies," he means it entirely, whereas when the speaker of "Credo" says, "No, there is not a glimmer, nor a call," he means it only for the time being, and by the end of the poem he rises out of such despair to say that he feels "the coming glory of the Light!" Similarly the paradox that "the dark will end the dark" employs Robinson's customary symbolic meanings, but it diametrically opposes his belief that the light will end the dark. No other phrase of the poem more plainly sets the speaker at odds with Robinson the moralist and seer. One or two familiar images in the poem present more of a problem. When the speaker says that the remembered kiss "blinds you to the way that you must go," he must be understood ironically, as in the manner of his speaking about trust and faith. In poems such as "The Children of the Night" and "The World," "blind" refers to spiritual blindness; but what "blinds" Havergal is a memory of love and life that may save him from suicide. Only a counselor of despair could call such a memory blindness.

The problems of interpreting "Luke Havergal" as a piece of deliberate degeneration are incidental ones. At most they suggest minor flaws of composition. But what of the poem as a whole: is not there a general defect in a poem that so consistently confuses its readers? Perhaps not; for in a way the poem has never been confusing. No critic who has commented on the tone of the poem has ever described it as anything but despairing. But instead of listening to that tone, looking steadily at the poem, most critics have turned away to find an interpretation consonant with Robinson's general philosophical outlook. At least two of them have admitted to being defeated by the tone: the interpretations they have arrived at seem to them less important than the melancholy tone. But that melancholy tone itself renders Robinson's intended meaning in a most powerful way.

Looking back now at "The House on the Hill," one might suspect that the bleak tone of the final version of the poem does not defeat Robinson's mystical intention, rather that the mystical intention refers only to the first version, and that in revising the poem Robinson undertook the same sort of task as in "Luke Havergal": to express a viewpoint totally at odds with his professed outlook. Consider such an attempt in the light of the moralistic poems. Broadly speaking, the moralistic poems take two paths: either they begin strongly and continue strongly to the end, as with most of the "Octaves" ("We thrill too strangely at the master's touch" is complemented by "Is always and unfailingly at hand"), or they begin in despair and rise to triumph, as with "Credo" ("I cannot find my way" yields to "I feel the coming glory of the Light!"). "The House on the Hill" and "Luke Havergal" might be described as experiments in writing only the first half of "Credo."

But both poems are too impressive to be regarded merely as experiments. In a letter to Smith of 17 April 1892, Robinson quotes a portion of "Supremacy," a moralistic poem that rises in the manner of "Credo" from a first line that reads, "There is a drear and lonely tract of Hell." Robinson remarks upon the poem: "I don't know how long this Hell business will last, but I may sigh out two or three more. It is a damned cheerful subject and my muse is merry whenever she gets into it" (60). "Merry" must mean "inspired," since Robinson's poetry is never merry; and Robinson must be recognizing the fact that his best poetry speaks of hell rather than of heaven.

III

Although Robinson's critics have not been hesitant about making final pronouncements upon him, there can be little doubt that the past thirty years have provided just the wrong sort of atmosphere for an adequate appraisal. "Verse that is to easie" was R. P. Blackmur's judgment upon *Talifer*, but what has been easier than the critical stance itself?[8] Everyone knows that morality and philosophy are not poetry, and even Robinson's most sympathetic critics invariably make apologies. But the present high critical tone was not always taken, and may not be in the future. One suspects that a preoccupation with symbolic meanings is not so far removed from an interest in explicit meanings as is often assumed. Suppose, though, that Robinson's poetry is indeed defective to the extent that it is philosophical and moral. Will the judgment have to be modified if the voice of the poetry is an opposing voice?

The Man against the Sky offers such a problem. As Robinson wrote to one of his friends, the purpose of the poem was "to cheer people up" (92), and the poem is a straightforward enough review of various philosophical attitudes available to man, with Robinson pointing out the sole satisfactory one. Ask, though, where the elevated moralistic voice is, and the answer is that it evidences itself in the seven lines (out of three hundred and fourteen) that describe the way to salvation: "But this we know...." Nothing more remains of the confident moralist of "The Children of the Night": the rest belongs, in a muted way, to the mood of "Luke Havergal," from the sunset image with which the poem opens to the final darkness of the last lines. Judge the poem to fail in fulfilling the poet's intention, to contradict its meaning in its voice, to be unpoetic insofar as it is philosophical and moralistic. Then imagine a critic who nevertheless regards the poem as the equal of any other American poem of comparable length: he listens to the discoursing melancholy voice, and is satisfied to hear it; he says that similarly he is unconcerned with the hope that T.S. Eliot constructs in *Ash Wednesday* but is moved by the accents of despair ("Because I do not hope"—"And let my cry come unto Thee").

It is tempting to say that the dilemma of Robinson's career was the struggle between true voice and false belief. The latter induced him to assume the false voice of the prophet; it also led him to see his poetic function in grandiose terms that made the long narrative poems inevitable. The true voice had at first to express itself in the ironical modulations of *Captain Craig* and "Richard Cory," in the opening of such poems as "Credo" and "Supremacy," and in the supposedly false belief of the poetry of opposites. It came ultimately to dominate his poetry, and to provide its richest occasions, not only "Luke Havergal" and *The Man against the Sky* but other lyric poems such as "For a Dead Lady" and passages such as the opening of *Cavender's House* and the close of *Tristram*.

Inevitably one is led to ask whether the dilemma explains Robinson's failure to be a great poet (for his failure preoccupies his critics). Had he understood himself and his poetry more clearly, he would not have cried, "Oh for a poet—for a beacon bright | To rift this changeless glimmer of dead gray,"[9] and he would not have made the mistake that most critics regard the long narratives as being: poems whose large intentions are flawed by a deficiency of energy. But what instead would he have done? He might, for one thing, have seen the uselessness of poetry itself, and been still less of a poet. At best he would have avoided the seven offending lines in *The Man against the Sky* and would have written several more lovely lyrics of despair in the manner of "Luke Havergal." His position in

American letters would not be significantly improved—and there would be readers to regret that he did not write the long poems that for all their defects have unforgettable passages.

R. P. Adams, in an article on Robinson in 1961, provides the alternative way out of the dilemma: Robinson should have abandoned despair rather than philosophy. As Adams describes his situation, Robinson was susceptible to the chill that late nineteenth-century science laid upon most thinking people, describing for them a universe that was mindless, aimless, dead. Robinson had enough wisdom to recognize the inadequacy of the scientific vision, but he lacked a strong alternative conviction. The consequence was that the access of creative energy that comes to the man of strong positive belief never came to Robinson; he was unable—in contrast, say, to Yeats—to rise out of malaise.[10] Adams's view has much to recommend it, but it does not take into account what for this critic is the central fact of Robinson's poetry: that it is always at its best when it is despairing. To make Robinson a greater poet by eliminating the characteristic quality of whatever greatness he does possess is to transform him into an altogether different poet.

We are left, perhaps, with a poet for whom a significantly different fate was not possible. In any event, his dilemma was not a simple one. In a letter to Smith of 7 December 1896 he writes, "I am an idealist. Perhaps idealism is the philosophy of desperation, but I do not think so" (264). He recognizes here the inescapably twofold vision of the idealist; he denies only that the vision of the actual world need be one of despair. Such a twofold vision implies, for a poet, a double voice. Rephrase Robinson's dilemma as a conflict between two true voices, or between two true visions, and there is no way out of it. The justification for regarding the dilemma as one between true voice and false belief is only that Robinson seems at once to have failed to see how somber and compelling the one voice and vision were, and to have overestimated the other voice and vision both poetically and philosophically. A poet, of course, is not required to see himself and his poetry clearly. Why should Robinson realize that his poetry of opposites was closest to his heart? Any stratagem is permissible to protect poetic self-confidence from despair or self-consciousness.

13 Religion, Science, and Philip Henry Gosse

THE CRISIS OF FAITH of Victorian England was one of the great crises of that age, and it is recorded nowhere more poignantly than in Edmund Gosse's *Father and Son*, written just after the age had closed. Therein is told the tale of a pious household of Plymouth Brethren at mid-century, and the falling away toward disbelief of the carefully nurtured son. Remarkably enough, the passage from Philip Henry's zealous faith to Edmund's loosely held piety was not lighted by either the higher criticism or the discoveries of Lyell, Darwin, and others. By the time young Edmund got around to mentioning the higher criticism to his father, the quarrel between them had all but finished its course. Rather, it appears that Edmund had a fatal lack of religious susceptibility from birth, and in his heart he could not have been saved had he lived two hundred years earlier. He described the difference in the way his father prayed and the way he as a child prayed.

> My father prayed in private in what I may almost call a spirit of violence. He entreated for spiritual guidance with nothing less than importunity. It might be said that he stormed the citadels of God's grace, refusing to be baffled....
> ....
>
> The poverty of my prayers had ... long been a source of distress to me, but I could not discover how to enrich them.... Then it was that my deadness made itself felt, in the mechanical address I put up, the emptiness of my language, the absence of all real unction. I never could contrive to ask God for spiritual gifts in the same voice and spirit in which I could ask a human being for objects....[1]

If it seems that too much of seriousness ought not to be expected of a child, compare Edmund's practice with the riches of his mother's childish piety, described by her in some private notes.

> I cannot recollect the time when I did not love religion.... If I must date my conversion from my first wish and trial to be holy, I may go back to infancy.... (6)

Emily Gosse herself grew up in a household that was indifferent to religion, and her piety came as naturally to her as Edmund's slackness of faith came to him.

It was otherwise with Philip Henry. His family background was pious nonconformity; his inclinations were the same; and he met the troubles of his maturity with profound faith. His special interest to a later age is that he opposed the claims of the new science and the old religion, and that he was trapped by the claims of both. He had no use for the scientifically conceived world in which there was no place for God or a purely perfunctory place, and yet he was a skilled scientist and followed and acquiesced to the sort of reasoning of the geologists. He had no use for institutionalized religion, and spoke to God informally and alone, and yet he subscribed to beliefs that were at one with those of the institution.

To see him with some justice it may be desirable first to discount the portrait that Edmund paints in *Father and Son*. That portrait followed by seventeen years his conventional *Life of Philip Henry Gosse, FRS*, and in the *Life* a somewhat different person appears, a man not so morose and seclusive, often gay, inclined to enjoy the company of small groups of scientists and amateur naturalists, leading a contented home life, and providing for his family rather more successfully than seems to be the case in *Father and Son*. The hazard of reading *Father and Son* alone is that the reader sees more strictly than in the other book from the son's perspective, and though Edmund makes disclaimers and qualifications, his perspective is made to look like the truth. But imagine the son as a weak, pathetic, and melancholy child who responded indifferently to much love and gaiety that surrounded him, and who nursed the grievances of childhood into adulthood, and it may be believed that in *Father and Son* he found occasion to cast his father into his own gloom. Such reservations about *Father and Son* were first expressed in an anonymous review of the book in the *Times Literary Supplement* in 1907. The reviewer seems to have been a family friend.[2]

I

Philip Henry Gosse was born in Worcester in 1810. His father Thomas, born in 1765, was one of a dozen children of a well-to-do cloth manufacturer who fell upon hard times. Young Thomas wanted to be an artist, and his father encouraged him. He trained at the Royal Academy, but he seems to have had more craft than art, and in the course of his career he descended to being an itinerant painter of miniatures. He was also a prolific and unpublished author of tales, epics, and dialogues, the later ones in the manner of Scott and Byron. He was a solitary and grave man, and underwent some sort of religious conversion to Wesleyan Methodism when he was twenty-five. He was walking in Fleet Street and suddenly saw "Christ as risen and received into heaven as my accepted Righteousness."[3] After his marriage, and during Philip Henry's youth, he was traveling on business as much as ten months of the year. He carried with him on his travels a Bible and a Theocritus. Of his wife Hannah much less is known. She was a yeoman's daughter, strong-willed and superstitious. She was about nineteen years younger than Thomas, and their marriage in 1807 was more to his liking than hers.

Philip Henry's youth was mainly spent in and around Poole, which in the second decade of the century had a population of six thousand. He seems to have lived the ordinary sensuous life of a country boy, with religion occupying his Sundays. He had one close companion, and the two of them were amateur zoologists and botanists in the way that many youths are. He was a great reader of Bunyan, Defoe, Byron, and other authors both edifying and frivolous. His habits were moral and serious.

The impression one gains from the *Life* and from other evidence is that his professional and religious destinies were not entirely manifest from his youth. The influences of father and mother and the experiences of Poole provided an entrance, but only an entrance, to what he became. At the age of fifteen, after some irregular schooling, he entered a counting house in Poole, and after a couple of years there he acquiesced to going out to the firm's office in Newfoundland to perform the same task. He was in Newfoundland for eight years, and then became a frontier farmer in southern Canada. He gave up farming after three years, though not before trying to persuade his family to come out and join him. He then traveled into the United States, and in the year 1838 he was teaching in Alabama. He returned to England and contemplated becoming an itinerant minister for the Wesleyan Methodists. He conducted a school in London from 1840 to 1843.

The one thing that is clear is that from youth onward he was an amateur naturalist, in the line of Gilbert White of Selborne, a quotation from whom provides the epigraph for his first published book, *The Canadian Naturalist* (1840). He was a lover of the things of the earth, and an ardent, acute, and patient observer of them. This love became profession by accident, and its transformation is visible in his scientific articles and treatises, but it remained love too, and is observable in other books that had their beginning as early as the journal-record he kept on his first trip to Newfoundland.

It would not do to make unusual claims for the artistic expression of his delighted interest in nature, but there was a certain development. Here is a passage from a letter home in the year 1833, when he was twenty-three years old.

> Before six this morning, I was on the shore of Little Beaver Pond, where I stood for a few moments in mere admiration of the day and quiet beauty of the scene. The black calm pond was sleeping below me, reflecting from its unruffled surface every tree and bush of the towering hill above, as in a perfect mirror. Stretching away to the east were other ponds, embosomed in the mountains, while further on in the same direction, between two distant peaks, the ocean with the golden sun above it, flashed forth in dazzling splendor. The low, unvarying, somewhat mournful note of the

snipes on the opposite hill, and, as one would occasionally fly across the water, the short quick flapping of his wings, seemed rather to increase than to diminish the general feeling of repose. The air seemed (perhaps from its extreme calmness) to have an extraordinary power of conveying sounds, for I could with perfect ease keep up a conversation with Sprague on the other side (not less than one-eighth of a mile off), without raising the voice above the pitch used in ordinary discourse.[4]

This relative ease in letter writing abandoned Philip Henry in *The Canadian Naturalist*. The book takes the reader through a Canadian year, month by month, and does so in the form of a dialogue between father and son. Here is the beginning of April.

> Father. Will you accompany me, Charles, on a walk? The late heavy rains have removed nearly all the snow, and the present fine weather is exhilarating to the spirits.
> Charles. Yes, it is indeed a beautiful morning, and the advances which all nature is making to a renewal of life and animation make it still more cheerful.
> Father. Let us lift our hearts to our beneficent Father in gratitude....
> Charles. What trumpet-like note is that?
> Father. It is the honk of the Wild Goose. Yonder is the bird, standing on the frozen river.[5]

Thirteen years later in *A Naturalist's Rambles on the Devonshire Coast* (1853), he found a less awkward public style. Here is the opening.

> "You are seriously ill, Henry," said my wife; "you have been in the study a great deal too much lately; you must throw it all up, and take a trip into the country."
> "Oh no," said I, "not bad enough for that, I hope; a few days' inaction, with God's blessing, will set me right. I do not want to leave London."
> But I got worse: sitting by the parlour fire, doing nothing, was dreary work; and it was not mended by traversing the gravel walks of the garden in my great coat.[6]

And then another twelve years later, after the death of his first wife and his remarriage, he published *A Year at the Shore*, which has the same month-by-month form as *The Canadian Naturalist*. Here is the beginning of April again.

> Shall we explore the sands today? A bright sandy beach well exposed to the sea is no bad hunting ground for the naturalist, bare as it looks, and proverbial as is its character for sterility.... So we make our way along the dusty highroad that leads from Torquay southward, skirting the shore, now and then getting peeps of the rocks and the retiring tide, over the massive sea-walls.... Wild hyacinths are peeping among the rank foliage of the arums and nettles; and harts-tongue ferns and primroses are everywhere, clustering in great masses, or studding the green banks in single stars; the bright rose-campion smiles, and the ever lovely germander speedwell, brightest, sweetest of spring flowers, gladdens us here and there, like "angels' eyes," as our rustics poetically call these pretty azure flowers.... We pause to wipe our foreheads....[7]

It was rather by chance that a cousin took an interest in the amateur's manuscript of *The Canadian Naturalist* and found a publisher for it, and then that two years later the Society for the Promotion of Christian Knowledge wanted to publish a semi-technical book on zoology, and the same cousin and the publisher happened to be on the advisory board, and the publisher said why not Philip Henry? So Philip Henry undertook the more technical work, and this led to still more technical work.

The progress of his religious life is obscure. Up to the age of twenty-two he appears to have been rather more interested in reading and writing poetry than in serving God, and the poetry was sensuous, romantic. Nevertheless, he was a moral young man, and he obeyed his mother's injunction to read his Bible daily when he went out to Newfoundland. His one close friend in Newfoundland was an irreverent and lighthearted young man, if not an entirely sceptical one. In 1832, Philip Henry learned that his sister Elizabeth was gravely ill, and he sailed home on leave. "My prominent thought in this crisis was legal," he says in some recollections published in the *Life*, "I wanted the Almighty to be my friend.... I knew he required me to be holy. He had said, 'My son, give Me thy heart.' I closed with Him, not hypocritically, but sincerely; intending henceforth to live a new, a holy life; to please and serve God" (74, 75). A few days later he said "damn," as had become his wont. He felt conscious of sin, and never said it again. When he went back to the new world he became friendly with a husband and wife who were serious Wesleyan Methodists, and he began to withdraw from friendships with people whose beliefs were radically different. However, he seems to have experienced some falling off of faith, for in 1838 when he was in Alabama he underwent a depression of spirits and following it a renewed religious feeling. He decided then that he must speak to people on the condition of their souls. On his return to England some months later he preached informally to the crew, despite considerable unease at doing so.

Little if any of this experience distinguishes Philip Henry from many another Protestant hardening into religious scruple, self-righteousness, and a ministerial calling. It does not prepare us, and did not prepare him (except in retrospect), for a signal occasion in 1842. It came when he was a teacher.

> One day... Mr. Habershon [father of one of Philip Henry's students and a writer on religious subjects] sent for my acceptance his *Dissertation on the Prophetic Scriptures....* It was in June... when the days were at the longest. I began to read it after my pupils were dismissed in the afternoon, and sat in the garden eagerly devouring the pages, and actually finishing the work (of four hundred octavo pages) before darkness set in. When I closed the book, I knew not where I was; I had become so wholly absorbed in the great subjects, that some minutes elapsed before I could recall my surroundings.... Of the Restoration of the Jews, I had received some dim inkling already...; but of the destruction of the Papacy, the end of Gentilism, the kingdom of God, the resurrection and rapture of the Church at the personal descent

of the Lord, and the imminency of this,—all came on me that evening like a flash of lightning. My heart drank it in with joy; I found no shrinking from the nearness of Jesus. It was indeed a revelation to a spirit prepared to accept it. I immediately began a practice, which I have pursued uninterruptedly for forty-six years, of constantly praying that I may be one of the favoured saints who shall never taste of death, but be alive and remain until the coming of the Lord. (375-76)

Perhaps there was some echo in the experience of his father's conversion, but it eventually led to a break with his father's creed, and more especially it had a character of exaltation and joy unrecorded in Philip Henry's previous years. This exaltation and joy remained with him, and even provided moments of despair, for he repeatedly calculated the day on which Christ would return to earth and the event repeatedly failed to occur. How personal his faith became is suggested by the fact that he presently took up with the Plymouth Brethren, a sect notable for its lack of ritual and formal leadership. Even within this group he seems largely to have gone his own way, having little to do with other groups.

II

Philip Henry Gosse believed deeply, thoroughly, and privately, and on two occasions, both ending in the year 1857, his belief drove him into trouble. The first came when his first wife, Emily, developed cancer of the breast. Their doctor examined her and recommended immediate excision. But the Gosses heard of an American who professed to cure without operation. He possessed a secret medication that killed the diseased tissue, which was then sloughed off. Supposedly there was 80 percent chance of cure by this method, 20 percent chance of recurrence with an operation necessary. The Gosses prayed to God to tell them what to do, and God told them to rely upon the American. During the next several months three ointments were applied to Emily Gosse's breast on successive days. One of the ointments was painful. There were no results. The American then decided to extract, and he accomplished the extraction over a period of three weeks by the following process. On the first day the diseased tissue was wetted with nitric acid, on the next day a slight incision was made, on the third day nitric acid was applied again, on the fourth the incision was deepened, and so on. There was no anesthesia, and the effect was painful in the extreme. For several hours after each treatment Emily Gosse could neither sit nor stand, but dragged herself around her room in agony. Two days after the operation was completed, there appeared to be new infection, and she underwent the same treatment for another three weeks. At the end of that time the American told her that the disease was in her blood, and he proposed to continue the procedure. The Gosses gave him up, but they both knew she was mortally ill. They found another doctor, and for the next several weeks until Emily's death she received drugs to ease her pain.

The account of the illness, in rather grimmer detail than is given here, was written by Philip Henry himself, and published later in the year of her death. In this little book, entitled *A Memorial of the Last Days on Earth of Emily Gosse*, he also records the happiness of married life that the illness blighted. "Many times she had said, 'How happy we are. Surely this cannot last.'" He records some of her words during her illness. "I love you—better than on my wedding day, better than when I was taken ill" and "My beloved Henry, gladly would I remain, if such were the Lord's will, and be your companion for the rest of your pilgrimage."[8] He also describes the spirit in which they chose the American, and how they felt afterward.

> We asked in confidence that we should not be denied; that peace *would* keep our hearts and minds, and that wisdom *would* be given us. And let it not be thought inconsistent with this latter promise, that the result of our acting was different from what we desired and expected; not even if it could be shown that the treatment resorted to did really (as I believe was the case) aggravate my beloved's sufferings, and hasten her death.... But God...had promised to give wisdom, and I must believe that He did give it; that the treatment we selected was the one which, *in this particular case*, He saw really best for us. He had his own end in view, and that was the removal of his beloved child to his own presence.... He has nowhere promised to grant his children all that their foolish hearts would like, but what He judges best for their real welfare. (10-12)

The other crisis for Philip Henry came with the publication of his book *Omphalos* a few months after *Memorial*. Philip Henry believed that the world was created six thousand years ago, as indicated by Biblical chronology, and he also believed it was created in six days—or six ages. But he was well aware of the growing body of geological evidence that the world was millions of years old, and he was also aware of the clash between religion and science that this evidence implied. He wrote his book as a scientist who was religious, in "an attempt to untie the geological knot" and reconcile science with the word of God.[9]

The book begins with a quotation from *Ivanhoe*: "'You have not allowed for the wind, Hubert,' said Locksley, 'or that had been a better shot'" (iii). The geologists have missed the mark because they have not allowed for the law of prochronism. The first hundred pages of the book, though, are devoted to the case for the geologists, and they are a notable effort to give the scientific argument its due. Then follows the counterargument, which Philip Henry recognizes to be based upon two assumptions, (1) the creation of matter out of nothing, and (2) the eternal fixity of species. It is also based upon the observation that the course of organic nature is a circle: the egg produces the chicken which produces the egg, the seed produces the flower which produces the seed. The argument is that at whatever point God creates, at whatever point he breaks into the circle of organic nature, the created object will bear an implied past form. If God creates an adult chicken, there is implied an earlier growth, even though there has been no growth. If he creates merely the egg, there is implied the chicken that laid the egg, even though no chicken laid it. If he creates the mature Adam, Adam will have his navel, his omphalos, even though he was not born of woman. Philip Henry takes notes of Sir Thomas Browne's opinion that Adam did not have a navel, and dismisses it. This is the law of prochronism: the apparent but unreal temporal past visible in any created organic form the moment it is created. Suppose a botanist comes along and inspects a bamboo tree the moment after God has created it. Will not the botanist find evidence, fallacious evidence, that the tree has been in existence for some while? Now, says Philip Henry, if the law of prochronism operates in the organic world, may it not in the inorganic? May not all the fossil records be like Adam's navel? He concludes with the Bible: "In six days Jehovah made heaven and earth, the sea, and all that in them is" (372).

The book was a laughingstock, and not only among scientists. Charles Kingsley, a close friend, wrote to say that he could not "give up the painful and slow conclusion of five and twenty years' study of geology, and believe that God has written on the rocks one enormous and superfluous lie." The reviewer in the *Athenaeum* suggested that Philip Henry extend his theory of prochronism to include the Egyptian pyramids. Even in a religious journal such as the *London Quarterly* it was felt that he had some more thinking to do. "During that grim season," says Edmund, "my Father was no lively companion."[10] But there was no recanting, just as there had been no regret over choosing the American doctor for Emily.

III

The description of Philip Henry Gosse that has stuck for many years is that of T. H. Huxley: "the honest hodman of science"—the man with no imagination, no ability to see the woods as well as the trees, the man who could observe sea anemones and rotifera minutely and accurately and provide the sort of detail with which the great scientist like Darwin could make his inductive leaps. But Huxley himself was a hodman of science who could say that he sat down before fact as a little child and who regarded scientific investigation as "the source of all human blessings and from which has sprung all human prosperity and progress." For him every question assumed a scientific standpoint. He looked at the novelists and artists about him, and observed their struggle for existence, and proclaimed that they were the highest type of man and that one could see within the nineteenth century itself the struggle that was constantly raising their quality and the quality of life generally. He could look back to savage life and reflect upon the refinement of the species in the ensuing millennia; he could look back to parliament in the seventeenth century and reflect upon its improvement since then. On the subject of free will he faced ambiguities, but in the main he was content to believe that it is an illusion, for everything happens under scientific laws of cause and effect, and whatever we do is determined thereby. He went so far as to say that a sufficiently wise intelligence of the year one million b.c. could have predicted the exact state of British flora and fauna of the year 1865 (and by implication the exact state of British society), for it would only be a matter of knowing and tracing the causes.[11]

For Philip Henry Gosse, every question assumed a divine standpoint. He lived in a moral, ordered world whose morality and order were God-made, and he saw that everything men think and do has relation to this fact, and that men are distinguished in this way from other animals. Insofar as anything conflicted with this fact—as the viewpoint of science began to—it must somehow be wrong. Philip Henry's mistake was to conduct his religious argument scientifically, to let his vision of God and the world be framed and thence trapped by logic and fact, but this was the understandable mistake of a man who was both religious and scientific. It will not serve him today to defend his vision scientifically, but it is worth observing that in the centennial year of the *Origin of Species* it was apparent to scientists that the missing link had never been found, that the theory of natural selection did not adequately account for the moral, spiritual, and aesthetic brain of man.

Philip Henry Gosse was a man of deep spirituality and otherworldliness, and at the same time he was a man with a great and simple pleasure in the sensuous world. He was not to be fundamentally deceived by the new science, even though he made a fool of himself and made pain for his wife in defending his wisdom.

14 Wilfred Owen's Poetic Development

THE OUTLINE OF Wilfred Owen's poetic development is memorably clear. Under the impact of horrifying experience he transformed himself from a priggish young Keatsian into a greatly original poet. But the details of the development are unclear. What was the chronology of his experimenting with off-rhyme, and at what point did the mature poet begin to appear? Critics have been free with their answers to these questions, but any assessment of their answers reveals contradictions. In his book on the poet, D.S.R. Welland suggests that the undated "Greater Love" may have been composed as early as May 1916, and he offers in evidence (1) that the view it expresses of war as a holy sacrifice is one that Owen later abandoned, and (2) that one draft of the poem appears on the reverse side of the page of a poem dated 10 May 1916. If "Greater Love" is one of Owen's finest poems—an opinion that Welland seems to share with most critics—such a date contradicts the familiar view that Owen came to maturity only with the experience of trench warfare in January 1917, a view that Welland himself seems to subscribe to elsewhere. Another critic, John H. Johnston, has looked at the development of Owen's religious views with some care, and he assumes that "Greater Love" dates from the spring or summer of 1918 on account of its casual treatment of God. The authors of the two most recent books on Owen, Dominic Hibberd and Jon Stallworthy, date Owen's maturity from the meeting with Siegfried Sassoon in August 1917, and they see Owen treating off-rhyme experimentally or ornamentally until then or later. Yet both authors are aware that earlier dating for both "Greater Love" and "Exposure" remains an open question and that Owen's interest in off-rhyme goes back several years. Stallworthy is preparing an edition of the complete poem, and his study of the manuscripts will solve many problems. In the meantime it may be possible to describe some aspects of Owen's development with certainty and to discuss others that even such an edition may not settle.[1]

I

The basic facts of Owen's development of off-rhyme are these: he was powerfully interested in rhyming and chiming from the outset of his career; one or more poems of the years 1914-16 display impressive skill at off-rhyme, and much of his subsequent poetry gives elaborate attention to it; and his later poetry, to the very end, is notable for the flexibility with which he moves between ordinary rhyme and off-rhyme.

The first indication of interest apparently comes in January 1912, with markings of off-rhyme that Owen makes in his copy of John Addington Symonds' *Shelley*. The second comes with the poem "The Imbecile," whose terminus ad quem appears to be the early months of the Bordeaux period, perhaps late 1913. The poem itself is heavily laden with internal full rhyme and with internal half-rhyme of consonance and assonance. In the first stanza there is *light-light-white, long-along, hair-fair-hair, light-shineth-white, long-falleth-all-along-wrong, shineth-falleth-length-knoweth, long-long-light, nothing-knoweth*. On the back of one of the drafts of the poem, a draft that Stallworthy dates from the same period, appears a list of off-rhymes for a poem that Stallworthy assumes is to be entitled "Nocturne." Here are the first four sets:

land	Ardour
learned	Odour
leaned	~~Harder~~
lined	Eider
brays	toll
browze	toil
breeze	tool

A poem much more characteristic of Owen in its sombre sensuousness is "Maundy Thursday," which Hibberd dates convincingly from the Bordeaux period, September 1913 to September 1915. Again the end-rhyme is conventional, and across the fourteen lines there is heavy chiming internally: *cross-kissed* (this word repeated several times)-*came-creed-Christ-crucifix-cold-cling*. Lines 2 and 6 are especially noteworthy: "The silver cross was offered to be kissed" and "Then mourning women knelt: meek mouths they had." In "Long Ages Past," which dates from October 1914, we have what at a glance is a piece of blank verse; but close inspection suggests that it is an early attempt at subdued off-rhyme, slightly more disguised than the off-rhyme in "The Parable of the Old Man and the Young" of several years later. The rhymes that do occur seem to be more frequent than chance would make probable: *beryl-idol, sacrifice-palace, ears-toys, beauty-wantonly, flower-lovers, mirror-pleasure*, and others. If "Long Ages Past" was meant to be blank verse, it is the only example of the form among the completed poems in *Collected Poems*. There are only two clearly unrhymed pieces of poetry in the collection: the fragment of ten irregular lines beginning

"Not one corner" and the fragment "Antaeus," which Owen describes in a letter as "a strong bit of Blank" that he wrote "to order." Almost all Owen's poetry is heavily rhymed, whether the rhyme is full or partial, whether the rhymes are obvious as in "Greater Love" and "The Last Laugh" or unobtrusive as in "The Parable of the Old Man and the Young" and perhaps "Long Ages Past."[2]

The first unmistakable example of off-rhyme comes with "Has Your Soul Sipped?" of 1916. This is a poem that some commentators find puerile and offensive in its irony, and Stallworthy sees in it an unpleasant suppressed homosexuality; yet it represents a clear progress from similar material in "Maundy Thursday" and "Long Ages Past"—with their debt to Wilde and Swinburne—toward the fulfillment of "Greater Love." Redder than girls' lips and sweeter than nightingales are the blood and smile of dead young men. With such a progress in view, the skill of the poem in its off-rhyme may perhaps more easily be acknowledged. In the first stanza the second and fourth lines present the contrast and irony of perception that the poem concerns, and the off-rhyme condenses them: *sweets-sweats*. Then for several stanzas the off-rhymes complement one another softly. With the ninth stanza Owen comes to his main clause and to his explicit irony, and the off-rhymes make his point precisely: *smile-small, myth-mouth*. The smile is small, the mouth a myth. To someone who has seen a wan worn smile of a dying person, the accuracy of Owen's description is notable: the line of the mouth is the only remaining recognisable trace of the countenance, and appears a mythic remnant. The off-rhymes of the rest of the poem are used with similar care.

It would seem that with "Has Your Soul Sipped?" Owen has mastered the technique of off-rhyme. In "Happiness," written several months later, he weaves across his conventional rhyme a pattern of off-rhymes: *s* sounds throughout the first stanza, *o* and *u* sounds throughout the second. Within another few months he writes the fragment "Bugles Sang" largely in off-rhyme. In August-September 1917 he elaborates and translates "Bugles Sang" into the conventionally rhymed "Anthem for Doomed Youth."

In this development over several years there are two other poems of considerable interest. The first, the exercise poem "From My Diary, July 1914," has usually been dated 1914, from the experience in France to which it refers. Such a date accords well with the account above: it comes midway between the noting of Shelley's off-rhymes of 1912 and "Has Your Soul Sipped?" of 1916. Aside from its off-rhymes, notably *flashes-fleshes* (which Owen uses again later in "Arms and the Boy"—and the phrase "starr'd nocturnal flowers" there is nothing but cliché in the poem (*quivering...passion, sighing...boughs*) and the most conventional alliteration, assonance, and end-rhyme (*murmuring-myriads-shimmering, cheerily-chirping, singing-summer, day-hay*). Stallworthy, though, dates the poem August 1917. If he is right, can the poem be anything more than an exercise written "to order"?

A similar problem arises with "The Unreturning." This too has commonly been dated 1914, but in a private communication Stallworthy dates it 1917. Stallworthy argues that the title probably derives from Sassoon's poem "Prelude: The Troops" which Owen could have seen in manuscript at Craiglockhart, and that one draft of the poem is on stationery Owen is thought to have used only at Craiglockart.[3] Further support for Stallworthy's date may lie with the striking similarity between this poem and two poems of 1918. At first glance the rhyming is conventional, but close inspection gives us off-rhyme in almost equal quantity: *hurled-walled-appalled-world* in the first stanza, *woke-called* in the second, and *dawn-minds-drained -withdrawn* in the third. The *walled-world* rhyme recurs in "Strange Meeting," and the sequence *dawn-minds-drained* reappears (but not as end-rhyme) in the fourth section of "Insensibility." The phrase "sick men's sighs are drained" reappears in "Insensibility" as "many sighs are drained." (Hibberd has noted this last recurrence independently.) The general subject of the poem, the speaker watching for the dead, is that of "Strange Meeting."

Two reservations can be entered against the argument for the 1917 date. The first is that Sassoon's word *unreturning* is not an original image in the context of war, even when yoked to the word *youth*. The one word alone appears in "The Unreturning," but both of them are used by Owen in "Happiness" of February 1917, well before Owen met Sassoon. The Bodleian draft of the poem reads: "But the old Happiness is unreturning. | Boys' griefs are not so grievous as youth's yearning." The other reservation is that Owen was accustomed to repeating rhymes and phrases in his work, occasionally at considerable distance in time. The most notable instances (except for "The Unreturning" and "Insensibility," if the former poem dates from 1914) occur with the phrase "autumn rots," repeated in "1914" four years after it appears in "Written in a Wood, September 1910" (the phrase being the only thing worth salvaging from the earlier poem), and with a few of the off-rhymes in "Has Your Soul Sipped?" repeated from the list of two years and perhaps some months earlier. The *ardour-odour* rhyme Owen uses again in "The Roads Also" of 1918. Such recurrences are in part easy to explain: Owen often kept his earlier poetry with him; when he was at Craiglockhart he had his mother send him a bundle of his earlier writing.

If "The Unreturning" dates from 1917, it is an unremarkable piece of work. Owen has already displayed his skill at off-rhyme, and the rhetoric of the poem alternates uneasily between the high-flown and the subdued. Compare the first line, "Suddenly night crushed out the day and hurled" with "sick men's sighs are drained." If the poem dates from 1914, it is at once the earliest obvious piece of off-rhyming and an unusually mature poem for that year. How close it is in character to the poem "1914" is evident from the first line of the latter poem: "War broke: and now the Winter of the world." "1914" also uses the *world-hurled* rhyme of "The Unreturning."

II

If Owen masters off-rhyme by 1916-17 or before, his clear maturity as a poet comes only in 1917. Several of the important war poems can be firmly dated in the latter part of 1917, and the chief question is whether one of the war poems, "Exposure," can be dated earlier in the year and whether "Greater Love" can be dated 1916. The earlier dates would serve to emphasize Owen's independence from Sassoon and the intimate links between the early poetry and the late. Hibberd remarks upon Owen's reliance upon romantic imagery and diction throughout his career, and the progress from "Long Ages Past" through "Has Your Soul Sipped?" to "Greater Love" illustrates his continuing reliance upon the Swinburnian-Wildean mode. Stallworthy observes that in 1912 Owen writes a phrase that "astonishingly anticipates his poems from the Western Front": "the stunning guns are dumb"; and "1914" and "Has your Soul Sipped?", if not "The Unreturning," move Owen along toward his final subject. Owen himself locates his maturity in the year 1917, in the famous remark to his mother at the end of the year, "I go out of this year a Poet, my dear Mother, as which I did not enter it," and also in a comment in a letter in August, wherein he says that the last three lines of "Happiness" are the first of his writing that "carry the stamp of maturity."[4] The last three lines of the poem, written in February, are dense with sombre chiming of sounds: "The former happiness is unreturning: | Boys' griefs are not so grievous as our yearning. | Boys have no sadness sadder than our hope." One sees the preparation for such tones in "Maundy Thursday" and "Long Ages Past."

The problem of dating "Greater Love" is set forth in partial detail at the beginning of the present essay. The more complex problem of "Exposure" is perhaps more interesting, and it may be useful to lay out the problem in its several aspects. The second of two known drafts of the poem bears the date February 1916, and Edmund Blunden in his edition of the poems assumes that this was a slip of the pen for 1917, the sort of slip that often happens at the beginning of a year, especially if a man is in battle for the first time in January. The poem presumably deals with this experience, and is in character with letters Owen wrote to his mother at the time. The argument for later dating has been advanced by several critics, including Welland, Hibberd, and Stallworthy. In his book, Welland argues that the poem's maturity of off-rhyme and perspective fairly certainly indicates substantial revision later in the year after Owen met Sassoon; he reports Sassoon telling him that although he never saw the poem in Owen's lifetime he believed Owen revised it at Craiglockhart after reading Henri Barbusse's *Under Fire*. There is some inaccuracy in this account insofar as Owen did not read *Under Fire* until December 1917, and he had left Craiglockhart in early November, not to return except for a brief visit at Christmas. Like Welland, Hibberd is convinced that the composition of so finished a poem indicates revision over a long period of time, and he thinks the manuscripts indicate this. He notes that the final MS is written on the same paper as a poem that fairly certainly dates from September 1918; he also notes that Owen quotes the title in a letter to his mother of April 1918. Long gestation also appeals to Stallworthy, who additionally believes there are traces of *Under Fire* visible in the poem; he assumes that 1916 is a slip for 1918. The reviewer of Hibberd's book in the *Times Literary Supplement* in 1973 is emphatic in dating the poem 1918, and points out that at the top of the manuscript of the fragment "Cramped in that funnelled hole," which itself is unquestionably influenced by *Under Fire*, appears a corrected line from "Exposure." The reviewer thinks that Owen's 6 in 1916 may be an uncompleted 8. Lastly, Welland returns to the argument, and this time gives more weight to earlier dating. In a letter published in the *Times Literary Supplement* in 1974, he provides further details of Sassoon's comments on the poem: "In some holograph notes written for me in December 1950 he accepted the date of February 1917 for the genesis of the poem as 'a certainty'." Genesis does not preclude substantial revision later under the influence of Sassoon and Barbusse, but Welland quotes Sassoon minimizing his own influence: " 'Exposure,' being dated previous to W. knowing me, provides proof that he was working on his own creative line before that (my influence on him having been exaggerated)."[5]

None of this argument is convincing one way or the other. One of the incidental puzzles is why Owen failed to show the poem to Sassoon if he had already written it. Soon after he met Sassoon, Owen brought him a sheaf of poems to read. They seem mainly to have consisted of earlier writing, and did not include anything about the war except "1914." Sassoon was not impressed with anything he saw then or later, until Owen showed him a draft of a new poem, "Anthem for Doomed Youth." Thereupon, Sassoon realized "that my little friend was much more than the promising minor poet I had hitherto adjudged him to be."[6] Interestingly enough, Owen composed at least five poems between February and August 1917 that either broadly or explicitly concern the war: "Happiness," "To My Friend," "Le Christianisme," "Conscious," and "The Fates." There is no evidence that Sassoon saw any of these small poems, let alone "Exposure." In his letter to the *Supplement* Welland quotes Sassoon as saying that until "Anthem for Doomed Youth" Owen "withheld the MSS of his most powerful poems ('Exposure' for one) possibly because he feared they would pain me." Owen may or may not have produced one or both of the known drafts of "Exposure" before he arrived at Craiglockhart; he may or may not have written or revised the poem there under the influence of Sassoon; he may or may not instead or additionally have written or revised it in December or later after reading Barbusse.

The two known manuscripts of "Exposure" are held at the British Museum. They are (1) an undated working draft of the poem, with two of the four sheets given to the final stanza, and (2) a later draft, dated February 1916, which again is heavily reworked. Assuming that Blunden is right that 1916 is a slip for 1917, the poem would have been written from first to last in January-February 1917. Aside from the final stanza, the two drafts are much the same poem, and could have been written within a few days of each other. If there was a considerable gap of time between them Owen's struggle with the final stanza would be reason enough for not showing the poem to Sassoon. It may be the most reworked stanza in all Owen's writing.

There are several interesting features to the drafts. First of all, the skill evidenced in the off-rhyme is complete in the first draft: the rewriting does not concern it significantly. The off-rhyme in the first stanza remains unchanged. In the following transcriptions I have put [?] after words I may have read wrongly, and [??] in the place of unreadable words.

    Our brains ache in the merciless iced east winds that knive us.

    Wearied we keep awake because the night is silent.

    ~~Strange~~ [?] ~~A few wan droops star shells haunt the ghastly~~
    A ~~feeble~~ [?] ~~pale light~~
    [??] drooping stars   confuse our memory of the salient.
    Sad
    [??]
               whisper
    Worried by silence, sentries ~~listen~~, curious, nervous,

    But nothing happens.

   . . . .

    Our brains ache in the merciless iced east winds that knive us...

    Wearied we keep awake because the night is silent....

    Low, drooping flares confuse our memory of the salient....

    Worried by silence, sentries whisper, curious, nervous,

    But nothing happens.

Later stanzas sometimes show more revision, but only the last stanza (or what may at one point have been intended as an additional stanza) is extensively reworked, and it is notable even here that the off-rhymes that Owen finally settles for are mainly the ones he begins with. His effort was instead to transform the nature of the poem in the last stanza. The poem in its published form gives an opening statement of the situation, a progress into dawn and renewed activity, thoughts of home, reflections upon the war, and in the last stanza a restatement of the continuing situation. The repetition of "But nothing happens" indicates the sense of suspended time, limbo, helplessness; and it keeps the last stanza very much on a plane with the earlier stanzas, suggesting that nothing is happening rhetorically to give the poem drama and movement that would be false to the reality it is depicting. (The accepted erroneous reading of *His* for *this* seems to go against this intention.) In several of the drafts of the final stanza Owen's aim is to translate the real into the apocalyptic by a description of the crater-house of the soldiers being blasted open and the men entering the earth. The final phrase of the poem would have been "And our door opens," transforming the image and implication of "the doors are closed" in the sixth stanza. Whether Owen abandoned the attempt because he finally felt he wanted the more modest rhetoric is impossible to tell. The attempt links the poem to other subterranean poems such as "The Unreturning," "Miners," and "Strange Meeting"; it is the work of the visionary, passionate poet. The final form is the work of the more detached observer who wrote poems like "S. I. W." Both sorts of poems appear early and late in 1917-18.[7]

III

Owen's use of off-rhyme is remarkable for its range, and some indication of the range may be useful, for most of his critics have discussed the subject with "Strange Meeting" chiefly in mind. John Middleton Murry in early comments on the poetry speaks of the "mournful, impressive, even oppressive quality" of 'Strange Meeting,' with its "single, low, muffled, subterranean" tone, and he sees that the poet developed off-rhyme to express the depths of his emotion: his off-rhymes "are the very modulation of his voice; you are in the presence of that rare achievement, a true poetic style." Blunden sees the expressiveness of off-rhyme from a more technical standpoint. "Strange Meeting" is once again the key poem, "but again and again by means of it he creates remoteness, darkness, emptiness, shock, echo, the last word." Welland sees that off-rhyme is less "poetical" than ordinary rhyme and therefore serves the unpoetical war poetry better; he thinks also that somehow off-rhyme reflects "the disintegration of values in the world" (reason why other poets of Owen's time and later found it congenial); but mainly he takes Murry's view and quotes him approvingly, and then he provides a modified interpretation: "it offered a unique and perfect expression to that diffidence and lack of self-confidence that all who knew him record, and at the same time it coincided with the hesitant sense of frustration that his poetry had to communicate." Johnston thinks that "the feeling of tension, monotony, and defeated expectation is reinforced by the device." Hibberd thinks that off-rhymes "produce an effect of dissonance and failure."[8]

Apply these visions of off-rhyme to the opening lines of "A Terre":

> Sit on the bed. I'm blind, and three parts shell.
> Be careful; can't shake hands now; never shall.
> Both arms have mutinied against me,—brutes.
> My fingers fidget like ten idle brats.

Apply them to "The Last Laugh," that altogether savage poem whose final stanza reads thus:

> "My love!" one moaned. Love-languid seemed his mood,
> Till, slowly lowered, his whole face kissed the mud.
> And the Bayonets' long teeth grinned;
> Rabbles of Shells hooted and groaned;
> And the Gas hissed.

They do not apply. At one extreme is the emphatic off-rhyme of passages such as these, calling attention to its ironies of sound and sense; at the other extreme is the subdued off-rhyme of "The Parable of the Old Man and the Young," so unobtrusive that the reader does not see it. In "The Parable of the Old Man and the Young" Owen quietly mingles off-rhyme with blank verse and full rhyme; in "A Terre" he moves from the harsh and humorous off-rhymes of the opening to the softer sounds that serve the anguish of the latter part of the poem (*sure-share-shower, winds-weaned-wounds*). It is certainly the case that Owen's best off-rhyme is in his war poetry, but that is because his best poetry is his war poetry. A good many of the war poems are in conventional rhyme, and the explanation for Owen's use of either off-rhyme or full rhyme in individual poems will not be easy to come by.

It is worth noting also that Owen did not "return" to traditional rhyme in his last poem, as indicated by C. Day Lewis in his comments in the *Collected Poems* (77n). The suggestion by Johnston that "At a Calvary Near Ancre" was composed in September 1918 leads one to suppose that it was written a day or more following the composition of "Smile, Smile, Smile," and is the last poem rather than "Smile, Smile, Smile," It is indeed written in full rhyme. "Smile, Smile, Smile" itself mixes off-rhyme in with full rhyme: *scanned-small-haul, done-homes-aerodromes, dead-died-stead*. Other late poems such as "Arms and the Boy," "The Roads Also," and "S.I.W." rely wholly or in some part on off-rhyme.

IV

For many critics "Strange Meeting" is the best of Owen, not merely in its use of off-rhyme but in its overall character. But one has only to look at "At a Calvary Near Ancre" to see another kind of poem of considerable importance.

> One ever hangs where shelled roads part.
> In this war He too lost a limb,
> But His disciples hide apart;
> And now the Soldiers bear with Him.
>
> Near Golgotha strolls many a priest,
> And in their faces there is pride
> That they were flesh-marked by the Beast
> By whom the gentle Christ's denied.
>
> The scribes on all the people shove
> And brawl allegiance to the state,
> But they who love the greater love
> Lay down their lives; they do not hate.

The Keatsian poet of "Strange Meeting," visionary, profound, bearing the wisdom and guilt of ages and art on his back, has gone away. Owen sets out his images casually and confidently in neat tetrameter quatrains, and he himself is hardly there. The poem has no expressive voice; it has only a light tone established by the regularity of rhythm and phrasing; and its impact and merit rest largely with the ironical contrast between the light tone and the surreal subject.

How unusual is the poem? With respect to voice, there are vernacular poems such as "The Letter" and "The Chances" that exclude the poet's presumed own voice just as completely, and there are other poems of dialogue, monologue, or quotation that do so to a lesser degree: "Inspection," "Smile, Smile, Smile," and most of the first half of "A Terre." The fact is that when one begins to classify Owen's poems, one sees considerable variety, and this variety makes difficult a description of his development in a straight line. For whether or not we take the view that he was a fully mature poet by the time of his death, we cannot see his beginnings with respect to a nearly fixed end. There are those such as Johnston who know the Owen they want, a seer with historical, epical sweep, and for Johnston "Strange Meeting" is merely a promise of a poem Owen might one day have produced. For most other critics "Strange Meeting" possesses visionary scope enough. But the poet who in 1918 was "above all... not concerned with Poetry" surely had other of his poems primarily in mind. [9]

Two of the most impressive examples of another sort of poetry are "A Terre," dating from December 1917, and "S.I.W.," undated but presumably written in 1918. "A Terre" begins in easy ordinary speech ("Sit on the bed"). The voice is distinctly not the voice of Owen or his alter ego in "Strange Meeting." In the course of the first five stanzas a more subdued and formal note comes in, not always successfully (as with "Less live than specks that in the sun-shafts turn"). Then in the first line of the sixth stanza a different voice speaks: "O Life, Life, let me breathe." This voice immediately disappears, and a humorous ironical voice takes over, though one distinct from the voice of the earlier stanzas. With stanza 7 there is another modulation, and we have the voice that comes across in "Dulce Et Decorum Est" (compare "Friend, be very sure" with "My friend, you would not tell"). Then with the close comes another shift to intense yet subdued ironical anguish, of a piece with the endings of "Insensibility" and "Apologia Pro Poemata Meo": "Carry my crying spirit till it's weaned | To do without what blood remained these wounds." The poem does not manage the shifts entirely well, and the easier task Owen sets himself in a similar way with "Dulce Et Decorum Est" produces a technically more satisfactory poem.

Owen meets the problem in another way in "S.I.W.," where he breaks the poem into four separate "pieces"—as he describes the sections in manuscript. The titles to the pieces make the artifice deliberate, ironical, final; and each piece is remarkable. "The Prologue" gives us light touches of patriotic rhetoric, and snatches of family letters, and moves easily into a light ironical description of the boy in the trench, deepening only at the end. "The Action" provides a summary account of the boy's death, with a touch of objective narrative ("One dawn, our wire patrol") and a glimpse of questions asked ("Not sniped?"). "The Poem" gives us the poet, and a poet whose tone seems to this reader to be as individual as Keats's changed tone in "To Autumn" is usually thought to be. It has no less the high poetic intention of "Strange Meeting," and high poetic vocabulary, but it is more restrained, more sure, and in its effect more devastating. Then in the two lines of "The Epilogue" Owen closes with an informal and understated piece of savage irony, giving the last words to an anonymous soldier. In the draft of the poem at the British Museum (which Lewis prints from) the sections were at first marked only by asterisks, with slightly different dividing points. At the end of the draft Owen notes that the poem is a "story" of four "pieces," and he identifies them thus:

 I   The Prologue   a satire
 II The Incident—narrative
 III The Apology—a poem
 IV The Epilogue—a cynicism.

"S.I.W." is to this reader the poem that hints of the postwar Owen, writing poetry not just profoundly expressive of himself and of the pity of war and life, but embracing a variety of tones, moods, attitudes, and perspectives, governing them with rich and various poetic power. This is the direction in which the experimenting leads. It makes poems such as "At a Calvary Near Ancre" and "The Letter" quite as important in Owen's career as "Strange Meeting"; it suggests that the detached ending Owen arrived at for "Exposure" was a conscious choice. Owen's visible development is one of experiment, increasingly mature. He deepens in objectivity as much as he deepens in subjectivity.

15 The Play that Oscar Wilde Failed to Write

OSCAR WILDE'S CAREER as a dramatist covered fifteen years, from the time he wrote *Vera* (1880) to the time he completed *The Importance of Being Earnest* (1894). But there was a long gap after *Vera* and *The Duchess of Padua* (1883) until the next play, *Lady Windermere's Fan* (1890), and only five years remained. In August 1894, a few weeks before he dashed off *The Importance of Being Earnest*, Wilde wrote to George Alexander about the plot of another play he had just conceived. He saw "great things in it," but he did not write it.[1] Likewise, he did not write other plays that he thought about after his release from prison. It is lucky for us that the crash did not come before *The Importance of Being Earnest*, and unlucky for us that it did come. What sort of play might Wilde have written had he gone on? What sort of play should he have written, given his talents? To some people, *The Importance of Being Earnest* seems as nearly perfect as any play is likely to be, and the appropriate culmination of Wilde's career. Perhaps he would have written a succession of such plays, rather in the manner of the succession of lovely early symphonies that Mozart wrote. But Mozart came to a better end. Why not Wilde?

I

In an article in the *Saturday Review* written at the time of Wilde's death in 1900, Max Beerbohm said that Wilde was not a born writer. He saw that Wilde's genius was indeed in his life, and the writing was merely an overflow of that genius. He noted the variety of literary forms that Wilde experimented in; and presumably thinking of *Lady Windermere's Fan* as the real start, he saw that Wilde had taken up playwriting rather late and "as a kind of afterthought." Nevertheless, he credited Wilde with abilities superior to those of most of the dramatists around him: great knowledge of the world, remarkable facility in dialogue, and flair for theatrical construction. Beerbohm's overall judgment seems a sound one, and it puts a qualification on any thoughts of what might have been. The record of work from the time of the crash forward is not significant, and the record of work without the crash might not have been either. We see the two courses exemplified in the Oscar Wildes of our own day—Joe Orton, cut off as he achieved success, and Tom Stoppard, seemingly content (even with *The Real Thing* in 1982) to let success slide. St. John Hankin echoed Beerbohm's views a few years later. He thought that Wilde despised the theater, and wrote for money. Had there been a national theater, said Hankin, Wilde's talents might have been nurtured, and he might have begun to take playwriting seriously.[2]

Seeing Wilde's further career is also made difficult by the fact of his imitativeness. The charge of imitation was leveled against his work from the time of the *Poems* (1881), and very few critics have failed to remark upon some aspect of it. Hankin gave attention to the Elizabethan-Jacobean pastiche that is *The Duchess of Padua*, the reviewer of *Salomé* in the *Pall Mall Gazette* in 1893 offered unkind details on the sources of that play, and the reviewers of the first three comedies were fairly well united in their condemnation of the hackneyed plots. A.B. Walkley examined the French sources for *Lady Windermere's Fan*, and noted the minor variations that Wilde undertook.[3] In among these comedies came the two unfinished plays, *La Sainte Courtisane* and *A Florentine Tragedy*, the first probably written in 1893-94, the second begun in 1893 and revised in 1897. All that need be said of them is that they were imitations of imitations, the one trying to do *Salomé* again, the other repeating *The Duchess of Padua*. With any other first-rate author, one would assume that these two plays were unfinished because the author could not bear so flagrantly to repeat himself. Not so with Wilde.

Various details of the first three comedies illustrate the tendency. To the question posed by Lord Darlington, "Do you think seriously that women who have committed what the world calls a fault should never be forgiven?", Lady Windermere replies, "I think they should never be forgiven." It is much the same reply that Hester Worsley gives to herself in *A Woman of No Importance* when she contemplates the same issue: "Let all women who have sinned be punished." Lady Chiltern in *An Ideal Husband* merely enlarges the scope of such self-righteousness in her words to the corrupt Mrs. Cheveley: "A person who has once been guilty of a dishonest and dishonourable action may be guilty of it a second time, and should be shunned."[4] Each woman has obviously something to learn about moral ambiguity, and each eventually learns it, and in language that makes them as much like one another at the end of the plays as they are at the beginning. They and other familiar types recur: the pure woman, the pure man, the woman with a past, the serious dandy, the bore, the cynic, and so forth. In the way of repeated plot mechanisms there are women hidden in rooms, misinterpreted bankbooks and letters, mislaid fan and bracelet, abandoned daughter and son. The fact that slightly different changes are rung from play to play does not hide the shabby similarity. And the new play of August 1894 in which Wilde saw great things was more of the same, along with a soupcon of tragedy in the manner of *The Duchess of Padua* and *Vera*. Subject: "a sheer flame of love between a man and a woman."⁵ Characters: pure wife, pure young lover, impure other woman, impure husband. Plot: a mix-up among them leading to a climactic scene in which husband and impure woman are hidden together in a room but the wife happens to be there as well and saves them (in the manner of Mrs. Erlynne saving Lady Windermere) when the woman's husband comes knocking at the door. The touch from *The Duchess of Padua* and *Vera* (in which plays the heroines commit noble suicide) is the sinning husband's suicide prior to a duel with the pure young lover. The great things Wilde saw in the play can only have been great sums of money. After his release from prison he contemplated the play again, and did indeed make money on it—in a tangle of an attempted collaboration with Frank Harris, who presently wrote the play under the title *Mr. and Mrs. Daventry*.

II

But in all this repetition and backsliding there was the progress to *The Importance of Being Earnest*. Arthur Symons in his review of the fourteen-volume edition of Wilde's works, issued in 1908, remarked upon "the curious movement, forward and backward, of a mind never fully certain of its direction," and he saw the progress as that of a man who began with the "desire to write tragedies, above all romantic tragedies in verse" and who only gradually discovered "that it was through the medium of the comic stage that he could best express his essential talent."⁶ In the main Symons's view is hardly to be denied, and one wonders why the great wit himself could not see from the outset that his best talent lay where it did. The easy answer (as people have observed, with a glance at "The Decay of Lying") is that Wilde in his person had an instinct for tragedy. His life imitated tragic art, and he recurrently tried to carry that tragic instinct into his writing. The fulfillment of tragedy in life offered no release, and he tried to get on with *The Florentine Tragedy* and did get on with *The Ballad of Reading Gaol*. Symons offered only a detail or two of his view of the progress, but here is the sort of elaboration he might have provided. The first two plays were murky melodramas of a familiar sort, with little to save them except an occasional flash of wit, one item of which in *Vera* ("Life is much too important a thing ever to talk seriously about it" [665]) Wilde resurrected ten years later for *Lady Windermere's Fan*, transferring it easily from the villainous Prince Paul to the charming Lord Darlington (390). *The Duchess of Padua* in particular was in a mode that had been dying a lingering death for three hundred years at the hands of some of England's most distinguished poets. The plays were failures in the theater. And so, although still hankering after tragedy (which he apparently could conceive only as melodrama), he came to the popular sentimental melodrama of the day, and here he found a congenial form and also public approval. The critics generally thought that he provided a good evening's entertainment, and that the best of it was the ample supply of wit with which the melodrama was leavened. A few were troubled by thoughts that the wit itself was imitative, consisting of familiar phrases turned upside down. The best critics laughed at the wit somewhat more heartily than they laughed at the melodrama.

But then there was *Salomé*, written just as Wilde was finishing or had finished *Lady Windermere's Fan*. Symons himself was uneasy about this work. He saw it as Wilde's last real effort at tragedy, and he granted it a "strange fascination," but overall he did not regard it as drama. It was a series of poses, "languid, and horrible, and frozen," and "a celebration of dark rites" (598). The work has indeed divided Wilde's critics more seriously than any other of his plays, some regarding it as an abomination, others as a piece of tinsel, others as bait for the Philistines, others as titillation for same, others as Wilde's finest work—sometimes excepting *The Importance of Being Earnest*, sometimes not. Hankin, who did regard it highly, said that Wilde wrote it without the theater in mind and that only the accident of Sarah Bernhardt's asking him in jest why he had never written anything for her led to its production (801). For the moment, the play is easiest to see as Symons sees it, inessestial to Wilde's progress, rather more a last gesture than a play, having neither character nor action in the ordinary sense but only voice and pose. The play survives on the stage today transmogrified as opera, and it seems to suggest no further dramatic direction, only repetition, as in *La Sainte Courtisane*.

It was in the three serious comedies that more obvious progress came. Ridicule by the critics was not in itself enough to make Wilde abandon his melodramatic plots. Far from it, as the new play of August 1894 shows. All the same, Wilde was responsive to criticism, and he took up the opposite charge that the third act of *Lady Windermere's Fan* lacked action. In the beginning of the act there is the melodrama of Lady Windermere alone and then with Mrs. Erlynne, and at the very end there is the melodrama of Lady Windermere's escape, but half an act lies in between, and that half is given over to miscellaneous banter among the men when they come in. Wilde's response was typical of him: he would do the impossible and write a whole act that had no action. The first act of *A Woman of No Importance* was the result. "In the act...," says Wilde, "there was absolutely no action at all. It was a perfect act."[7] As usual he exaggerated, but the act does sustain itself almost entirely on witty repartee, and the plotting is slender. We learn of Gerald's being taken up by Lord Illingworth, we learn that the unseen Mrs. Arbuthnot will appear in the evening, we are invited to think about what Hester might do if Illingworth offers to kiss her, and we may be piqued to know why Mrs. Arbuthnot is unimportant. How different these titbits are from the crisis, mysteries, and revelations that convulse the first act of *Lady Windermere's Fan* and the latter part of the first act of *An Ideal Husband!* How different is the soft close (Illingworth throwing away the title-line) from Lord Windermere's violent despair and Sir Robert's quieter despair! We have momentarily arrived at *The Importance of Being Earnest*, in which during the whole play (to exaggerate a little) no one talks anything but nonsense, no one does anything, and no one brings the curtain down with a crash. That Wilde did not progress immediately from the perfect act to the perfect play may again indicate the uncertainty of his development. He also had other things to develop, notably his witty but nice young men and women. In *Lady Windermere's Fan* Lord Darlington is a wit and something of a rake during most of act 1, but he is a solemn moralist in act 3, and the aspects of his character do not hang together. His successor, improved, is Lord Goring in *An Ideal Husband*, who is witty and serious at the same time, and solemnly moralistic only at the end. In *Lady Windermere's Fan* and *A Woman of No Importance* all the best people are prigs who make and serve the melodrama. In *An Ideal Husband* the best people are nicely moral, and they either help to restrain the melodrama (Lord Goring) or have nothing to do with it (Lord Caversham, Mabel Chiltern). When Lord Goring and Mabel Chiltern are on their own they have an amusing conversation quite in the spirit of *The Importance of Being Earnest*.

> Lord Goring: I have something very particular to say to you.
> Mabel Chiltern (rapturously): Oh! is it a proposal?
> Lord Goring (somewhat taken aback): Well, yes, it is—I am bound to say it is.
> Mabel Chiltern (with a sigh of pleasure): I am so glad. That makes the second today.
> Lord Goring (indignantly): The second today? What conceited ass has been impertinent enough to dare to propose to you before I had proposed to you?
> Mabel Chiltern: Tommy Trafford, of course. It is one of Tommy's days for proposing. He always proposes on Tuesdays and Thursdays, during the Season.
> Lord Goring: You didn't accept him, I hope?
> Mabel Chiltern: I make it a rule never to accept Tommy. That is why he goes on proposing. (541)

The way was now open for a play in which the wit flows freely throughout, unhindered by melodrama, moralists, or moral points.

So *The Importance of Being Earnest* was the end to which the would-be tragedian naturally came. It was, though, an end with complications, or seeming complications. Critics have been divided over whether the end was a trifle or a criticism of life. William Archer said that "it imitates nothing, represents nothing, means nothing, is nothing, except a sort of *rondo capriccioso*, in which the artist's fingers run with crisp irresponsibility up and down the keyboard of life." A.B. Walkley turned Archer's censure into highest praise: "it is with no ironic intention that I declare Mr. Oscar Wilde to have 'found himself,' at last, as an artist of sheer nonsense." St. John Hankin mediated between the two: it "is only a joke, though an amazingly brilliant one."[8] More recent critics, of an academic sort, have taken the play more seriously. Eric Bentley in a cursory discussion in 1946 saw that the apparently frivolous humor touches upon all the serious issues of life: class and caste, morality, love, money, death, and so forth. Richard Foster, in 1956, wanted to show that the play is "an intellectual tour de force of the first order," notably in its parodies of literary forms and conventions. L. A. Poague, in 1973, attempted to unveil "verbal irony so dense" that the playgoer might be hard put to it to keep up with the play intellectually (400 examples of irony at a count). Poague reviewed this modern academic estimate of the play, and decided that it was the right one.[9] If so, *The Importance of Being Earnest* represented an end that was rather more a transformation or a beginning, perhaps offering in itself very little clue to the future except to warn readers and spectators that hereafter they would have to keep on their intellectual toes.

It seems more sensible, though, to see the play mainly in relation to the earlier plays, and a glance at a couple of aspects of the relationship suggests the rightness of the view that it is a masterly trifle. The major faults of the serious comedies are absurd plotting and inconsistent characterization and speech. How is it that an upright and loving husband such as Lord Windermere can demand so peremptorily that his gentle wife invite the notorious Mrs. Erlynne to her birthday party, or that the gentle and loyal wife can suddenly go through her husband's bankbooks and forthwith believe the worst and aim to abandon herself to another man, or that the notorious Mrs. Erlynne can suddenly find her maternal instinct after twenty years and as suddenly lose it again? Most of the speeches of the play ring false in consequence, and the passionate outbursts of Lady Windermere and Mrs. Erlynne sound exactly alike. The problem extends to small moments of conversation, as when in act 2 Lady Windermere says to Lord Windermere, "London is full of women who trust their husbands. One can always recognize them. They look so thoroughly unhappy" (400). She has not hitherto shown herself to be a wit, nor has she displayed either the knowledge or the cynicism to warrant her expressing such a view. The line properly belongs to someone like Lord Darlington—except that he too is witty or solemn according to the whim of his author. *Lady Windermere's Fan* is full of such irresponsibility, and the other two serious comedies repeat it. The most ridiculous piece of plotting surely comes with Mrs. Cheveley's broach in *An Ideal Husband*.

What *The Importance of Being Earnest* does is to make a virtue of these defects. Richard Foster's display of Wilde's skill at parody in the play should begin with self-parody—the inveterate imitator achieving his great success when he parodies himself. Abandoned daughter in *Lady Windermere's Fan* and abandoned son in *An Ideal Husband* become mislaid son in *The Importance of Being Earnest*, and the whole melodramatic apparatus that seems necessary to bind first act to last in the one sort of play becomes an elaborate joke at the end of the other. Characters who are unbelievable become characters who do not ask to be believed. Characters who are alike in spite of themselves become characters who freely exchange identities. Is it Jack or Algernon who says, "If ever I get married I'll certainly try to forget the fact"? It happens to be Algernon, who has just said, apropos of Lane's remarking that his family life was not interesting, "Lane's views on marriage seem somewhat lax." Is it Gwendolyn or Cecily who says, "There is something in that name that inspires absolute confidence"? Of course it is both, except that Cecily says "seems to inspire." Is it Miss Prism who says of novels, "The good ended happily, and the bad unhappily. That is what Fiction means"? No, it is the author, who is lurking somewhere behind her. And who is it who offers the puzzling observation that "All women become like their mothers. That is their tragedy. No man does. That's his"? It is Algernon again, who steals it from Lord Illingworth and Mrs. Allonby in *An Ideal Husband*.[10] The perfect play emerges when melodrama dissolves into mischief, when character becomes agreeable charade, and when wit is distributed genially and freely, if not quite indiscriminately—when the carelessly or unintentionally absurd becomes the deliberately absurd. To call the play a criticism of life is to imply that the serious comedies are criticisms of life as well—criticisms hampered by problems of dramaturgy.

III

As a last preliminary we need to ask what Wilde himself thought of his progress. In the abstract are the views of art expressed in "The Decay of Lying" and the preface to *The Picture of Dorian Gray*, both of which works were published just at the time that Wilde was writing *Lady Windermere's Fan* and *Salomé*. The preface states the views succinctly: "no artist desires to prove anything," "no artist has ethical sympathies," and "all art is quite useless" (17). With such standards, Wilde could have passed only the two plays that certain early critics described as trifles—*Salomé* and *The Importance of Being Earnest*—and he must have deplored the others. In *Salomé* we stand distant from the virtue of Jokanaan and from the individual viciousness of Herod, Herodias, and Salomé. The resolution of the play is spectacular and narrative, rather than moral or immoral, and offers no clue to conduct for ourselves. Similarly, *The Importance of Being Earnest* is a piece of nonsense that jests at sense. Jack and Algernon say it all in the close of the first act in lines that are as lightly detached from morality and immorality as the whole of *Salomé* is melodramatically detached:

Jack: Oh, that's nonsense, Algy. You never talk anything but nonsense.
Algernon: Nobody ever does. (339)

As Wilde says, the play is a trivial comedy for serious people.

In contrast, all the other plays present serious moral problems that are brought to explicit moral resolutions. One can, of course, judge them to be useless in achievement of their intentions, and one can equally judge Wilde to have been lightly cynical in his intentions. Such judgments are different matters. There is, though, one way in which all the plays sit happily together in Wilde's abstract considerations. "The artist," he says in the first line of the preface, "is the creator of beautiful things." *Salomé* is perhaps the most splendid visually, *The Importance of Being Earnest* the most splendid verbally, but the other plays aim at comparable effects, and in this light they may even be said to share to some degree the uselessness of the first two. Lady Windermere and Mrs. Erlynne, Mrs. Arbuthnot and Lord Illingworth, Lady Chiltern and Mrs. Cheveley can be seen as beautiful exemplars of individual qualities, and Lady Windermere's sanctimonious virtue may seem quite as beautiful in its way as her compassionate virtue. In *The Decay of Lying* Wilde distinguishes between the "unimaginative realism" of Zola's characters and the "imaginative reality" of Balzac's, and suggests that "a steady course of Balzac reduces one's living friends to shadows" (976). It is perhaps to make the best of Wilde's intentions in his plays to say that in all of them he did aim to create some sort of beauty of heightened imaginative reality. If, then, one asks where in the plays are to be found characterizations most successful in this way, one might answer: in Salomé and Herod and Jokanaan, in Lord Illingworth and Mrs. Allonby, and in Lord Goring. Such an answer would affect the description of Wilde's further career.

Of equal interest are Wilde's individual views on the plays as he wrote them or reflected upon them later. Not surprisingly, these views contradict in large part the abstract views. *Vera* was to him a play with a purpose consonant with his belief in socialism. It was not political, he said in a letter to Marie Prescott of July 1883, but "I have tried to express within the limits of art that Titan cry of the peoples for liberty, which in the Europe of our day is threatening thrones." In a letter to Richard D'Oyly Carte of March 1882 he said that the stage sets should show "realistic not operatic conspiracy." He saw *The Duchess of Padua* somewhat similarly, remarking in a letter to Mary Anderson of March 1883 that sympathy for the London poor would be stirred by certain of the sixteenth century material of the play. But to a much greater extent than with *Vera* he showed himself to be interested in the manipulation of the audience, as though vice and virtue were coming to be mere instruments that he played upon. The same letter indicated as much, and concluded with the observation that "all art must be capable of scientific analysis, if it is not merely prettiness." Wilde began the letter with the observation that the play was "my masterpiece thus far," but in July 1898 he wrote to Robert Ross that "the *Duchess* is unfit for publication—the only one of my works that comes under that category."[11]

Among the serious comedies, Wilde made useful comments only on *Lady Windermere's Fan*. They suggest some preoccupation with unimaginative realism, stock characterization, stage tricksiness, and primitive audience sympathies rather than with high artistic uselessness and beauty. In a letter to George Alexander in February 1891 while he was writing the play, he said, "I can't get a grip of the play yet; I can't make my people real." A year later, when the play was in rehearsal, he wrote to Alexander to reject Alexander's suggestion that the revelation of Mrs. Erlynne's identity should be moved forward from act 4 to act 2. Such a change, Wilde argued, would necessitate drastic changes in characterization and incident. In the context of act 2 a woman who was known to have abandoned her daughter would have to be perceived as a horrid woman, and even so the audience would be repelled at the thought that the daughter might have struck her own mother. Furthermore, Mrs. Erlynne's self-sacrificial cry at the end of act 3, "It is I who am lost," would also be "repulsive" from a woman known to be Lady Windermere's mother rather than believed to be merely an adventuress. In contrast, revelation of Mrs. Erlynne's identity in act 4 would bring no repugnance, for by then an oblique reconciliation would have occurred between mother and daughter.[12] Eventually, Wilde yielded to Alexander's wished-for change, and it was no great matter, and he found that he did not have to change the rest of the play. Of course anyone who listens to certain information dropped by Lords Darlington and Windermere in act 1 can guess the whole silly situation well before the revelation comes.

There remain *Salomé* and *The Importance of Being Earnest*, and it is these plays that Wilde commented on in a way that corresponds with his abstract views of art. His brief allusions to *Salomé* here and there in his letters mentioned its "tragic beauty," and its "color and cadence"; it is "beautiful, colored, musical," a "terrible colored little tragedy." In a letter to the *Times* of about 1 March 1893 he corrected the mistaken opinion that he wrote the play for Sarah Bernhardt. "I have never written a play for any actor or actress, nor shall I ever do so. Such work is for the artisan in literature, not for the artist." (He did write *The Duchess of Padua* for Mary Anderson.) In the great long letter to Lord Alfred Douglas of January-March 1897 he recalled an occasion years earlier at Oxford when he expressed to a friend a desire "to eat of the fruit of all the trees in the garden of the world." He then went into the world but kept to the "sun-gilt" side of the garden, shunning the other side, having only a glimmering sense that "the other half of the garden had its secrets for me also." In *Salomé*, he said, he expressed that desire, experience, and glimmering knowledge: these "recurring *motifs* make *Salomé* so like a piece of music and bind it as a ballad."[13]

Wilde commented on *The Importance of Being Earnest* just before, during, and after writing it. His remarks suggest higher uselessness and beauty. To George Alexander in July 1894 he wrote, "The real charm of the play, if it is to have charm, must be in the dialogue." To Douglas in August he wrote, "My play is really very funny: I am quite delighted with it. But it is not shaped yet. It lies in Sybilline leaves about the room, and Arthur [the butler] has twice made a chaos of it by 'tidying up.' The result, however, was rather dramatic. I am inclined to think that Chaos is a stronger evidence for an Intelligent Creator than Kosmos is:

the view might be expanded." To Alexander in September he wrote, "My play, though the dialogue is sheer comedy, and the best I have ever written, is of course in idea farcical." Five years later the play was published for the first time, and Wilde's life and view of life were now transformed. He regarded the play with some regret, some Arnoldian sense of failure. In February 1899 he wrote about it to friends. To Reginald Turner: "It was extraordinary reading the play over. How I used to toy with that tiger Life!" To Louis Wilkinson: "It is a fanciful, absurd comedy, written when I was playing with the tiger Life." To Frank Harris: "so trivial, so irresponsible..., mocking at morals." And to Robert Ross: "I only wish it was a more wonderful work of art—of higher seriousness of intent—but it has some amusing things in it, and I think the tone and temper of the whole thing bright and happy."[14]

IV

What play more wonderful and with higher seriousness than *The Importance of Being Earnest* could Wilde have written—without backsliding into melodrama, unbelievable characters, and general fraudulence? As the letter to Ross suggests, the answer will exhibit some compromise between earlier abstract ideals of art and the lessons of life.

i

We begin with a play rather like *The Importance of Being Earnest*, perhaps involving love and marriage (like most of Wilde's plays), but with a subject beyond it for the wit to play upon. In *The Importance of Being Earnest* Algernon remarks that "more than half of modern culture depends on what one shouldn't read," and he also notes that "truth is rarely pure and never simple [and] modern life would be very tedious if it were either, and modern literature a complete impossibility" (324, 326). To these remarks on literature can be added Miss Prism's definition of fiction and comments by Gwendolyn and Cecily on sensational diaries. As a subject, literature has to share attention with a few dozen other subjects in the play, and the witticisms about each are lovely bubbles that burst and are forgotten in our admiration of other bubbles bursting about them. The new play must have a single subject.

The subject is ready to hand in *A Woman of No Importance* in the light satire on Englishman versus foreigner. The first several minutes of the play are given over to a delicious examination of the American Hester Worsley by Lady Caroline Pontefract. Hester's patriotism, her morality, her democratic virtue, her naive perception of character, are all held up to agreeable ridicule, while at the same time Lady Caroline herself is made laughable amid amusing remarks by herself on English character. Later in the act Lord Illingworth and Mr. Kelvil comment wittily on America, and toward the end of the act Hester and Mrs. Allonby show their national colors in a brief exchange:

Hester: I dislike London dinner-parties.
Mrs. Allonby: I adore them. The clever people never listen, and the stupid people never talk.
Hester: I think the stupid people talk a great deal.
Mrs. Allonby: Ah, I never listen! (441)

Superficial honors in the exchange go to Mrs. Allonby, but Hester's point is not lost. Then in act 2 Hester delivers her passionate attack on the English. It is impolitely rude, in contrast to the polite rudeness of her hosts, and it exhibits American faults as clearly as it names English faults. It is not answered in kind. Lady Caroline merely stops her in full flow by saying, "Might I, dear Miss Worsley, as you are standing up, ask you for my cotton that is just behind you? Thank you" (450).

There, except for a phrase or two, the lovely subject collapses, and presently the play itself collapses into melodrama. In act 4 Hester joins forces with Mrs. Arbuthnot, and the two of them together quite outdo Hester's earlier moralizings, and no one is present to say, "Might I, dear Mr. Wilde, as you are sitting down, ask you for a lovely piece of wit to deride them?" How happily he could have obliged! How cheaply he failed! Nevertheless *A Woman of No Importance* offers a solid portion of the English-foreigner play, and additional bits appear in *Lady Windermere's Fan* and *An Ideal Husband*. In *Lady Windermere's Fan* we have the Duchess of Berwick trying to snare the rich Australian Mr. Hopper for daughter Agatha, and prepared all the while to say outrageous things about the physical shape of the country and the quality of the canned food that Mr. Hopper's father made his fortune on. Regrettably, we see little of Mr. Hopper, who turns the Duchess's wit back upon her nicely and who has an amusing thing or two to say about London society. In *An Ideal Husband* the English-foreigner humor is of another sort, having mainly to do with the malapropisms and misplaced manners of the Vicomte de Nanjac, "a young attaché known for his neckties and his Anglomania" (483). The material is slight, but it is in Wilde's best vein, vivacious and easy. There is also in the play an occasional comment by Mrs. Cheveley on English society. She has been out of England for some years, and she offers detached observations on the English gentleman, English newspapers, English pragmatism. Unfortunately, she belongs to the melodrama of the play, and her observations lose force and focus in the general confusion of perspective that the play surrenders to. Her observations remind us, though, that the melodramatic parts of all three serious comedies do involve criticism of English society—its moral hypocrisy on the one hand and its superficiality and cynicism on the other. The criticism is trivialized by the melodrama, and we see again that the happy artistic solution must be to dissolve seriousness in laughter. How readily Wilde could have assembled a cast of English fortune hunters, hypocrites, fops, matrons, and gentlemen, matched them with American and Australian moralists, materialists, and title hunters (stealing bits and pieces from the serious Mr. Henry James), tossed in among them a French dandy, an African princess, and a Chinese sage, shaken them all together in a laughable plot, and served them up with glittering wit and wisdom!

Of course we see too that it might have meant nothing more than an irresponsible running of fingers up and down the international keyboard. So Wilde must introduce one character into the play who is not a figure of fun but a spirit of comedy, who will give to the international frolic an agreeable meaning above itself. That character is Lord Goring. As we see him in *An Ideal Husband* he is in part no better than Lord Darlington or Algernon and Jack. His conversation with Phipps the butler is a first version of Algernon's with Lane, and not nearly so clever. His flippancy with his father, his pleasantries with Mabel, his moralizing with Lady Chiltern, all stand against him, and so does the phrase by which Wilde initially describes him, "He plays with life" (488). But from the outset there is a hint of individual intelligence. To the Vicomte de Nanjac's praise of English newspapers he replies, "Then, my dear Nanjac, you must certainly read between the lines" (489). To Mabel's question of whether he is coming into the music room he replies, "Not if there is any music going on, Miss Mabel" (489).

It is mainly in the opening scene of act 2 that he distinguishes himself from the other merely amusing or moralistic people about him and from similar types in the other plays. By now the play has begun its descent into melodrama, and Sir Robert Chiltern is in distress over Mrs. Cheveley's attempted blackmail. Lord Goring has to be counsellor and moralist, and he achieves the unique success of restraining himself. Some of his responses to Chiltern are altogether plain. To Chiltern's words, "And after all, whom did I wrong by what I did? No one," he merely replies, "Except yourself, Robert" (504). When Chiltern identifies Baron Arnheim as the instigator of his downfall, he says, "Damned scoundrel!" (505) When Chiltern elaborates the vision of power that Arnheim unfolded to him, he says, "A thoroughly shallow creed" (505). Elsewhere he displays humor and irony in keeping with such plain words and with the true wit we have seen from him earlier. Sir Robert defends Arnheim: "A man of culture, charm, and distinction. One of the most intellectual men I ever met." Goring replies, "Ah! I prefer a gentlemanly fool any day. There is more to be said for stupidity than people imagine" (505). When Sir Robert says that Arnheim made three quarters of a million pounds from their dealings and he himself a hundred and ten thousand, he replies, "You were worth more, Robert" (506).

His best moment comes at the very beginning of the scene, with Sir Robert's eulogy of Lady Chiltern. He replies, "Is Lady Chiltern as perfect as all that?" Sir Robert is affronted: "Yes, my wife is as perfect as all that." "What a pity!" says Goring—taking off his left-hand glove, as Wilde directs (503). He apologizes to

Chiltern for being frivolous, but the whole labored meaning of the play and of *Lady Windermere's Fan* and *A Woman of No Importance* is caught in his easy phrase. Suppose now that Lord Goring were cast in among an international set of naifs and knaves and all that lie in between. Suppose that he were a Liberal peer with Socialist wit. Might he not expose aristocratic-capitalistic-democratic pretensions and chicanery in true comic light, and send playgoers home seeing themselves and their world anew?

ii

It is the irony of Wilde's life that he who was a critic of his world in so many ways, who stood outside the social norms in part of his private life, and who was put out of the world into prison should have been so largely a conventional moralist. Love, compassion, and forgiveness are what the serious comedies preach and also what the long letter to Lord Alfred Douglas preaches. Possibly love, compassion, and forgiveness are what we all must or ought to come to, and the complaint against Wilde can be only that his representation of their condition in life is superficial. What we want of him rather more than an international frolic wrapped up in Socialist love is a brilliant dramatization of one kind of hazard in which love, compassion, and forgiveness find their uneasy way. We see the basis of it in Lord Illingworth, and to a lesser degree in Mrs. Allonby (and also in Mrs. Cheveley).

Illingworth is Wilde's most impressive character. He derives in part from Lord Darlington and other lightly cynical young men in *Lady Windermere's Fan*, and in part he is no better than they are. He derives more significantly from Lord Henry Wotton in *The Picture of Dorian Gray*, and picks up at least a half dozen of Wotton's witticisms. But whereas Wotton is predominantly a hedonist, Illingworth at his best is a thoughtful man. That Wilde dismissed him at the end of the play with a slap in the face by an unimportant moralist is a disgrace to Wilde. Here is the problem of the new play: Illingworth represents some kind of intellectual corrosion and despair, and he must be defeated; but he also represents some kind of integrity and wisdom, and he must not be defeated cheaply. How Wilde will achieve his end we cannot say. What we can show is Illingworth's brilliance in certain scenes. It will be necessary to omit one merely hedonistic remark that he repeats from Wotton, and also necessary to retain a couple of more thoughtful observations that he draws from him. One or two of Mrs. Allonby's remarks in these passages come from Wotton as well.

In act 1 we see Illingworth in conversation with Mr. Kelvil, a member of Parliament. Kelvil expresses surprise that Illingworth takes no side in politics.

Lord Illingworth: One should never take sides in anything, Mr. Kelvil. Taking sides is the beginning of sincerity, and earnestness follows shortly

afterwards, and the human being becomes a bore. However the House of Commons really does very little harm. You can't make people good by Act of Parliament—that is something.
Kelvil: You cannot deny that the House of Commons has always shown great sympathy with the sufferings of the poor.
Lord Illingworth: That is its special vice. That is the special vice of the age...
Kelvil: Still our East End is a very important problem.
Lord Illingworth: Quite so. It is the problem of slavery. And we are trying to solve it by amusing the slaves...
Kelvil: May I ask, Lord Illingworth, if you regard the House of Lords as a better institution than the House of Commons?
Lord Illingworth: A much better institution, of course. We in the House of Lords are never in touch with public opinion. That makes us a civilized body.
Kelvil: Are you serious in putting forward such a view?
Lord Illingworth: Quite serious, Mr. Kelvil. (To Mrs. Allonby): Vulgar habit that people have nowadays of asking... whether one is serious or not. Nothing is serious except passion. The intellect is not a serious thing, and never has been. (437-38)

In act 3 Illingworth offers advice to Gerald about the conduct of life, and Wilde fails him to a degree, except for the closing line, which Illingworth offers as Mrs. Arbuthnot enters: "I want you to know about life. For the world has been made by fools that wise men should live in it" (461). General conversation ensues, and people come and go, and Mrs. Arbuthnot makes a veiled allusion to the damage done to her by Illingworth. Lady Hunstanton replies complacently, and in so doing instigates a series of comments on the secret of life.

Lady Hunstanton: I think on the whole that the secret of life is to take things very, very easily.
Mrs. Allonby: The secret of life is never to have an emotion that is unbecoming.
Lady Stutfield: The secret of life is to appreciate the pleasure of being terribly, terribly deceived.
Kelvil: The secret of life is to resist temptation, Lady Stutfield.
Lord Illingworth: There is no secret of life. Life's aim, if it has one, is simply to be always looking for temptations. There are not nearly enough. I sometimes pass a whole day without coming across a single one. It is quite dreadful. It makes one so nervous about the future.
Lady Hunstanton (shakes her fan at him): I don't know how it is, Lord Illingworth, but everything you have said today seems to me excessively immoral. It has ben most interesting listening to you.

> Lord Illingworth: All thought is immoral. Its very essence is destruction. If you think of anything, you kill it. (464)

Illingworth is the one character who resists an easy epigram on the secret of life. His denial of a secret and his comment on an uncertain aim imply the dullness of the people about him and the dullness of life itself, and his further observation that thought is destructive implies personal malaise. Whether one can go back to his conversations with Gerald and with Mr. Kelvil to show that his comments on thought, wise men, and intellect are consistent with one another need not detain us. We glimpse in all three passages a radical cynicism about society and humankind. It is compelling, and it demands to be answered compellingly.

Illingworth's other brilliant moments in the play are shared with Mrs. Allonby. In act 1 the two of them begin a conversation on the lawn with allusion to Hester Worsley, whom Mrs. Allonby describes as a Puritan.

> Lord Illingworth: Ah, that is inexcusable. I don't mind plain women being Puritans. It is the only excuse they have for being plain. But she is decidedly pretty. I admire her immensely. (Looks steadfastly at Mrs. Allonby).
> Mrs. Allonby: What a thoroughly bad man you must be!
> Lord Illingworth: What do you call a bad man?
> Mrs. Allonby: The sort of man who admires innocence.
> Lord Illingworth: And a bad woman?
> Mrs. Allonby: Oh! The sort of woman a man never gets tired of.
> Lord Illingworth: You are severe—on yourself.
> Mrs. Allonby: Define us as a sex.
> Lord Illingworth: Sphinxes without secrets.
> Mrs. Allonby: Does that include the Puritan women?
> Lord Illingworth: Do you know, I don't believe in the existence of Puritan women? I don't think there is a woman in the world who would not be a little flattered if one made love to her. (441-42)

The conversation continues with other more diffuse observations, and ends with Lord Illingworth suggesting that they go in to tea.

> Mrs. Allonby: Do you like such simple pleasures?
> Lord Illingworth: I adore simple pleasures. They are the last refuge of the complex. But, if you wish, let us stay here. Yes, let us stay here. The Book of Life begins with a man and a woman in a garden.
> Mrs. Allonby: It ends with Revelations.
> Lord Illingworth: You fence divinely. But the button has come off your foil.
> Mrs. Allonby: I have still the mask.
> Lord Illingworth: It makes your eyes lovelier.
> Mrs. Allonby: Thank you. Come. (443)

Another equally fine moment in the play is in act 3 just after the conversation about the secret of life. If one takes Illingworth and Mrs. Allonby at their best, the moment is poignant, bitter, and beautiful.

Mrs. Allonby (goes over to Lord Illingworth): There is a beautiful moon tonight.
Lord Illingworth: Let us go and look at it. To look at anything that is inconstant is charming nowadays.
Mrs. Allonby: You have your looking-glass.
Lord Illingworth: It is unkind. It merely shows me my wrinkles.
Mrs. Allonby: Mine is better behaved. It never tells me the truth.
Lord Illingworth: Then it is in love with you. (465)

It is the case that Wilde did not know what to do with Illingworth. That he failed to give adequate expression to his seriousness reflects his own lack of seriousness. Eventually he delivered himself into the hands of unimportant moralists, and perhaps at the time of writing the play he was unconsciously content to see (or consciously pretending to see) that the world and the end of the play must be made by fools. But a new play with a more serious Illingworth would hardly have been beyond his talent and compass, and perhaps a lucky escape to the continent before the moralists caught him would have given him occasion to contemplate his situation anew. The play would stand in emblematic relation to his life: it would present an impressive Illingworth in a significant action, and it would deliver him into the hands of wiser love.

iii

Wilde's last play is the tragedy that he failed to write except in his own person. Like the international play and the Illingworth play, it has literary prefiguration, notably in *Salomé*, but it finds perspective and depth in the crisis of his life.

Insofar as the play requires the crisis, it is much less likely to have been written than the other plays. Prison and its aftermath seem fairly certainly to have dammed up or destroyed the creative overflow that Beerbohm saw Wilde's writing to be. Time and again after his release he planned to write a new play or other large work, but the conceptions seem uniformly to have been trivial, and they came to nothing. Comments in various letters suggest the true case. To Frank Harris in February 1898: "As regards a comedy, my dear Frank, I have lost the mainspring of life and art, *La joie de vivre*; it is dreadful. I have pleasures and passions, but the joy of life is gone." On 9 March 1898 he wrote the same thing to Carlos Blacker, and added a phrase that looks forward to the final comments on *The Importance of Being Earnest*: "Life, that I loved so much—too much—has torn me like a tiger." To Robert Ross on 17 March 1898: "My writing has gone to bits—like my character." To Ross again on 16 August 1898: "Something is killed in me. I feel no desire to write. I am unconscious of power." Hesketh Pearson is concerned to show in his biography that Wilde was the same gay, humorous, and enchanting conversationalist after prison that he was before, but very little writing overflowed.[15]

It is in the long letter to Lord Alfred Douglas that Wilde gives an indication of the sort of play he will write afterward if he is "able to re-create my creative faculty" (468). His aim here is consonant with the one aim that covers all his writing, to "produce even one more beautiful work of art" (470), but the particular quality of beauty he describes consorts with the beauty of *Salomé*. "Something must come into my work, of fuller harmony of words perhaps, of richer cadences, of more curious color-effects, of simpler architectural-order"; "a deeper note, one of greater unity of passion, and directness of impulse" (489-90). Pearson remarks that during the prison years Wilde sketched in his head the action of two plays like *Salomé*, one about Pharaoh and the other about Ahab and Jezebel, and that later he often told the tales in conversation; but in the long letter to Douglas the subject of the new play is Christ, and the play has high seriousness that there is no evidence for in these two other plays.

The long letter itself is devoted in its first part to the most bitter denunciation of Douglas for having ruined Wilde, and ruined a great artist. Douglas's selfishness and his shallowness, his lack of imagination, are the key terms of the indictment. Then Wilde admits that there is nothing to do but to forgive Douglas and to take upon himself the full blame for his ruin. He sees that he himself turned the good things of his life to evil, and that now he must turn evil into good. He will find personal and artistic salvation in Christ-like love. Pearson in his biography discusses the letter chiefly to say that Douglas emerges in it as Judas, and he discounts the letter as a piece of melodramatic anguish inspired by Robert Ross's malice against Douglas—Ross succeeding for a time in poisoning Wilde's mind against Douglas, and the letter resulting. But for all its defects the letter is more substantial than Pearson allows it to be. The following account concerns the latter half of the letter, and occasionally picks up Wilde's language.

His new art, Wilde says, will deal with sorrow, for sorrow is the supreme emotion, and suffering is the secret of life. It was once the case that happiness was his natural condition; and though he told himself that he wanted to explore every part of the garden of life, he shunned the unhappy side. He saw suffering, and thought that only a heartless deity and heartless men could allow it. He was wrong, and now he sees that suffering is the condition in which one learns humility and thence love. In his own suffering, in his own humiliation, he has learned humility and love. But he cannot construct his new art out of the immediate circumstances of his suffering, and he turns to Christ as the great example.

Christ's life, he says, is a greater tragedy than the Greek tragedies, greater in its pity and terror, and it shows that Aristotle was wrong in saying that the hero of great tragedy could not be a blameless man. The supreme tragic circumstance is the last act of Christ's passion, with its betrayal, its supper, its loneliness, its sorrow, its submission, its crucifixion. But before the last act—so united is sorrow with beauty—Christ's life is an idyll. The wonderful shepherd performs miracles that bring peace and love to men out of the pain and darkness of their lives. In every aspect of his life, moreover, Christ is the supreme individualist, romanticist, and artist. The humility that Christ exhibits is not self-abnegation but self-realization on the path to perfection. Christ's concern is the development of the soul of man, and the imaginative sympathy that derives from his humility is the secret of all creativity. Imagination and love are one: they are what Douglas lacks and must acquire; they are the guide henceforth for Wilde in life and art.

It is easy enough to disparage the letter. Wilde has lost his sense of humor in it, and his discussion of Christ as man and artist shows more rhetorical excess than sustained thought. (For the sake of irony it might be noted that the description of Christ looks more like Douglas than Wilde, and one recalls that in a letter to Douglas just before going to prison, Wilde said that he thought of him "as a golden-haired boy with Christ's own heart" [397].) Moreover, everything that the letter looks forward to came to naught. Wilde sees in the letter that he has much to do artistically and that literary expression is necessary for him. He longs for the simple life, the sea, the sun, nature; he will be content in himself. He will meet Douglas in sorrow and humility, to teach him about sorrow and beauty. He faces a supreme task, in which religion, morality, and reason cannot help, of absorbing and accepting all that he has done and all that has been done to him, of repossessing and realizing himself, of climbing steeper hills and passing through darker valleys than he has yet faced. How sadly and excusably these intentions crashed is indicated in a letter to Ross of 16 November 1897.

> I cannot live alone, and Bosie is the only one of my friends who is either able or willing to give me his companionship.... It seemed to me to be the only gate to any life. (673)

But genius surprises us, and why should not Wilde have written his play about Christ? He had surprised us once before, though we hardly knew it—writing that loveliest of celebrations of heterosexual love in the midst of the corruption that his homosexuality entailed. Now with his life in ruins he might have contemplated good and evil with greater artistic seriousness than before, and elaborated more profoundly the polarities of *Salomé*, of *The Picture of Dorian Gray*, of Goring at his best against Illingworth at his best, and of much else. With his command of colorful cadence, with his dramatic skills, he might have created from dreadful experience figures more impressive than Salomé, Herod, and Jokanaan—perhaps shadowy still, but owning a heightened reality of emblematic truth. No doubt the play would have tended more toward melodrama than toward high tragedy, and its characterization of Christ would have narrowly escaped seeming that of a pretty young man of artistic temperament. No doubt some critics would have been mightily offended. The rest of us, though, would have been glad that the great artist had not been destroyed either by himself or by society.

III Personal Sketches

16 Where Arnold Bennett Went Wrong

IT IS TOLD of Arnold Bennett that in his dying moment he imagined he was at a hotel and called for his hotel bill. Such a story would do for Balzac too, and would never do for someone like Goethe. It is apparently untrue. What is true (I think) is that Bennett's last journal entry concludes with the sum that he tipped a waiter. So anyone who dislikes Bennett has his choice of a true or an untrue story for his symbol.

When I first began to read Bennett seriously, I saw him as the critics wanted me to see him; for I was a graduate student in English literature, and I read the critics first, and then read Bennett, and everything they said was fact. Admittedly my literary politics at the time prepared the way. I knew that D. H. Lawrence was God; or if not Lawrence, then Joyce. I knew that realism was a low grade of art, and that a man whose career had taken him from the industrial Midlands to the Savoy had gone from bad to worse.

Four years earlier I had read *Imperial Palace* in an army library, with only the vaguest idea who Arnold Bennett was. I thought it was full of the savor of life; I thought it was gay, wise, and sensuous; I read it avidly. Four years later the critics told me it was an "epic of dullness," and they were right. Well, the terrible thing is that I stayed with Bennett long enough to think they were wrong. I blinded myself to his defects, as a scholar must who gives several years of his life to an author. It took a recent trip to the Potteries for me to realize again that Bennett had indeed gone wrong, just like the critics.

I first went to the Potteries in the summer of 1958. By that time I was living intimately with Constance and Sophia Baines and Edwin Clayhanger. I knew what the houses and streets looked like—mean, higgledy-piggledy, smoke-laden. I had even seen photographs. So when I came to St. John's Square, Burslem, it was like coming home. I looked across the square just as Sophia looked across it when she came home after the long lonely years abroad, and I thought how pitifully small it was and how terrifying the passage of years. A great novel, this, that seizes the details of life, and composes them into a scene that shows us life's essence. Or one essence. Bennett himself lived the first twenty-one years of his life in the district without composing the scene. He had to go away to London and come back when a friend of the family died before he began to see it:

> During this week... when I have been traversing the district after dark, the grim and original beauty of certain aspects of the Potteries... has fully revealed itself for the first time.... It is *not* beautiful in detail, but the smoke transforms its ugliness into a beauty transcending the work of architects and of time...; it thrills and reverberates with the romance... of our fight against nature, of the gradual taming of the earth's secret forces. And surrounding the town on every side are the long straight smoke and steam wreaths, the dull red flames, and all the visible evidences of the immense secular struggle for existence.

Most of the novels of the next fifteen years try to render the scene. When Bennett turned from the Potteries to portray modern London and Paris, he did so with the same eye.

Of course I got filthy dirty in the Potteries. During the day I traipsed around identifying the places where Dick Povey had gone downhill on the boneshaker and Denry Machin and Ruth Erp had crashed into the canal, and at night I came back to my hotel (where Charles Fearns of *Whom God Hath Joined* had seduced his housekeeper) and washed the soot off. In *The Old Wives' Tale* the Baines shop yields to the Povey shop which yields to the Midland Clothiers Company, all within the space of forty-five years; but I visited shops that looked as though they hadn't yielded to anything except dirt in the last fifty-eight years. What an incredible town, I said to myself, trying unsuccessfully to flush the toilet at the hotel. "I'm going to get out of this," Bennett told a friend when he was young. Years later he passed by the district on his way from Manchester to London, and "the sight... gave me a shudder." Filled with the romance of the Potteries, I myself returned thankfully to London. Bennett had taken me in too.

In thinking about how Bennett went wrong, I used to pay especial attention to his many gifts. Eugene Goossens said that he knew more about music than any English author except Shaw. Someone else could have said similar things about his knowledge of architecture, painting, English politics, literature. H. G. Wells told him he had "the best mind in Europe (in many respects)," and though Wells was a friend and had gone wrong himself, I was inclined to believe it. In thirty-five years he produced thirty-five novels, twenty plays, a hundred and fifty short stories, a few thousand articles, and upwards of a hundred thousand letters. Admitting it all to be undistinguished, the display of energy was extraordinary, and the man found time to paint, make music, and go to concerts. A short while before he began to write *The Old Wives' Tale* he took up the hobby of calligraphy, and he decided to write the novel itself in an elegant script. In eight months he produced two hundred thousand elegant words. They comprise what may be the handsomest-least-corrected-most-quickly-produced manuscript of a long novel in existence.

Against his gifts of mind and person, though, I weighed certain other things, and the other things began to loom so large that I wondered how Bennett managed to go right at all. He came of an undistinguished family and grew up in an undistinguished town. Writing of that undistinguished young man of the Potteries, Edwin Clayhanger, he says:

> In that head of his a flame burnt that was like an altar-fire, a miraculous and beautiful phenomenon, than which nothing is more miraculous nor more beautiful over the whole earth. Whence had it suddenly sprung, that flame?... There is little to encourage it. The very architecture of the streets shows that environment has done naught for it: ragged brickwork, walls finished anyhow with saggers and slag; narrow uneven alleys leading to higgledy-piggledy workshops....

How could Bennett escape what Edwin Clayhanger failed to escape? He got out of the Potteries. But where did he go? He became a clerk in a law office in London for four years, and turned from that to other literary hackwork. Some of his writing he regarded with loathing. *The Old Wives' Tale* itself came seven years after the ten years of office drudgery. It was immediately preceded by the writing of two potboilers and was interrupted for another. Moreover, Bennett had just contracted a disastrous marriage, and may already have been feeling its ravages. The only part of the enterprise that seems to have had dignity was the calligraphy. He must have taken it up in desperation.

So doubt entered my mind. Perhaps Bennett hadn't gone wrong. He may not have been the greatest novelist of the twentieth century, but given what he had to contend with, he did well enough. Not that he was a Titan overcoming adversity, any more than he was a Titan living above the world. Not that he was a Kafkaesque figure, whose genius was in his aches and pains. But an unusually clever and good man, who managed to write some unusually clever and good books. It doesn't always happen.

Eight years later I went to the Potteries again. Charles Fearns's house was gone, and a petrol station stood in its place. The air was cleaner. Outside the City Museum was a sculpture of a miner, done in white stone and looking like a woman. (That must be a piece of irony, I thought.) I went up Mow Cop and looked across green plains to the Welsh Hills, and across other plains to where the Jodrell Bank telescope was sitting on its side. Then I walked along the back streets of Burslem by myself. A few of the old potbanks remained with their bottle-shaped ovens; and I imagined the town a hundred years earlier, a panorama of houses and bottles. The bottles rose a story or more above the houses, and they had graceful curves that complemented the square masses of houses. The old brick was lovely too, soft black and brown and red. I walked along sooty alleys between the backs of houses, where there was no grass, but cobblestones, walls, and sheds. The architectural masses and angularities had great weight and softness, great variety and unity. The scene was beautiful, and a hundred years ago, with the bottle ovens everywhere, it must have been more beautiful. Then it was not a street here and there, uninvaded by petrol stations and plastic shop fronts, but a whole town, and six towns. I suppose that in the middle of the nineteenth century the Potteries must have been uniquely beautiful. "Yes," a pottery manufacturer said to me later, "the place is getting cleaner and uglier every day."

Bennett failed to see this beauty. He had to have the Potteries in the blur of industrial history. When he looked closely, he allowed only two or three buildings in the whole place to pass the test of beauty. One of them was Hill Top Pottery, an elegant Georgian building. In *Clayhanger* Osmond Orgreave shows the building to Edwin, and provides the occasion for Edwin's spirit to burn most brightly. Bennett thought that he himself had more esthetic sense than Edwin, and got out of the Potteries, and I decided while I walked the back streets of Burslem that this was where Bennett went wrong.

Whenever I think of Bennett's mind as a means of intelligence and perception, divorced from soul and character, I see it as a fine mechanism. In an essay on his religious experience, he remarked upon his awareness of a separation between soul and mind, and saw the former giving orders that the latter ought to carry out like clockwork (in a well regulated person). He was a man who plotted the course of his day, laid out the structures of his novels, counted every word he wrote, made his home in an elegant Georgian house. Such a mind, were it free to choose the form of art most congenial to it, might choose eighteenth-century music or architecture—assuredly not realistic fiction.

But the mind was not free. The man was born in a country whose particular genius is literature and drama, those most civilized arts, which forbid the mind to meditate in a void, but set it the task of seeing life and creating beauty out of almost intractable materials, and offer the reward of the richest and most diverse expression of human existence. Furthermore, the man was born in an age whose esthetic creed put severe limitations upon formalizing capacities. His soul and character were English ("I am an Englishman and become daily more English," he said during his sojourn in France), and he set himself the task of seeing life in the literary mode of realism. Thus the confusion. His mind drove him away from the Potteries because it could not find there a sort of beauty congruent with itself; and his soul and character brought him back to create another sort of beauty. How much greater a writer he might have been had he been born alongside Alexander Pope; how much greater if he had forced himself to stay in the Potteries.

But take him as he is, and more and more I am conscious of his unrealistic side: his orderliness, wit, reserve, and controlled energy. I think of some of the delightful passages in *The Old Wives' Tale*. The pious John Baines offers the Reverend Mr. Murley a new suit of clothes. "Mr. Murley, who had a genuine medieval passion for souls, and who spent his money and health freely in gratifying the passion, had accepted the offer strictly on behalf of Christ, and had carefully explained to Mr. Povey Christ's use for multifarious pockets." Then there is Archibald Jones, celebrated religious intellectual, whose Christian name is "a luscious, resounding mouthful for admirers." He has a love affair with a dessicated spinster. "It must be a union of intellects! He had been impressed by hers, and she by his, and then their intellects had kissed. Within a week fifty thousand women in forty counties had pictured to themselves this osculation of intellects, and shrugged their shoulders, and decided once more that men were incomprehensible." I could go on for pages, as Bennett does, never faltering.

I think too, of some of his plays, which are usually seen as the mistakes of a man whose mode was the realistic novel. They are; and what gay and wise mistakes! Not the realistic or pseudo-realistic plays such as *Cupid and Commonsense* and *Milestones*, which tell the same tale as the novels and with less success, but *What the Public Wants* and *The Honeymoon*. The latter plays make a nod to realism but are mainly comedies of morals and manners, in the tradition of the well-made play. In *The Honeymoon* Cedric Haslam and Flora Lloyd have just gone from their marriage ceremony to a seaside hotel in Essex. The year is 1911. He is a famous aviator, and she is a famous beauty, and they have ahead of them a month in which to celebrate their union. But he reads in the evening paper that a German aviator is on his way to England to be the first man to fly over Snowdon. No, he tells Flora, he doesn't care about the ten thousand pounds prize money that is being offered to the first man over Snowdon. It's for the honor of Great Britain, for his own honor; and the honeymoon will have to be postponed.

Cedric. Now just listen to me, Fluff. I'm really thinking at least as much of you as of myself. This affair is bound to have an influence on my career.
Flora. And what about its influence on mine?
Cedric. Same thing. I suppose our interests are identical.
Flora. My poor simple boy, do you really believe that?
Cedric. Well, dash it, aren't you my wife?
Flora. So far as I'm concerned, it would be more correct to say that you're my husband. In fact you've got a career as my husband.
Cedric (*anxious to be fair*). Certainly. And you as my wife. But...
Flora. One second, dearest. You're unique as an aviator, aren't you?
Cedric (*conventionally modest*). Oh... well...
Flora. Now. Man to man. Give your modesty a rest. Really don't you consider you've proved yourself unique in your line?
Cedric (*hesitatingly, chivalrously*). I suppose I'm just about as unique in my line as you are in yours, my dear.
Flora. Now that's very nice of you.
Cedric. Not at all.
Flora. Yes, it is, because it's exactly what I wanted you to say. You've often said that I'm unique, and I just wanted you to say it again at this identical particular instant.... Now look here, Cedric, don't you think it would be a pity to stop this creature, who is so unique in her line, from giving a full exhibition of her unique powers at a unique moment; at the very height of

her career. You know, she'll never have another opportunity like this of proving that she really is unique in her line.

Cedric. What do you call her line? Let's be clear.

Flora (*quietly, off-handedly, after a pause*). To charm. Merely that.

Cedric. By God! She can do that. But (*winningly, but half to himself*), I hardly know how to put it.

Flora. I think you do, dearest; but you're so nice, you don't like to. You wanted to make a comparison between the importance of your line and the importance of mine. I admit all that. I'm quite humble. I fully admit that if Hyde Park were full of aviators and Battersea Park were full of charming young women, rather pretty and ...er...chic...(*gesture to show off her frock*)...I fully admit that not a man among you would ever *dream*...of crossing the river. I fully admit that if every aviator in Europe gave up business tomorrow the entire world would go into mourning, whereas if all the charming women retired from business they'd never be missed. Still...

Cedric (appreciative). You're a witty girl...

Flora. We're both rather witty, aren't we, at times?

Cedric. But the fact is I wasn't going to make any comparison at all between our respective lines. I was only going to point out that you can keep on being charming all the time. You're always charming; you're always doing *your* line. Whereas for my line I have to choose times and seasons...or rather I don't choose 'em, they're chosen for me, as, for instance, just now. Wherever we are, honeymoon or no honeymoon, you're...well, you're giving an exhibition flight.

Flora. Now, Cedric, your good nature's getting the better of your sincerity. I'm *not* always charming. And I don't *want* to be always charming. Who would? As for exhibition flights, you've never seen me give one. You think you have, but what you've seen up to now is nothing. I don't mind telling you that I had arranged a rather sensational exhibition flight for the next month. It would last just thirty-one days. I don't mind telling you that I've thought a good deal about it, and made all my elaborate preparations. It really would be a pity to interfere with it. And you know it can't be postponed. I don't choose time and season any more than you do....

Cedric (a little coldly). Say no more, Snowdon is chucked. Of course, my position is impossible. You have only to insist.

Flora (*losing her self-control*). Insist? *Insist* that you neglect an aeroplane so that you can stay with me? My dear boy, I'm incapable of taking such a mean advantage of an aeroplane. An aeroplane can't insist. And I can assure you I shan't.

At this juncture Cedric's family arrive at the hotel to inform the pair that they have been married by a bogus curate. The plot takes its conventional turn, and the action proceeds apace, with undiminished verve. It is a public sort of play, with certain true emotions artificially refined for appearance at a hotel. And it makes me think that I would be satisfied if Bennett had called for his hotel bill with his last breath. Such a gesture would have shown his particular sense of life: his detachment, irony, wit.

17 Dirty Words, Clean Poetry

MANY YEARS AGO when I was a new critic I had to teach Dryden's *Mac Flecknoe*, and I discovered in the poem a piece of humor that I supposed no one had seen before—not since Dryden had put it there three hundred years earlier. In the last four lines of the poem Flecknoe is surrendering his reign to his son and heir:

> Sinking he left his Drugget robe behind,
> Borne upwards by a subterranean wind.
> The Mantle fell to the young prophet's part,
> With double portion of his Father's art.

Others before me would have seen that the subterranean wind is the divine afflatus of the likes of Flecknoe, and not only the word "behind" but allusions earlier in the poem make it obvious:

> From dusty shops neglected Authors come,
> Martyrs of Pies and Reliques of the Bum.
> Much *Heywood, Shirley, Ogleby* there lay,
> But loads of *Sh*-- almost choakt the way.

My unique discovery was to see that Dryden names the wind. In the last two lines of the poem the *f*-sounds in "fell," "prophet," and "father" combine with "art" in both lines to give "fart."

Of course the discovery was a negligible matter, but it illustrated the new critical principle that if you stare at a poem long enough you will see something no one has seen before. Ever since that time I have told my students about it, and last year I had the pleasure of telling a young Renaissance-Restoration friend and seeing him march off to tell his students too. This is called the advancement of learning, and the upshot of it was that recently my young friend came back to me with a discovery of his own. He had been teaching Donne, and he suddenly saw that "sucked on country pleasures" in "The Good Morrow" has a rude meaning. Think of Hamlet's "country matters," he said. I thought. Did I agree? Good God, no, I said; the sense and tone of the poem are against it—Donne's not talking about gross physical desire; the reference of "sucked' is to "weaned" in the preceding line and to "childishly" at the end of its own line; the image is playful, rough; it serves the contrasting poignancy of the succeeding lines:

> If ever any beauty I did see
> Which I desired, and got, 'twas but a dream of thee.

But my young friend was not to be deprived of his discovery, and I myself was to blame for having encouraged it with *Mac Flecknoe*. We stood there arguing, and I mentioned "A Valediction Forbidding Mourning" as a clearer case. In the image of the compass, Donne's wife is the "fixed foot" that "leans and harkens" after Donne the traveling foot, and she "grows erect as that comes home." If, I said, you introduce the sexual meaning of "erect," the image becomes ludicrous—the erection being on the wrong foot: the poem is about spiritual love, and it's the two souls that are the compass, not the fleshly man and wife. But no, he liked the sexual meaning here too. At this juncture another Renaissance expert (female) came along, and we put the matter to her because she and we were frank and mature people; and she said she thought the notion of erection was relevant to the poem in a loose way, and was intended by Donne. I thereupon shut up. I was not going to ask her about "The Good Morrow." After she left, my young friend admitted that in spite of his maturity he himself felt some constraint. But suppose I had asked her. God knows she would have responded in a frank, mature, and absurd way.

Since then I have been in a quandary. Was my discovery about *Mac Flecknoe* the folly of youth? Is my horror about "The Good Morrow" the reaction of age? If Jack Donne was a sexy man, mustn't he—or must he?—think of cunt every time he says country? Have I stumbled upon a literary problem to which there has hitherto been no name but which my wife suggests may be given a name drawn from painting—inadvertent imagery?

I do realize that the issue has floated across my mind many times before. I remember John Unterecker telling me years ago (*Reader's Guide to Yeats*) that in "Leda and the Swan" the word "laid" ("And how can body, laid in that white rush") has its usual sexual meaning, for the scene is explicitly sexual. I remember hearing that Eugene Field, sentimental writer about little toy soldiers, was actually a dirty old man whose collected dirty works are held at Harvard. I remember (rather recently) the editors of *The Oxford Anthology of English Literature* telling me that Tennyson "fell in love" with Arthur Hallam at Cambridge and that both *In Memoriam* and *The Wasteland* are "poems of repressed homosexual passion," and I knew beforehand (from a source I cannot recall) that the chief dirty word excised by Tennyson from *In Memoriam* is "his" in section 95, in which Tennyson describes his sense of union with the dead Hallam upon reading the volume of Hallam's letters. Tennyson substitutes "this" for "his" so that neither he himself nor his reader will think a dirty thought:

> And all at once it seemed at last
> The living soul was flashed on mine,
>
> And mine in this was wound, and whirled
> About empyreal heights of thought....

Most especially I remember being given a copy of *Playboy* in which appeared several decorous drawings of two women nibbling at each other sexually, in illustration of an article on the repressed Victorian sexuality of Christina Rossetti in *Goblin Market*. The chief relevant passage of the poem goes thus:

> She cried "Laura" up the garden,
> "Did you miss me?
> Come and kiss me.
> Never mind my bruises,
> Hug me, kiss me, suck my juices."

Such memories! And surely it is amusing to see the low-minded editors of *Playboy* thinking the same sorts of thoughts as the high-minded editors of *The Oxford Anthology of English Literature*. They all could trade jobs, and no one would know the difference. Long years ago, before I became a new critic, any sensible person would have known what to do with the likes of *Playboy* (what Dryden did with Shadwell); but in *PMLA* in 1958 Lona Mosk Packer saw that the goblin feast in Christina Rossetti's poem was "obviously an invitation to erotic pleasure," and about 1968 the British Musuem began subscribing to *Playboy*, and today you and I and the editors of all the sex magazines have joined hands in the advancement of learning about our bodies and souls.

Isn't it a quandary? Yes, it is. And I have found the way out by reconsidering a series of exchanges in the *Times Literary Supplement* from 1974. The series began with an article on Shakespeare's sonnets by John Bayley in which it was argued that the "man right fair" of the later sonnets was not the Earl of Southampton but Shakespeare's penis. A new and surprising interpretation it might seem, and Bayley admitted he had never met with it before; and yet the Earl of Southampton himself was doubtless acquainted with it, said Bayley, and must have enjoyed the droll image of Shakespeare picking up venereal disease from the dark lady: the man right fair, the good angel of sonnet 144, is in the bad angel's hell (cant term for pudendum), and may be turned fiend¡i.e., infected. To the reader of Bayley's article, the real surprise ought to have been that a meaning so obvious to Southampton could have got lost so thoroughly for four hundred years.

Two weeks later Martin Green wrote in to applaud Bayley's general argument and to suggest that it was overextended. If the man right fair was Shakespeare's penis, how could Shakespeare only guess that it was in the dark lady's vagina ("I guess one angel in another's hell")? The solution for Green was not to be too single-minded in assigning meanings. Shakespeare's language is "impregnated with phallic imagery," and *cherchez la verge*; but multiple meaning is everything and everywhere, and please read my forthcoming book entitled *The Labyrinth of Shakespeare's Sonnets* in which I reveal all. In due course Bayley made a gracious reply to Green, and suggested that Green himself might be carrying things a bit far in believing Shakespeare to be obsessed with phallic imagery. In the main, he and Green were in agreement: Shakespeare is the master of quibble and pun and ambiguity. In a still later letter Bayley capped his argument with a rhetorical question: "Can we imagine *Shakespeare* punning inadvertently?"

And there is the first large issue of the exchanges: the issue of inadvertence. Can we believe that the chief wizard of words ever fails to make conscious use of the multiple meanings he knows and invents for every word? Can we believe that a lesser wizard such as Donne ever fails when the word lies within his special province of sex? Can we believe that Keats, who according to Christopher Ricks had a masterly understanding of embarrassment (*Keats and Embarrassment*) is ever inadvertently embarrassing? Answer yes to the last question if your name is John Bayley (who argues thus in *The Uses of Division*). The issue of inadvertent imagery is the old problem of intentional fallacy in special costume. Can a great artist ever intend less than we discover in him? Can he want to? If he wants to, can his readers' fuller meanings be denied? Can his readers be smarter than he is?

The other issue developing from Bayley's article was itself a piece of inadvertence. Along with Martin Green's response there appeared a letter from John Sparrow, who was inspired by Bayley's efforts to undertake similar scrutiny of Milton's sonnet "When I Consider How My Light Is spent." Sparrow offered chronological evidence to show that the poem could not concern either Milton's blindness or his long deferred epic, and he adduced other evidence to suggest that it instead concerned the thwarting of Milton's procreative powers in the disastrous first months of his first marriage and in the enforced celibacy after his first wife's death. The poem ends in sexual stoicism: "They also serve who only stand and wait." Sparrow's discussion was an excellent piece of mockery, but it was not taken to be such by some readers, who doubtless feeling insult added to injury chose to attack him rather than Bayley. In the following weeks Alistair Smart successfully reestablished the conventional reading of the poem, and David Knowles and Helen Gardner offered supporting evidence. Knowles suspected that Sparrow was jesting, and Helen Gardner was certain. What Helen Gardner deplored was that Sparrow should choose so noble a poem to make his jest with. Might he not inadvertently debase its meaning among young people, who find so much else debased about them?

And there is our second issue: what should be our strategy of defense against the sexologists of literature? Polite and high-minded silence a la Helen Gardner, or ridicule a la John Sparrow? Doubtless both strategies, and other strategies as well. I have in mind that the next time I pick up a scholarly edition of Thomas Campion's works and read,

> I care not for these ladies
> That must be wooed and prayed
> Give me kind Amaryllis
> The wanton country maid,

and the editor informs me that "country" makes "the common obscene pun (see *Hamlet*, III, ii, 123), a pun reinforced by the alliteration on c and the assonance of words in l. 9" ("But when we come where comfort is")—why when that happens I am going to ask God's forgiveness for having thought about alliteration in *Mac Flecknoe*, and then I am going to write a letter to that editor and say: "Dear Sir, You have a vulgar, dirty mind; go edit a sex magazine for the rest of your life." But also I am going to prepare myself beforehand for such people. The real service that John Sparrow performed was to get in there ahead of the sexologists and so prevent them from doing a job on Milton. Thus I know already that "The Lady of Shalott" concerns the feminine predicament in the exact sense of menstrual helplessness: "'The curse is come upon me,' cried | The Lady of Shalott." (Some thought of Tennyson the transvestite will help here; see *In Memoriam*, section 60, in which he describes himself as a girl.) I also know that prim Miss Austen enjoys the occasional playful innuendo: "In winter his private balls were numerous enough for any young lady who was not suffering under the insatiable appetite of fifteen" (*Sense and Sensibility*). I also know—everyone knows—about Housman:

> Ere the wholesome flesh decay,
> And the willing nerve be numb,
> And the lips lack breath to say,
> "No, my lad, I cannot come."

Yes, of course, the best way out of the quandary is to get in there first with the sexual meaning. Laugh the sexologists away with the breeze. To this happy result I recommend a little anthology by Edward Gathorne-Hardy entitled *An Adult's Garden of Bloomers*, published by the Bodley Head in 1966. It offers several dozen illustrations of sexual imagery, including those by Tennyson, Austen, and Housman I have just given. I conclude with a last example, drawn from the master (Henry James himself), who in his supreme consciousness of his craft provided Gathorne-Hardy with more passages than anyone else: "'Oh, I can't explain!' cried Roderick impatiently, returning to his work. 'I've only one way of expressing my deepest feelings—it's this.' And he swung his tool."

18 Thomas Hardy among the Americans

PERHAPS IF YOU ARE ENGLISH you know all about these things, and don't care, and perhaps if you are American you have to learn about them diligently, and don't care either. The first time I passed the signpost to Stinsford on the A35 out of Dorchester I said to myself, "Isn't that where Hardy lived?" and sped on my way. I had been reading Hardy for forty years, but reading his novels and poems rather than his life, and knowing him in that abstract way so inevitable and appropriate to the foreigner. Had I known certainly that Stinsford was the place where his heart was buried, I would have turned off the road a quarter of a mile to pay my respects along with the other foreigners. Now, two years later, I have come back to redeem my carelessness. I have brought with me a half dozen American students, and for six weeks we are doing Thomas Hardy to a fare-thee-well. It is very affecting.

Imagine the Sunday afternoon pouring with rain. Young Dick Dewy has been to a funeral, and he walks home to Upper Mellstock by way of Lower Mellstock so that he might see Fancy Day. He does see her, but she won't let him into the house (the schoolhouse), and she will not lean out the window for him to give her a kiss because she would get her hair wet. The window is too high for him to reach up to kiss her, so she puts her hand down to him. Then Dick goes off in the rain again, and handsome Mr. Maybold comes into view from the direction of Mellstock Church. When my students and I stood in front of the schoolhouse—now a private dwelling but with the schoolbell still in place—we were able to see that *Under the Greenwood Tree* was a literal translation from life. "Which window," cried the teacher, "must have been the window too high except for a hand down from it?" "That window!" cried the students, getting their A's with ease.

Truth to tell, people have been going the rounds of the novels for eighty years, and any number of guides have been published to help them. *Under the Greenwood Tree* is especially well served by a pamphlet by M.R. Skilling, available from the Thomas Hardy Society. Happily, the scenes of *Under the Greenwood Tree* are, of all the novels, the scenes that survive least damaged, least changed by time. They are the scenes most intimately connected with

Hardy's life. Mellstock Church is Stinsford Church, and Tranter Dewy's cottage in Upper Mellstock is Hardy's home in Higher Bockhampton, and Fancy Day's schoolhouse in Lower Mellstock is the schoolhouse in Lower Bockhampton to which Hardy walked as a frail young boy of eight. If you love *Under the Greenwood Tree* for its gay and sweet celebration of rural Dorset life in the 1840s, you cannot help being touched, being amazed, that you can walk back into that time. Scene by scene the novel is there before you, and you forget the car and the tarmac and all the other visual ugliness that modern England has inflicted upon itself, and you forget as well all the other aches of modernity, and you see the world that Hardy lived in, cared for, and helped to keep in mind. Regrettably, my students did not like *Under the Greenwood Tree*. They found it boring, and they told me Fancy Day was an unconscionable young woman like Scarlett O'Hara. So they didn't feel my emotions, and I was glad enough to pack them into the car again and take them back to our hotel in Dorchester.

After *Under the Greenwood Tree*, *The Mayor of Casterbridge* is the novel whose scenes one can visit most successfully, and then *The Return of the Native*. We stood on Rainbarrow, a half mile above Hardy's cottage, and surveyed the Frome Valley from Blooms-End past the Quiet Woman to Shadwater Weir. Perhaps we could have seen as far as Alderworth (where Clym and Eustacia lived) had not the Forestry Commission replaced heath with plantations of tall pine. In the novel Hardy tells us that the heath is eternal: it was there before the Romans, and it will resist modern cultivation. But the Dorset County Museum tells us that the heath was man-made (rising from the destruction of great forests) and is fast being man-destroyed. Egdon Heath, the chief character of the novel, is gone, and what remains are landmarks in and around it. Rainbarrow is most notable. Eustacia stood there as Queen of the Night. Hardy stood there. We stand there. Anglo-Saxons, Romans, and true Britons stood there. On Rainbarrow literature and life and cultures coalesce. Eustacia Vye can't stand on Rainbarrow alone. Neither can Thomas Hardy. Romans come along to destroy things, then Forestry Commissions, then Americans. Nostalgia, pillage, and resignation go hand in hand.

Back at the hotel my students are enjoying themselves. They put their feet up on the coffee table in the lounge. They even put their feet up where their heads belong (heads and upper backs on the floor). They play football in one of their rooms. When the weather clears they climb out onto the roof to sun themselves. The manager protests, I protest, and they go their merry way. I come upon them several times watching American films on television. "Is this what you came to England for?" Not that it follows that such films are for English eyes alone. What can they know of English television who only English programs know?

It seems possible to me that my students will make themselves generally objectionable, and I say to myself, so be it. But I am wrong. They find friends among the hotel staff, one or another of whom wants to visit Disneyland. And up on the High Street they are welcome customers at the Royal Oak pub. On our very first evening in Dorchester we ate supper at the Royal Oak, and presently found ourselves listening to an English entertainer sing "American Pie" in an American accent. Englishmen at the bar joined in, my students joined in, and I joined in. My students were ten years old when the song was written, and I alone of all the people at the Royal Oak knew its references intimately. I was there, in Kingston, Rhode Island, the day the music died—the day John Kennedy was shot. I had delivered papers and driven Chevies in years before, and I had stood in high school gyms and watched girls and boys kick off their shoes to dance. What is more, I knew that it was tawdry music—that the America I grew up in did not match the nostalgia I felt for it. The odd fact of my life is that I lived in England for several years, liking English civilization more than my own. When I went back home to a job in 1972 I heard "American Pie" for the first time, and was strangely overcome by remembrance of my past. Why should I imagine—as I do—that rural Dorset of the 1840s is more deserving of remembrance? Perhaps Hardy plays a trick on all of us who love his novel.

The great night at the Royal Oak was luckily a night that I missed—Cowboy night. My students went in their jeans, expecting merely a sing-along, and found the English customers fitted out in cowboy boots, ten-gallon hats, and cap-firing six-shooters, with much fringe and studwork. The music was general American rather than cowboy, and the English customers knew the words better than my students (so the students said). The evening ended late with a shoot-out, in the bars and then on the deserted streets of the ancient Roman city.

During these six weeks I have gone to Hardy's cottage three times. The first time was with my students, and we compared the cottage with Tranter Dewy's cottage, and we looked with some pleasure and some chagrin at the large ugly stone behind the cottage "erected to the memory of Thomas Hardy by some of his American admirers." The second time I went with one of my bright students of past years, and in front of us was a loud American who took pictures of everything, including the caretaker's cat. "Why do Americans have to act like that?" said my student. The third time I took my wife. We went upstairs to the bedroom where Hardy sat at a window to write *Under the Greenwood Tree*. It seemed to us like the right place for the imaginative life.

19 Visiting Robert Frost in England

IT IS ODD TO THINK of Robert Frost in England. In fact he sat in a suburban English garden without an apple tree or a birch tree or a wall to mend, and he wrote there those quintessentially American poems of his—"After Apple-Picking," "Birches," and "Mending Wall." He went to England in 1912, with wife and four children, and lived in a bungalow in Reynolds Road in Beaconsfield New Town for nineteen months, and did not like its suburban atmosphere, and left to live briefly in Gloucestershire. Before he returned home in 1915, he expressed an American thought about his English experience. "The fortunate monopolise too much here. The fortunate are very delightful people to meet, they afford so many of the virtues and graces. But one cannot help seeing the unfortunate.... I should want my children to grow up in America." Today there is an apple tree in the garden at the bungalow in Reynolds Road, and a Japanese professor recently took a photograph of it. Tomorrow there may be a Frost plaque at the door. But one's sense in visiting the place is that Frost made no mark on it, and it left no mark on him.

He himself returned to Reynolds Road in 1957 in the company of his biographer Lawrance Thompson, and he could not identify the bungalow. In 1912 the Road had made a long curve away from the high street, and subsequently the curve was extended into a loop. There also were—and had been—other bungalows along the Road like his: plain white stucco. If he remembered the red-osier dogwood trees that had lined one side of his garden, they seemed to be gone in 1957, hidden behind a house that was built when part of his garden was sold off. If he remembered the high laurel hedge that lined the other side of his garden, it was seemingly gone too, cut back so drastically at that time that perhaps he did not see it.

I myself went recently to Beaconsfield to find the bungalow, armed with a description of it from one of Frost's letters home in 1912. I stopped at the Beaconsfield Public Library first, for possible assistance. Happily enough, the Library was in Reynolds Road, but the people there could not identify the bungalow. They knew it was somewhere up the Road, and they offered me Thompson's biography for help, and also a map of Beaconsfield (1926) and a Kelley's Directory (1939). These were of no use. I read two histories of

Beaconsfield, and learned that Edmund Waller, Milton, Burke, Disraeli, and Chesterton lived or worked there, but not Robert Frost.

So I walked up the Road. I had one further piece of possibly useful information, namely that the bungalow was called "The Bungalow." In letters home Frost called it "the bung hole." I looked for names on the gates of several white stucco bungalows, but they all had numbers. I stopped a young man and asked him if he knew of "The Bungalow." He was an estate agent and had come to Beaconsfield a few months earlier, and he could not help, though he offered to let me look at maps in his office. I stopped a woman pushing a grocery cart, and she had lived in the Road for twenty-six years, and she could not help. I told her that the loop had once been a curve.

"The loop's always been here," she said.

"Not in 1912," I said. Then I came to the last bungalow, and saw the laurel hedge, now high again.

I wasn't absolutely certain, though, so I went up and rang the doorbell. No one answered. I went away and looked for other laurel hedges and for red-osier dogwood, and walked round the rest of the loop. I came back and rang the doorbell again in vain. Then, just as I was ready to give up and go back to West Sussex, a car drove in the driveway. "Of course it's where Robert Frost lived!" the woman said to me when she got out of the car, and she trotted round into the garden and fetched the owner of the bungalow, who had been sitting in the garden all the while. They brought out chairs and sat me down and fed me tea, and we talked about Robert Frost and about his friends among the Georgian poets and other literary things.

The owner bought the bungalow in 1957. She did not know until later that Frost had lived there. When he died in 1963, someone came knocking on the door and told her. She was not surprised, for from the first there seemed to be something special about the place. She then read everything she could about Frost, and she loved his poetry. She thought about putting up a plaque, and exhibiting the bungalow, with a recording of Frost reciting his poems. But her son did not want people trampling the flowers in the garden. She satisfied herself with occasional visitors.

In due course she and her friend took me through the bungalow. They showed me the side door through which the Frost family had first entered, the grate at which Frost had burned some of his poems, the electricity meter that had once sat in plain view in the sitting room. People were proud to have electricity in early days, they said. (But I wondered whether "The Bungalow" would have had electricity in 1912.) They also explained about the invisible dogwood and the low laurel hedge.

But where was Robert Frost? As an American myself, I thought that I ought to be able to smell him out in his English setting. I could not. The easy civility and liveliness of the conversation, the manners of the tea, the elaborateness of the garden (made by the owner herself) all seemed quintessentially English, and opposed to the quality of the American poet—gruff, untidy, homely, flat-voiced. He said after six months in Beaconsfield, "I never knew how much of a Yankee I was till I had been out of New Hampshire a few months." He was there only by not being there.

Eventually the three of us talked generally about America and England, and the owner of the bungalow said, "With all due respect, the Americans..."

Her friend, alarmed that English civility might be in jeopardy, put in, "Now you can't generalize about national characteristics."

"Of course you can," the owner said firmly to me, and added, "She's Irish, and the Irish are crazy."

"What about the Americans?" I said.

"With all due respect, the Americans aren't a literary people."

I thought she was right, in a certain English way, just as a German might be right in saying that the English are not a musical people (though a musical German friend tells me that the Germans are not really musical, in contrast to the Czechs). We talked about the matter, and I wondered whether some very clever person from Mars could confront an unlabeled bag of poems by Frost, Edward Thomas, and Thomas Hardy and sort out the nonliterary American ones from the literary English.

When Frost went to England in the summer of 1912 he was pretty much a failed poet, thirty-eight years old and without a book to his name. He knew no one in England, and he went without letters of introduction. Nevertheless he got himself acquainted with a considerable number of poets there, impressed them, influenced one of them notably (Edward Thomas), and found a publisher for his first two books. When he returned home early in 1915 he was on the verge of international fame. It seemed clear to me as I drank my tea that had he never left home he would have achieved the same fame in his same provincial voice. I thought of his little poem "The Pasture" that is characteristically placed at the head of collections of his poems. He apparently wrote it at Beaconsfield.

> I'm going out to clean the pasture spring;
> I'll only stop to rake the leaves away
> (And wait to watch the water clear, I may):
> I shan't be gone long.—You come too.
>
> I'm going out to fetch the little calf
> That's standing by the mother. It's so young
> It totters when she licks it with her tongue.
> I shan't be gone long... —You come too.

Viola Meynell, of the literary Meynell family, used the poem as the epigraph of her artful pastoral novel *Columbine* published in January 1915. So we apparently have a nonliterary person affecting literary persons without being affected himself.

Notes

1. Deeper Chaos and Larger Order: Freudian Science and Art

1. *The Standard Edition of the Complete Psychological Works of Sigmund Freud*, vol. 13 (London: Hogarth Press, 1953), 211, 213.
2. Ernest Jones, *The Life and Work of Sigmund Freud*, vol. 2 (New York: Basic Books, 1955), 365n. Jones quotes the German from a letter to Martha Freud of 6 September 1901.
3. Theodor Reik, *Surprise and the Psychoanalyst* (New York: E.P. Dutton, 1937), 29.
4. Sir Kenneth Clark, *Leonardo da Vinci* (Baltimore: Penguin Books, 1967), 20.
5. Simon O. Lesser, *Fiction and the Unconscious* (Chicago: University of Chicago Press, 1957), 14, 46, 125.
6. Louis Fraiberg, *Psychoanalysis and American Literary Criticism* (Detroit: Wayne State University Press, 1960), 91, 104.
7. Joseph Schillinger, *The Mathematical Basis of the Arts* (New York: Philosophical Library, 1948), 3.
8. Edmund Bergler, "On a Five-layer Structure in Sublimation," *Psychoanalytic Quarterly* 14 (1945): 81-82.
9. Isador H. Coriat, "Some Aspects of a Psychoanalytic Interpretation of Music," *Psychoanalytic Review* 32 (1945): 408; Heinz Kohut and Siegmund Levarie, "On the Enjoyment of Listening to Music," *Psychoanalytic Quarterly* 19 (1950): 64-87—a summary of their views.
10. William Arrowsmith, *Euripides*, vol. 5 (Chicago: Chicago University Press, 1959), 142.

2. Stopping by Robert Frost

1. William Rose Benét, "Wise Old Woodchuck," *Saturday Review of Literature* 14 (30 May 1936): 6; Lionel Trilling, "A Speech on Robert Frost: A Cultural Episode," *Partisan Review* 26 (1959): 451; Robert Langbaum, "The New Nature Poetry," *American Scholar* 28 (1959): 327; Yvor Winters, *The Function of Criticism* (Denver: Alan Swallow, 1957), 159-87; Hyatt H. Waggoner, *The Heel Of Elohim* (Norman: University of Oklahoma Press, 1950), 41; James M. Cox, "Robert Frost and the Edge of the Clearing," *Virginia Quarterly Review* 35 (1959): 78, 83.
2. Lawrance Thompson, *Fire and Ice* (New York: Henry Holt, 1942), Leonard Unger

and William Van O'Connor, *Poems for Study* (New York: Rinehart, 1953); John Ciardi, "Robert Frost: The Way to the Poem," *Saturday Review of Literature* 41 (12 April 1958): 13-15, 65-67. All quotations from Frost's poems come from *The Poetry of Robert Frost*, ed. Edward Connery Latham (New York: Holt, Rinehart and Winston, 1969).

3. Reginald L. Cook, "Frost on Frost: The Making of Poems," *American Literature* 27 (1956): 66.

4. *Selected Prose of Robert Frost*, ed. Hyde Cox and Edward Connery Latham (New York: Holt, Rinehart and Winston, 1966), 45, 26, 18.

5. Such suggestiveness is called natural symbolism by René Wellek and Austin Warren in *Theory of Literature* (New York: Harcourt, Brace, 1949), 194-95. They refer to "Stopping by Woods" to warn of the hazard of such symbolism to both poet and critic. Sleep, they say, naturally calls to mind death; and thus the poet must ask himself whether he wants to use this suggestiveness in his poem or whether, if he does not want to, he can avoid it; and by the same token the critic must be careful not to assume that the natural symbolic meaning is the actual symbolic meaning that the poet achieves, and he must decide whether there is any confusion between such meanings in the poem. That there may be a confusion of meanings in "Come In" need not detain us in the present discussion. If there is any, it is not, in the opinion of this critic, a significant confusion, since it does not damage the tone of the poem. In this respect, Frost employs with complete success the natural symbolic association of the stars with loneliness and isolation. Consider the similar confidence with which Keats, in "Bright Star," and Byron, in *Childe Harold*, rely upon the natural association in beginning two apostrophes to melancholy: "Bright star! would I were steadfast as thou art—| Not in lone splendour hung aloft the night" and "Ye stars! which are the poetry of heaven! |If in your bright leaves we would read the fate| Of men and empires..."

6. Amy Lowell, *Recognition of Robert Frost*, ed. Richard Thornton (New York: Holt, 1937), 48. For Coffin's opinion see *New Poetry of New England* (Baltimore: Johns Hopkins Press, 1938) 11-24.

7. Charles A. McLaughlin, "Two Views of Poetic Unity," *University of Kansas City Review* 22 (1956): 316, 313.

8. John Ciardi, "Letter to Letter-Writers," *Saturday Review of Literature* 41 (17 May 1958): 15.

9. Quoted in an untitled note by Cecilia Hennel Hendricks in *Explicator* 1 (1943): 58.

3. Keats's Foster-Child and the Problem of Criticism

1. Cleanth Brooks, *The Well Wrought Urn* (New York: Reynal & Hitchcock, 1947), 143; E.C. Pettet, *On the Poetry of Keats* (Cambridge: Cambridge University Press, 1957), 322; Earl Wasserman, *The Finer Tone* (Baltimore: Johns Hopkins Press, 1953), 16. All passages from Keats's poems are quoted from *The Poetical Works of John Keats*, ed. H.W. Garrod, 2nd ed. (Oxford: Clarendon Press, 1958).

2. Jacob Wigod, "Keats's Ideal in the 'Ode on a Grecian Urn,'" *PMLA* 72 (1957): 113n, 113n, 117n, 117n.

3. Leo Spitzer, "The 'Ode on a Grecian Urn,' or Content vs. Metagrammar," *Comparative Literature* 7 (1955): 206-8.

4. John Middleton Murry, *Keats* (New York: Minerva Press, 1968), 217-18; Werner William Beyer, *Keats and the Daemon King* (New York: Oxford University Press, 1947), 261-62; Wasserman, 49; David Perkins, *The Quest for Permanence* (Cambridge: Harvard University Press, 1969), 242.

5. *The Letters of John Keats*, ed. Hyder Edward Rollins, vol. 1 (Cambridge: Harvard University Press, 1958), 183-87.

6. *The Prose Works of William Wordsworth*, ed. W.J.B. Owen and Jane Worthington Smyser, vol. 1 (Oxford: Clarendon Press, 1974), 140; *The Complete Works of Percy Bysshe Shelley*, ed. Roger Ingpen and Walter E. Peck, vol. 7 (New York: Gordian Press, 1965), lll; *The Complete Prose Works of Matthew Arnold*, ed. R.H. Super, vol. 9 (Ann Arbor: University of Michigan Press, 1973), 213; *The Arnold Bennett Calendar* (London: Frank Palmer, 1911), 41.

7. Alvin Whitley, "The Message of the Grecian Urn," *Keats-Shelley Memorial Bulletin* 5 (1953): 3; Jack Stillinger, "Keats's Grecian Urn and the Evidence of Transcripts," *PMLA* 73 (1958): 447-48; Robert Berkelman, "Keats and the Urn," *South Atlantic Quarterly* 57 (1958), 354-58; Robert Adams, "*Trompe L'Oeil* in Shakespeare and Keats," *Sewanee Review* 61 (1953): 253; C.M. Bowra, *The Romantic Imagination* (Cambridge: Harvard University Press, 1949), Chapter 6.

4. Swinburne Corrupted

1. John S. Mayfield, *Swinburne's Boo* (Washington: Goetz, 1954), originally published in *English Miscellany* 4 (1953): 161-78, issued by the British Council in Rome; Edmund Gosse, *The Life of Algernon Charles Swinburne* (London: Macmillan, 1917); *The Swinburne Letters*, ed. Cecil Lang, vol. 1 (New Haven: Yale University Press, 1959), 67. All references to Swinburne's letters are to Lang's edition.

2. Cecil Lang, "Swinburne's Lost Love," *PMLA* 74 (1959): 124.

3. All quotations from Swinburne's poetry follow *The Poems of Algernon Charles Swinburne* (London: Chatto & Windus, 1904).

4. Jean Overton Fuller, *Swinburne, A Critical Biography* (London: Chatto & Windus, 1968).

5. F.A.C. Wilson's articles include "Swinburne's Sicilian Blade," *North Dakota Quarterly* 36 (1968): 5-18; "Swinburne and Mary Gordon," *Times Literary Supplement* (16 January 1969): 62; "Swinburne's 'Dearest Cousin,'" *Literature and Psychology* 19 (1969): 89-99; "Swinburne in Love," *Texas Studies in Literature and Language* 11 (1970): 1415-26; "Fabrication and Fact in Swinburne's *The Sisters*" and "Swinburne's Prose Heroines and Mary's *Femmes Fatales*," *Victorian Poetry* 9 (1971): 237-48, 249-56. Philip Henderson, *Swinburne, Portrait of a Poet* (New York: Macmillan, 1974). See also Jerome McGann, *Swinburne, An Experiment in Criticism* (Chicago: University of Chicago Press, 1972). McGann imagines that Mary Gordon "may even have visited upon her willing cousin a few friendly whippings" (211).

6. "Notes on Poems and Reviews" appeared in the *Spectator* in 1866 and was published separately by John Camden Hotten in the same year. See pages 12 and 15 of the Hotten text.

7. Gosse's essay is printed in *Letters*, vol. 6. The quoted passage appears on page 243.

Swinburne's letter to D.G. Rossetti of 1 March 1870, *Letters*, 1: 105, is a fine example of mingled homosexual and heterosexual interests.

8. *Life*, 26, 319, 321, 321-22, 187-88.

9. Ford Madox Ford, *Mightier Than the Sword* (London: Allen & Unwin, 1938), 250, and Violet Hunt, *The Wife of Rossetti* (London: John Lane, 1932), 258.

10. The manuscript of "A Vigil" is held at the British Museum, as part of the Ashley Library. Clyde K. Hyder, "The Medieval Background of Swinburne's 'The Leper,'" *PMLA* 46 (1931): 1280-88, discusses medieval sources for "The Leper." Robert A. Greenberg, "Gosse's *Swinburne*, 'The Triumph of Time,' and the Context of 'Les Noyades,'" *Victorian Poetry* 9 (1971): 95-110.

11. Oswald Doughty, *A Victorian Romantic* (London: Frederick Miller, 1949), 118-28.

12. *The Novels of A.C. Swinburne* (Westport, Connecticut: Greenwood Press, 1978), 106, 107.

13. Cecil Lang, "A Manuscript, A Mare's Nest, and a Mystery," *Yale University Library Gazette* 31 (April 1957): 163-71; Clyde K. Hyder, "Algernon Charles Swinburne," *The Victorian Poets*, ed. Frederic Faverty (Cambridge: Harvard University Press, 1968), 235, 229, 232.

5. Tennyson the Sadist

1. Robert Stange, "Tennyson's Garden of Art," *PMLA* 67 (1952): 737.

2. Flavia Alaya, "Tennyson's 'The Lady of Shalott,'" *Victorian Poetry* 8 (1970): 273-89.

3. All passages are quoted from *The Poems of Tennyson*, ed. Christopher Ricks (London: Longmans, 1969).

4. Hallam, Lord Tennyson, *Alfred Lord Tennyson, A Memoir*, vol. 1 (New York: Macmillan, 1898), 193n.

5. *Memoir*, 1: 304.

6. The task has been partly accomplished by Susan Shatto and Marion Shaw, ed., *In Memoriam* (Oxford: Clarendon Press, 1982).

7. A.C. Bradley, *A Commentary on In Memoriam* (London: Macmillan, 1901), and Eleanor B. Mattes, *In Memoriam: The Way of a Soul* (New York: Exposition Press, 1951).

8. Bradley, 30-35; James Knowles, "Aspects of Tennyson," *Nineteenth Century* 33 (1893): 182; Martin J. Svaglic, "A Framework for Tennyson's *In Memoriam*," *JEGP* 61 (1962): 810-25; T.S. Eliot, *Essays Ancient and Modern* (New York: Harcourt, Brace, 1936), 190, 195, 196.

9. E.D.H. Johnson, "*In Memoriam*: the Way of the Poet," *Victorian Studies* 2 (1958): 137-48.

10. Jerome Buckley, *Tennyson, the Growth of a Poet* (Cambridge: Harvard Unversity Press, 1960); James G. Taaffe, "Circle Imagery in Tennyson's *In Memoriam*," *Victorian Poetry* 1 (1963): 123-31. Richard Monckton Milnes's lines are quoted by Buckley, lll.

11. *Memoir*, 1: 196; Knowles, 182.

12. *Memoir*, 1: 17, 35; *The Letters of Edward FitzGerald*, ed. Alfred McKinley Terhume and Annabelle Burdick Terhume, vol. 1 (Princeton: Princeton University Press, 1980), 211.

13. *Memoir*, 1: 304.

6. A Shot at the Verbal Icon

1. Geoffrey Hartman, *Beyond Formalism* (New Haven: Yale University Press, 1970), 56.

2. W.K. Wimsatt, *The Verbal Icon* (Louisville: University of Kentucky Press, 1954), 50.

3. W.K. Wimsatt, *Hateful Contraries* (Louisville: University of Kentucky Press, 1965), 36.

4. T.S. Eliot, *Essays Ancient and Modern* (New York: Harcourt, Brace, 1936), 195, 186, 191-92.

5. "What to say about a Poem," *Hateful Contraries*, 238, and "Genesis: A Fallacy Revisited," in Peter Demetz et al., ed., *The Disciplines of Criticism* (New Haven: Yale University Press, 1968), 218.

6. Leon Edel, ed., *The Ambassadors* (Boston: Houghton Mifflin, 1960), vi; F.R. Leavis, *The Great Tradition* (London: Penguin Books, 1962), 20, 31, 142; Ian Watt, "The First Paragraph of *The Ambassadors*: An Explication," in *The Ambassadors*, ed. S.P. Rosenbaum (New York: W.W. Norton, 1964), 476.

7. James Hepburn, "Disarming and Uncanny Visions," *Literature and Psychology* 9 (Winter 1959): 9-12.

8. A modified version of my argument appears in my book *The Art of Arnold Bennett* (Bloomington: Indiana University Press, 1963).

7. Mr. Pooter and the Little Tradition

1. F.R. Leavis, *The Great Tradition* (London: Penguin Books, 1962).

2. Lord Roseberry's words accompany various editions of *The Diary of a Nobody*. They are reprinted in part on the back cover of the Penguin edition published in New York in 1983. Lord Roseberry is said there to have stated his opinion in August 1910.

3. Walter Houghton, ed., *The Wellesley Index to Victorian Periodicals*, vol. 1 (Toronto: University of Toronto Press, 1960), xv.

4. Bonamy Dobrée and Edith Batho, *The Victorians and After* (New York: R.M. McBride, 1938), 356.

5. *The Journal of Arnold Bennett* (New York: Viking Press, 1933), 407.

6. These verses are taken from sheet music held at the British Museum. So are the words for George Grossmith's songs.

7. *The Diary of a Nobody* (New York: Penguin Books, 1983), 64. All quotations are from this edition, whose appearance eleven years after I wrote this essay may not end American ignorance of the book.

8. B.W. Findon, "Memoir of George and Weedon Grossmith," in the fifth edition of *The Diary of a Nobody* (London, 1920).

9. *The Complete Prose Works of Matthew Arnold*, ed. R.H. Super, vol. 11 (Ann Arbor: University of Michigan Press, 1978), 358.

10. Ebenezer Elliott, "The People's Anthem," *Poetical Works* (London: H.S. King, 1876), 70.

8. Ottoline the Terrible

1. *Memoirs of Lady Ottoline Morrell,* ed. Robert Gathorne-Hardy, vol. 1 (New York: Alfred A. Knopf, 1964), *Ottoline at Garsington, Memoirs of Lady Ottoline Morrell,* vol. 2 (New York: Alfred A. Knopf, 1973), 131; Sandra Jobson Darroch, *Ottoline* (New York: Coward, McCann & Geoghegan, 1975), 152.
2. *The Autobiography of Bertrand Russell* (London: George Allen & Unwin, 1967), 148.
3. *The Collected Letters of D.H. Lawrence,* ed. Harry T. Moore, vol. 1 (New York: Viking, 1962), 367.
4. Moore, 1: 620; Bertrand Russell, *Portraits from Memory* (New York: Simon & Schuster, 1956), lll.

9. Leda and the Dumbledore

1. *The Collected Poems of W.B. Yeats* (New York: Macmillan, 1956); *The Complete Poems of Thomas Hardy,* ed. James Gibson (New York: Macmillan, 1976). All quotations are from these two editions.
2. R.P. Blackmur, "The Shorter Poems of Thomas Hardy," and F.R. Leavis, "Hardy the Poet," *Southern Review* 6 (1940): 20-48, 87-98. Blackmur's phrases appear on page 48. Donald Davie, *Thomas Hardy and British Poetry* (New York: Oxford University Press, 1972), 18, 26.
3. W.H. Auden, "A Literary Transference," *Southern Review* 6 (1940): 78.

10. The Notebook for *Riceyman Steps*

1. J.B. Atkins, *Incidents and Reflections* (London: Christophers, 1947), 177; George Doran, *Chronicles of Barrabas* (New York: Harcourt, Brace, 1935), 142; Arnold Bennett, *Journal of Things New and Old* (New York: Doubleday, Doran, 1930), 213.
2. The notebook for *Riceyman Steps* is held in the Henry W. and Albert A. Berg Collection of the New York Public Library. I am grateful to the Library for permission to use it. The letter to Richmond Temple is likewise held in the Berg Collection.
3. *Riceyman Steps* (New York: Doran, 1923), 86. All references to the novel are to this, the first American edition.
4. H.G. Wells, *Experiment in Autobiography* (New York: Macmillan, 1934), 536; *Arnold Bennett and H.G. Wells,* ed. Harris Wilson (Urbana. University of Illinois Press, 1960), 182.
5. *The Journal of Arnold Bennett* (New York: Viking Press, 1933), 346, 349, 357.
6. Dorothy Cheston Bennett, "Arnold Bennett's Unfinished Novel," *Bookman* (New York) 75 (September 1930): 497-500; *Arnold Bennett's Letters to His Nephew* (New York: Harcourt, Brace, 1935), 333.
7. *The OLd Wives' Tale* (London: Benn, and New York: Doran, 1927), v. The edition is a facsimile reproduction of the original manuscript, which is now held at the Library at Indiana University. The manuscript of *Riceyman Steps* is held in the Berg Collection.

11. Some Curious Realism in Riceyman Steps

1. S.R., "An Old London Book Shop," *Notes and Queries*, n. s. 3 (1956): 310-11; E.C. Hales in a letter to the editors of the *Staffordshire Sentinel*, 27 July 1944; Reginald Pound, *Arnold Bennett* (New York: Harcourt, Brace, 1953), 301.

2. *Riceyman Steps* (New York: Doran, 1923), 18. All references to the novel are to this, the first American edition.

3. Virginia Woolf, *Mr. Bennett and Mrs. Brown* (London: Hogarth Press, 1928), 18.

4. Frank Swinnerton, *The Bookman's London* (London: Allan Wingate, 1951). 3; *The Old Wives' Tale* (New York: Doubleday, Doran, 1936), viii.

5. William J. Pink, *History of Clerkenwell* (London: Pickburn, 1865).

6. Edward Knoblock, *Round the Room* (London: Chapman & Hall, 1939), 314; F. Somner Merryweather, *Lives and Anecdotes of Misers* (London: Simpkin, Marshall, 1850); quoted by Pound, 301.

7. *The Author's Craft* (New York: Doran, 1914). 60-61.

12. E. A. Robinson's System of Opposites

1. *Untriangulated Stars: Letters of Edwin Arlington Robinson to Harry de Forest Smith*, ed. Denham Sutcliffe (Cambridge: Harvard University Press, 1947), 161.

2. Louis Coxe, *Edwin Arlington Robinson* (Minneapolis: University of Minnesota Press, 1962), ll.

3. *Selected Letters of Edwin Arlington Robinson*, ed. Ridgely Torrence (New York: Macmillan, 1940), ll. See also page 50. All letters not to Harry de Forest Smith are quoted from this collection.

4. Except as otherwise noted, all quotations of Robinson's early poetry follow the texts of the first editions of *The Torrent and the Night Before* and *The Children of the Night, A Book of Poems* as reproduced in *Edwin Arlington Robinson, Selected Early Poems and Letters*, edited by Charles T. Davis (New York: Holt, Rinehart & Winston, 1960).

5. Daniel Gregory Mason, "Early Letters of Edwin Arlington Robinson," *Virginia Quarterly Review* 13 (1937): 57.

6. Theodore Roosevelt, "Children of the Night," *Outlook* 30 (12 August 1905): 913-14; Robert Stevick, "E. A. Robinson's Principles and Practice of Poetry," (Ph.D. diss. University of Wisconsin, 1956), 124, 126; Yvor Winters, *Edwin Arlington Robinson* (Norfolk, Conn.: New Directions, 1946). 35.

7. Octave XIX.

8. R.P. Blackmur, "Verse that is to Easie," *Poetry* 43 (January 1934), 221.

9. "Sonnet," from *The Children of the Night*.

10. R.P. Adams, "The Failure of Edwin Arlington Robinson," *Tulane Studies in English* ll (1961): 131-34.

13. Religion, Science, and Philip Henry Gosse

1. Edmund Gosse, *Father and Son* (London: Oxford University Press, 1974), 123-24. All references are to this edition.

2. Some of the discrepancies between *Father and Son* and the *Life* are detailed in my Explanatory Notes to the 1974 edition of *Father and Son*. The *Times Literary Supplement* review appeared on 14 November 1907.
  3. Raymond Lister, *Thomas Gosse* (Cambridge: privately printed, 1953).
  4. Edmund Gosse, *The Life of Philip Henry Gosse* (London: Kegan Paul, 1890), 78-79.
  5. *The Canadian Naturalist* (London: John Van Voorst, 1840), 67, 76.
  6. *A Naturalist's Rambles* (London: John Van Voorst, 1853), 1-2.
  7. *A Year at the Shore* (London: Alexander Strahan, 1865), 85-86.
  8. *A Memorial of the Last Days on Earth of Emily Gosse* (London: J. Nisbet, 1857), 5, 53.
  9. *Omphalos: An Attempt to Untie the Geological Knot* (London: John Van Voorst, 1857).
  10. Kingsley is quoted in the *Life*, 281, *Father and Son*, 62; Gosse is speaking in *Father and Son*, 62.
  11. Huxley's description of Philip Henry is quoted in *Father and Son*, 68. For Huxley's scientism see *Collected Essays*, vol. 2 (New York: D. Appleton, 1894). See page 110 for his confidence about the causal chain, page 360 for the quoted passage.

14. Wilfred Owen's Poetic Development

  1. D.S.R. Welland, *Wilfred Owen* (London: Chatto & Windus, 1960), 192; John H. Johnston, *English Poetry of the First World War* (Princeton: Princeton University Press, 1964), 151; Dominic Hibberd, *Wilfred Owen* (London: Chatto & Windus, 1973), 28; Jon Stallworthy, *Wilfred Owen* (London: Oxford University Press, 1974), 211. I use the term off-rhyme to cover the half-rhyme (*old-bald, boys-suppose*), pararhyme (*shell-shall, brutes-brats*), and other imperfect end-rhymes (*brutes-use-disease*) that Owen employed. I do not know that it would be useful to make distinctions among them in discussion. Hibberd discusses the matter briefly, 82-83. (Stallworthy's edition of the *Complete Poems* has just now appeared, with my own book in press.)
  2. Unless otherwise indicated, all quotations from Owen's poems follow *Collected Poems of Wilfred Owen*, ed. C. Day Lewis (London: Chatto & Windus, 1963). The phrase from Owen's letter comes from *Wilfred Owen, Collected Letters,* ed. Harold Owen and John Bell (London: Oxford University Press, 1967), 478.
  3. Personal communication. I would like to thank Mr. Stallworthy for reading this essay in an earlier form and for providing me with information about the dating of several poems. I have indicated where my dating remains in disagreement with his.
  The ensuing discussion in the text discusses repeated phrases in Owen's poems. A possibly related repetition is suggested by the editors of the *Collected Letters*, 106n. In a letter to his sister Mary in January 1912 Owen remarks that "at 3 a.m. our life ebbs at its lowest; that is 'the hour when sick men die.'" The editors note the likeness of the thought—and its phrase from Sir Lewis Morris—to "The weak-limned hour when sick men's sighs are drained" in "The Unreturning." If the connection is more than accidental and if "The Unreturning" dates from 1917 as Stallworthy thinks, the repetition covers five years instead of the two that a 1914 date for "The Unreturning" would give.
  4. Stallworthy, 79; *Collected Letters*, 521, 482.

5. *Times Literary Supplement*, 21 December 1973: 1562; 18 January 1974: 55; 25 January 1974: 81.
6. *Siegfried's Journey* (London: Faber, 1945), 59-60.
7. I would like to thank the Trustees of the British Museum and Messrs. John Bell and Jon Stallworthy for permission to quote from the drafts of Owen's poems held in the British Museum.
8. J.M. Murry, in his review of Owen's *Poems, Nation and Athenaeum* 28 (19 February 1921): 706; Edmund Blunden, ed., *The Poems of Wilfred Owen* (London: Chatto & Windus, 1931), 29; Welland, 32; Johnston, 169; Hibberd, 34.
9. *Collected Poems*, 31.

15. The Play that Oscar Wilde Failed to Write

1. *The Letters of Oscar Wilde,* ed. Rupert Hart-Davis (London: Rupert Hart-Davis, 1962), 362.
2. Max Beerbohm, "A Satire on Romantic Drama," *Saturday Review* 90 (8 December 1900): 720, and St. John Hankin, "The Collected Plays of Oscar Wilde," *Fortnightly Review* 83, n.s. (1 May 1908): 791-802. Both pieces are reprinted in *Oscar Wilde, the Critical Heritage,* ed. Karl Beckson (New York: Barnes & Noble, 1970).
3. Unsigned review, *Pall Mall Gazette* (27 February 1893): 3; A.B. Walkley, "Lady Windermere's Fan," *Speaker* 5 (27 February 1892): 257-58. Both are reprinted in Beckson.
4. *Complete Works of Oscar Wilde* (London: Collins, 1971), 388, 449, 519. All quotations from both plays and prose are from this edition.
5. *Letters*, 361-62.
6. Arthur Symons, in an unsigned review, *Athenaeum* (16 May 1908): 598-600. Reprinted in Beckson.
7. Quoted by Archibald Henderson, "The Dramas of Oscar Wilde," *Arena* 38 (August 1907): 134-39. Reprinted in Beckson.
8. William Archer, in his review in *World* (20 February 1895):57; A.B. Walkley, in *Speaker* 4 (23 February 1895): 212-13; Hankin, 801-2. All reprinted in Beckson.
9. Eric Bentley, *The Playwright as Thinker* (New York: Reynal & Hitchcock, 1946), 172-77; Richard Foster, "Wilde as Parodist," *College English* 18 (1956): 23; L.A. Poague, "*The Importance of Being Earnest*: the Texture of Wilde's Irony," *Modern Drama* 16 (1973): 257. For an English estimate of a similar sort see Geoffrey Stone, "Serious Bunburyism," *Essays in Criticism* 26 (1976): 28-41.
10. *Complete Works*, 323, 322, 330, 360, 341, 335, 453.
11. *Letters*, 148, 104, 137, 142, 757.
12. *Letters*, 282, 308-9.
13. *Letters*, 328, 433, 492, 333, 336, 475.
14. *Letters*, 359, 362, 369, 778, 779, 780, 783.
15. *Letters*, 708, 715, 717, 760. Hesketh Pearson, *Oscar Wilde* (New York: Harper, 1946).

16. Where Arnold Bennett Went Wrong

P. 201. EPIC OF DULLNESS: Walter Allen, *Arnold Bennett* (Denver: Alan Swallow, 1949), 35.

P. 202. DURING THIS WEEK...: The *Journal of Arnold Bennett* (New York: Viking Press, 1933), 49.

P. 202. I'M GOING TO...: Margaret Locherbie-Goff, *La Jeunesse d'Arnold Bennett* (Avesne-sur-Helpe: Editions de L'Observateur, 1939), 113.

P. 202. THE SIGHT GAVE...: *Journal*, 983.

P. 202. THE BEST MIND....: *Arnold Bennett and H.G. Wells*, ed. Harris Wilson (Urbana: University of Illinois Press, 1960), 182.

P. 203. IN THAT HEAD...: *Clayhanger* (New York: E.P. Dutton, 1910), 17.

P. 204. I AM AN ENGLISHMAN...: *Letters of Arnold Bennett*, ed. James Hepburn, vol. 1 (London and New York: Oxford University Press, 1966), 115.

P. 204. MR. MURLEY, WHO...: *The Old Wives' Tale* (New York: Doubleday, Doran, 1936), 43.

Pp. 204-05. A LUSCIOUS RESOUNDING MOUTHFUL...; IT MUST BE...: *The Old Wives' Tale*, 65.

Pp. 205-06. CEDRIC. NOW JUST LISTEN...: *The Honeymoon* (New York: Doran, n.d.), 29-34.

17. Dirty Words, Clean Poetry

P. 209. SINKING HE LEFT...: The passage is quoted from *The Works of John Dryden*, ed. H.T. Swedenberg, Jr., vol. 2 (Berkeley: University of California Press, 1972).

P. 210. FELL IN LOVE...: *The Oxford Anthology of English Literature*, vol. 2 (New York: Oxford University Press, 1973), 1180.

P. 211. AND ALL AT ONCE...: The passage is quoted from *The Poems of Tennyson*, ed. Christopher Ricks (London: Longmans, 1969).

P. 211. SHE CRIED, "LAURA...: The passage is quoted from *The Complete Poems of Christina Rossetti*, ed. R.W. Crump, vol. 1. (Baton Rouge: Louisiana State University Press, 1979).

P. 211. OBVIOUSLY AN INVITATION...: Lona Mosk Packer, "Symbol and Reality in Christina Rossetti's *Goblin Market*," *PMLA* 73 (1958): 378.

Pp. 211-12. SERIES OF EXCHANGES...: John Bayley, "Who was the 'man right fair' of the Sonnets?" *Times Literary Supplement* (4 January 1974): 15; with responses by Martin Green and John Sparrow on 18 January: 54; a response by Alistair Smart on 25 January: 81; Bayley's first reply on 1 February: 108, with letters from David Knowles and Helen Gardner on the same page; a second response from Smart on 8 February: 134; and Bayley's second reply on 15 February: 158.

18. Thomas Hardy among the Americans

P. 217. THE DAY THE MUSIC DIED: Since writing the article, I have been told on good authority that Don McLean himself, composer of the song, has said that the day refers to the death of the singer Buddy Holly, who was killed in an airplane crash in 1959. So I have gone back to my original authority, my niece Lorraine Protheroe, who gave me my recording, and she says that she and her friends assumed that the reference is to Kennedy's death. I am left with an ambiguous postscript to a question posed in "Dirty Words, Clean Poetry": Can Shakespeare's readers be smarter than he was? Can we be smarter than Don McLean?

19. Visiting Robert Frost in England

P. 219. THE FORTUNATE MONOPOLIZE...: *Selected Letters of Robert Frost,* ed. Lawrance Thompson (New York: Holt, Rinehart and Winston, 1964), 118.

P. 221. I NEVER KNEW...: *Selected Letters,* 73-74.

Index

Adams, J. Donald 85, 86
Adams, Richard P. 155, 229
Adams, Robert M. 30, 225
Alaya, Flavia 62 226
Alexander, George 179, 187, 188
Allen, Walter (201), 232
Anderson, Mary 186
Anderson, Sherwood, 88-89, 90, 227
Archer, William 183, 231
Aristotle, 76-77
Arnold, Matthew 29, 94, 105, 188, 225, 227
Arrowsmith, William 13, 223
Atkins, J.B. 127, 132, 228
Auden, W.H. 119, 123, 228
Austen, Jane 93, 94, 135, 213

Bailey, Benjamin 28
Balzac, Honoré de 201
Barbusse, Henri 171, 172
Batho, Edith 96-97, 227
Bayley, John 211-12, 232
Beerbohm, Max 104, 179-80, 194, 231
Beethoven, Ludvig van 94
Benét, William Rose 15, 223
Bennett, Arnold 29, 89-90, 91-92, 98, 111, 127-33, 135-42, 201-07, 225, 227, 228, 229
Bennett, Dorothy Cheston, 132, 228
Bentley, Eric, 184, 231
Bergler, Edmund, 12, 223
Berkelman, Robert, 29, 225
Betjeman, Sir John, 87, 97
Beyer, Werner William (28), 225
Bird, Alice 50
Blacker, Carlos 194
Blackmur, R.P. 116-17, 119, 153, 228, 229
Blake, William 80-81, 84, 85-86
Blind, Mathilde 52

Blunden, Edmund 171, 173, 174, 231
Bowra, C.M. 30, 225
Bradley, A.C. 13, 66-67, 68, 69
Brooks, Cleanth, 23, 24, 25, 27, 29, 224
Browne, Sir Thomas 164
Browning, Robert 86, 94
Buckley, Jerome 68, 226
Burke, Kenneth 28
Burne Jones, Lady 54
Burney, Fanny 93
Byron, Lord 64

Campion, Thomas 213
Carrington, Dora 112
Chambers, Jessie 106
Christian imagery 89-90, 195-97
Ciardi, John 15, 17-18, 20, 224
Clark, Sir Kenneth 5, 223
Coffin, R.P. Tristram 19, 224
Conrad, Joseph 93, 94, 96, 97-99, 100
Cook, Reginald L. 16, 224
Coriat, Isador H. (12), 223
Cox, James M. 15, 18-19, 223
Coxe, Louis 144

Daiches, David 85
Darroch, Sandra Jobson 109, 111-12, 113, 227
Darwin, Charles 157
Davie, Donald 116, 228
de Lara, Isadore 101
Dickens, Charles 73, 95
Dobrée, Bonamy 96-97, 227
Donne, John 84, 209-10
Doran, George 127, 132, 228
Dostoevsky, Feodor 10, 96
Doughty, Oswald 54, 226
Douglas, Lord Alfred 187-88, 191, 195-96
D'Oyly Carte, Richard 186
Dryden, John 209, 210, 211, 213, 232

Edel, Leon 83, 227
Eliot, George 93, 127
Eliot, T.S. 65, 67, 68, 73, 79, 95, 113, 154, 155, 210, 226
Elliott, Ebenezer 93, 106, 227
Euripides 13

Faulkner, Jane 33, 48, 51, 52, 58
Faverty, Frederic 59, 226
Fenichel, Otto 88
Field, Eugene 210
FitzGerald, Edward 72, 226
Fliess, Wilhelm 4
Ford, F.M. 52, 54, 226
Foster, Richard 184, 231
Fraiberg, Louis 9-10, 14, 223
Freud, Sigmund 3-14, 89, 91, 223
Freudian critics and criticism 3-14, 81-82, 88-90, 91, 144, 223
Frost, Robert 15-21, 219-21, 223-24, 233
Fry, Roger 110, 111
Frye, Northrop 75, 82
Fuller, Jean Overton 35-37, 38, 41, 43-44, 45, 49, 55, 58, 59, 92, 225

Gardner, Helen 212, 213, 232
Gaskell, Elizabeth 93
Gathorne-Hardy, Edward 213
Gittings, Robert 123
Gledhill, Arthur 144
Goethe, J.W.v. 201
Goossens, Eugene 202
Gordon, Mary 34-38, 42, 43, 51-58, 225
Gosse, Edmund 33-34, 35, 40, 42, 43, 44, 45, 47, 48, 49-50, 52, 54, 58-59, 85, 87, 92, 157, 158, 225, 229, 230
Gosse, Emily 157-58, 162-63, 230
Gosse, Philip Henry 157-65, 229-30
Gosse, Thomas 158-59, 230
Green, Martin 111, 212, 232
Greenberg, Robert A. 54, 226
Grossmith, George 94, 96-107, 227
Grossmith, Weedon 94, 96-107, 227

Hales, E.C. (135), (136), 229
Hallam, Arthur 64, 66, 67, 68, 71, 210-11
Hankin, St. John 180, 182, 184, 231
Hardy, Thomas 87, 94, 95, 106, 115-24, 215-17, 221, 228
Harris, Frank 181, 188, 194
Hartman, Geoffrey 75, 82, 227
Henderson, Philip 37, 225
Hendrick, Cecilia Hennel 224
Hepburn, James 227

Hibberd, Dominic 167, 168, 170, 171-72, 175, 230, 231
Homer 94
Hood, Thomas 88, 106
Hopkins, G.M. 94, 95
Houghton, Walter 96, 227
Housman, A.E. 213
Hughes, Thomas 99-100
Hugo, Victor 144
Hunt, Violet 52, 53, 54, 57, 226
Huxley, Aldous 109, 111, 112
Huxley, T.H. 164-65, 230
Hyder, Clyde K. 59, 226

James, Henry 83-84, 93, 94, 104, 190, 213, 227
John, Augustus 110, 111
Johnson, E.D.H. 67-68, 226
Johnston, John H. 167, 174-75, 176, 230, 231
Jones, Ernest 4, 6-7, 8, 13, 14, 223
Joyce, James 201
Jung, Carl 6, 14

Kafka, Franz 203
Keats, John 23-31, 73, 83, 167, 176, 177, 212, 224-25
Kingsley, Charles 93, 94, 164, 230
Knoblock, Edward 139, 229
Knowles, David 212, 232
Knowles, James 67, 226
Kohut, Heinz (12), 223
Kris, Ernst 9

Lamb, Henry 110, 111
Lang, Cecil 33-35, 36, 37, 38, 40, 41, 42-43, 44, 45, 47, 48, 49, 55, 58, 59, 225, 226
Langbaum, Robert 15, 19, 223
Lawrence, D.H. 93, 106, 109, 111, 113, 123, 133, 201, 227
Lawrence, Frieda 111
Lear, Edward 88
Leavis, F.R. 83-84, 93-94, 97, 104, 116, 123, 227, 228
Lesser, Simon O. 9, 11, 223
Levarie, Siegmund (12), 223
Lewis, C. Day 175, 177, 230
Lowell, Amy 19, 224
Lyell, Sir Charles 66, 157

Mann, Thomas 13
Mansfield, Katherine 109, 111, 113
Mason, Daniel Gregory 145, 151, 229
Mattes, Eleanor B. 66, 226
Mayfield, John S. 33, 35, 48, 225

Index

McGann, Jerome 225
McLaughlin, Charles A. 20, 224
McLean, Don 232-33
Menken, Adah 47, 52
Meredith, George 94
Merryweather, F. Somner 139-42, 229
Meynell, Viola 221
Milnes, Richard Monckton 33, 55, 68, 226
Milton, John 68, 88, 212, 213
Morrell, Ottoline 109-14, 228
Morrell, Philip, 110, 112
Murry, John Middleton (27), 30, 109, 11, 174, 225, 231
Music Hall 94
Nichol, John 56
Nicolson, Harold 72
Nordau, Max 151

O'Connor, William van 15, 20, 224
Orton, Joe 180
Owen, Mary 230
Owen, Susan 171
Owen, Wilfred 167-78, 230-31

Packer, Lona Mosk 211, 232
Pearson, Hesketh 195, 231
Perkins, David (28), 30, 225
Pettet, E.C. 23, 25, 224
Pink, William J. 128, 138, 229
Poague, L.A. 184, 231
Pope, Alexander 204
Pound, Reginald 91, 136, 229
Powell, George 35, 38
Prescott, Marie 186
Protheroe, Lorraine 233

Quiller-Couch, Sir Arthur 85

Reik, Theodor 5, 223
Richards, I.A. 25, 27, 76, 77
Ricks, Christopher 66, 72, 212
Rilke, Rainer Maria 12
Robinson, E.A. 90-91, 143-55, 229
Roosevelt, Theodore 150, 229
Rosebery, Lord 96, 227
Ross, Robert 186, 188, 194-95
Rossetti, Christina 106, 211, 232
Rossetti, D.G. 34, 36, 38, 40, 47, 49, 52, 53, 54, 55, 57, 58, 59, 226
Ruskin, John 43
Russell, Bertrand 109, 110, 111, 112-13, 227

Saintsbury, George 85
Sassoon, Siegfried 110, 113, 167, 170, 171, 172, 173, 231
Schillinger, Joseph 11, 223
Schlegel, Friedrich von 13
Schnitzler, Arthur 7
Scott, Clement 101, 102, 106-07
Scott, Sir Walter 163
Shakespeare, William 11, 13, 64, 76, 78, 80, 84, 94, 209, 211-12, 213, 233
Shapiro, Karl 85
Shatto, Susan 226
Shaw, G.B. 202
Shaw, Marion 226
Shelley, Percy Bysshe 25, 29, 51, 68, 168, 169, 225
Siddal, Elizabeth (43), 52-58
Smart, Alistair 212, 232
Smith, Harry de Forest 143, 144, 145, 146-47, 148-49, 151, 153, 155, 229
Solomon, Simeon 38
Sparrow, John 212, 213, 232
Spitzer, Leo 26-27, 224
Stallworthy, Jon 167, 168, 169, 170, 171, 172, 230, 231
Stange, Robert 61, 226
Steiner, George 96
Stevick, Robert David 150, 229
Stillinger, Jack 29, 225
Stone, Geoffrey 231
Stoppard, Tom 180
Strachey, James 6
Strachey, Lytton 110, 112
Svaglic, Martin J. (67), 226
Swinburne, A.C. 33-59, 91, 151, 169, 171, 225-26
Swinnerton, Frank 138, 229
Symons, Arthur 181, 182, 231

Taaffe, James G. (68), 226
Taylor, John 28
Temple, Richmond 128, 129, 228
Tennyson, Alfred Lord 61-73, 79, 86, 94, 210-11, 213, 227, 232
Tennyson, Arthur 72
Tennyson, Edward 64
Tennyson, Hallam 86
Thackeray, W.M. 84, 94
Thomas, Edward 221
Thompson, Lawrance 15, 17, 219, 223
Tolstoy, Leo 94
Trilling, Lionel 15, 19, 223
Trollope, Anthony 93
Turner, Reginald 188
Twain, Mark 99, 105

Unger, Leonard 15, 20, 223-24
Unterecker, John 210

Waggoner, Hyatt H. 15, 223
Walkley, A.B. 180, 183-84, 231
Warren, Austin 224
Wasserman, Earl 24, 25-26, 27, 28, 29, 30, 31, 83, 224
Watt, Ian, 83, 227
Welland, D.S.R. 167, 171, 172, 174, 230, 231
Wellek, René 224
Wells, H.G. 132, 202, 228, 232
White, Gilbert 159
Whitley, Alvin 29, 30, 225
Wigod, Jacob 26, 224
Wilde, Oscar 169, 171, 179-97, 231

Wilkinson, Louis 188
Wilson, F.A.C. 37, 38, 41, 49, 59, 225
Wimsatt, W.K. 75-92, 227
Winters, Yvor 15, 19-20, 151, 223, 229
Woolf, Virginia 137, 229
Wordsworth, William 24, 25, 28-29, 73, 225

Yeats, W.B. 92, 95, 115-16, 117, 118-19, 120-24, 155, 210, 228
Yonge, Charlotte 94

Zola, Emile 127, 143, 151